THE HOUR OF TELEVISION:

critical approaches

by
N.D. BATRA

The Scarecrow Press, Inc.
Metuchen, N.J., & London
1987

The author gratefully acknowledges permission to use the research findings published by the A. C. Nielsen Company in their 1985 Nielsen Report on Television.

Library of Congress Cataloging-in-Publication Data

Batra, N. D. (Narayan Dass), 1937–
　The hour of television.

　Bibliography: p.
　Includes index.
　1. Television programs.　2. Television broadcasting.
3. Television criticism.　4. Television.　I. Title.
PN1992.5.B36　1987　　791.45'0973　　87-4315
ISBN 0-8108-1989-9

Copyright © 1987 by N. D. Batra
Manufactured in the United States of America

To

My Father

J. R. BATRA

In Memoriam

For a nation that is afraid to let its people judge the truth and falsehood in an open market is a nation that's afraid of its people.

John F. Kennedy

The best test of truth is the power of the thought to get itself accepted in the competition of the market.

Justice Oliver Wendell Holmes

CONTENTS

Acknowledgments	ix
Introduction	xi

1. CRITICAL APPROACHES TO TELEVISION — 1
    - Literary Criticism Approach — 2
    - Semiological-Structural Approach — 6
    - Marxist Approach — 11
    - Psychoanalytical Model — 14
    - Sociological Analysis — 17

2. THE TELEVISION MODE — 24
    - The Dramatic Mode — 27
    - Television as Erotica — 30
    - News That Entertains — 32
    - Why Is Television So Amusing? — 33
    - Psychology of Television Watching — 35

3. EMERGING TELEVISION TECHNOLOGIES AND THE CULTURAL LAG — 40
    - Satellites — 42
    - Cable TV — 44
    - Subscription TV — 46
    - MDS and SMATV — 47
    - Direct Broadcast Satellite — 48
    - Translators, LPTV, etc. — 49
    - Videocassettes/disks — 49
    - Teletext and Videotex — 51
    - Cultural Lag — 52
    - Privacy — 54
    - Free Speech and the Fairness Doctrine — 56

4. FORM AND STRUCTURE OF TELEVISION DRAMA — 62
    - Screen Realism — 63

	Formulaic Conventions of Television Series Drama	64
	Plot and Characterization	65
	Cliffhangers	67
	Topicality	69
	Commercial-punctuated Action	70
	"Hill Street Blues": The Case of Recombinant Progeny	74
5.	DRAMATIC SERIAL: PRIME TIME AND DAYTIME	82
	Origin, Form and Structure	82
	Structural Characteristics	86
	Inside Soap Opera Today	88
	Prime-time Series and Serials	89
	"Dallas" to "Dynasty"	92
	"Guiding Light"	96
6.	SITCOM: THE HALF-HOUR COMEDY	101
	A Typology of Sitcom	104
	The Early Phase	105
	First Phase: Television Sitcoms of Traditional Families	106
	Second Phase: Back-to-Nature Sitcoms	107
	Third Phase: Social Problem Sitcoms	108
	"M*A*S*H"	108
	"The Mary Tyler Moore Show"	112
	"All in the Family"	115
	Fourth Phase: Sitcoms Which Delight and Instruct	118
	Bill Cosby: The Comic Godfather of America	118
7.	THE COLLECTIVE AS CREATOR	123
	Negotiated Creativity	123
	The Role of the Producer	128
	Grant Tinker's MTM	132
	Norman Lear and the Dramatization of Resentment	137
8.	NEWS AND NEWSCASTERS	143
	Structure of the Newscast	150
	TV News as Business, as Show Business	152
	Can Television Be Fair?	156

9. TELEVISION DOCUMENTARY IN AMERICAN
   CULTURE   164

   Flaherty, Grierson, Vertov   165
   "March of Time"   168
   Documentary as Combat-Exposé: "See It Now"   170
   Documentary as Judgment   172
   Documentary as an Epic   173
   Massaging the Message: "The Times of
      Harvey Milk"   175
   Minidocumentaries and Counter-documentaries   176
   The Nation's Conscience Keeper   178

10. THE POETICS AND RHETORIC OF DOCUDRAMA   184

    The Roots of Docudrama   185
    The Fear of the Genre   189

11. MINI-SERIES: EPIC IN THE AGE OF
    TELEVISION   198

    The Problem of Adaptation   202
    The Narrative Structure of the Mini-series   206
    "The Jewel in the Crown" and the American
       Audience   211
    The Narrator as an Intruder, as a Noise   213
    "The Thorn Birds": An Epic of Sin and
       Suffering in the Vatican Backyard   215

12. TELEVISION CRITIC AS A SOCIAL PROPHET   218

    The Issues   218
    Standards and Practices of a Good Critic   222
    Ideology, Idealism and Ideal Types   225

13. THE WAYS OF NIELSEN   228

    Television Audiences as Markets of Taste   228
    Ratings   233
    What Ratings Measure and Measure Not   241
    Guardians of Public Taste   244
    Some Facts About American Television   246

14. CONCLUSION   249

Selected Bibliography   255

Index   263

ACKNOWLEDGMENTS

I am indeed very fortunate that an internationally known scholar, Professor Martin Esslin of Stanford University, critiqued my manuscript. His advice proved very valuable. Professor John G. Cawelti of the University of Kentucky read the chapter on sitcom. I found his comments very insightful. Professor Philip Palmgreen, also of the University of Kentucky, made valuable suggestions about the chapter on communications technology and the cultural lag. Professor Joseph R. Dominick of the University of Georgia made interesting observations about the chapter on audience analysis and rating methodology. Professor Arthur Asa Berger of San Francisco State University made very candid comments about the chapter on critical approaches to television. Mr. Malcolm M. MacDonald, Director of The University of Alabama Press, made incisive observations about the manuscript that proved very helpful. I am thankful to Dr. David Burg for his help in polishing the manuscript.

My intellectual life has been much influenced by the scholarly works of Professor J.L. Styan of Northwestern University and Professor R.A. Malagi of Gujarat University. I am also indebted to many other scholars whose work I have quoted in support of my arguments.

It is my good wife, Varsha, and our two children, Shefali and Nikhil, who have given me their moral support and love, without which I could not have survived my self-doubts.

I stand on the shoulders of others.

INTRODUCTION

Television is a repository of a nation's collective consciousness, its dreams, fears, obsessions, hopes, and aspirations. A platform for the marketman and poet, auctioneer and artist, it is "open sesame" to a nation's heart and soul, meriting study by the land's most enlightened minds. But its very profusion--its gigantic appetite for all kinds of materials to captivate viewers from hour to hour and grab a fair share of the statistician's normal curve in order to "make a buck," and its accessibility to advertisers with the "bucks" to spend--has created a pervasive, thoughtless, and contemptuous disregard for its achievements, with gloating over its unfortunate failings. It deserves better attention.

The immensity of American television coextends and correlates with the pervasiveness of the free marketplace of goods and ideas that constitutes the controlling center, the core, of American civilization. All organized societies have a stabilizing center, a dynamic core which diffuses energy to all the constituent members. When this core, or central symbol, is threatened, society's existence is placed in jeopardy. If a collapsed centralizing symbol is not replaced by another controlling symbol embodying a new vision, the society breaks up, as happened in the South Asian subcontinent when the symbolic British Raj collapsed and there was nothing to replace it. A threat to the free marketplace is therefore a threat to every American, as occurred in the 1930s. If this controlling symbol in American society were to be replaced by a cultist ideology, America, as we know it, would cease to exist.

Television as a cultural core in America exists in dynamic relationship with the free marketplace of goods and ideas; their symbiotic existence gives us a world view, a mode of consciousness quite different from the Japanese world vision, the French mode of consciousness, or the British "structure of feeling." Are we prisoners of our own mode of consciousness? We are redeemed by the autonomy of human imagination and the restless human spirit that lead to constant innovations and technological revolution, which in turn bring about structural changes in society. The search for better forms of television affects the way we market and the way we exercise our free speech, which in turn change television and our mode of consciousness and the way we experience reality.

Television, because of its multi-focus and multi-locus monitoring capacities, redeems reality in a way that no other medium of communication has ever done before. Its redemptive functions are matched only by its oracular powers, because television, being correlated with the free marketplace of goods and ideas in American society, reveals influence by the same predictive functions as the free market, within the realm of probability and measurable risks.

On the basis of such premises, this study explores both the fictional world heir to Aristotle and Shakespeare, and the mundane, empirical, and technologically accessible world of the marketplace, Nielsens, Ropers, Magids, et al. It looks at television phenomena humanistically and empirically, offering a kind of cross checking for greater understanding of reality. Each method of reality testing gives a partial view of reality, leaving much to be desired. Humanists and empiricists in their own way search for significance and meaning in cultural phenomena by asking different sets of questions engendered by their methods and standards. Briefly, the ultimate measure in humanistic research is authority--of an individual or of an ideal. In empiricism the final authority is probability (curve). All evidence is tested against chance. "Do you see what I see?" is the question empiricists ask with a scale in their hands. If an empiricist were to encounter Helen of Troy, instead of rhapsodizing, "Was this the face that launched a thousand ships and burnt the topless towers of Ilium?" he would call a panel of judges, factor beauty, and average the panel's scores. In the process he would strip a woman naked, almost, but isn't that one way of appreciating a woman's beauty? Don't forget the empiricist's norms of rigor, objectivity, and controlled measurement. What is not measurable is not worth the research, he seems to be saying, and

Introduction xiii

he challenges you: "Replicate and prove me wrong." He is certain that all knowledge is tentative and therefore uncertain. To quote (slightly out of context) a judge of the Second Court of Appeals, Learned Hand:

> ... that knowledge is hard to get, that man must break through again and again the thin crust on which he walks, that the certainties of today may become the superstitions of tomorrow; that we have no warrant of assurance save by everlasting readiness to test and test again."[1]

This sums up the empiricist credo.

The qualitative approaches of humanism--also called les sciences, humane Geisteswissen-schaften, critical theory, interpretive social science, hermeneutics, cultural science--include Marx, Weber, Freud, James, Dewey, Tocqueville, Vladimir Propp, Lévi-Strauss, Roland Barthes, the Chicago School, and many others of different philosophical and ideological orientations. Humanists study patterns, creative processes, symbols, and systems of meanings which humans create to make their lives meaningful. Humanism's purpose is interpretation. A humanist seeks naturalistic observation "to set up a poetic resonance with the native interpretation"; contextualization "in which the phenomena can be observed naturally rather than arranging them to happen under contrived conditions"; maximized comparisons of social wholes; and sensitized concepts "to capture original meanings validly, yet explicate them on a level that gives the results maximum impact."[2]

Empiricists also use these criteria (with different questions in hand); but instead of resting on authority or looking for "touchstones," as Matthew Arnold suggested, they test and test again and consult their tables of significance to explain and predict through probability. Empiricism is the predominant mode of thought and inquiry in America, separating Americans from Europeans. Americans in general are in the habit of indexing, quantifying, and computing for comparisons and predictions. As Nobel prize winner Sir Peter Medawar said in "Advice to a Young Scientist": "Quantification as such has no meaning except in so far as it helps to solve problems. To quantify is not be a scientist, but goodness, it does help."

Television needs to be studied from such different perspectives to save ourselves from the embarrassment of the blind men probing an elephant. But this study does not attempt to resolve "incommensurable positions" and to become a translator;[3] rather, it recognizes the value of plurality in understanding the complexity of television as a cultural core. The reader will find an absence of messianic and evangelical spirit because the purpose of this study is not to proselyte the reader into a particular school of thought but to explain and appreciate television from multiple stances. To unravel the generic formula of a police story or to understand its aesthetics should not exclude one from analyzing its content empirically and asking, "How is it that most of the criminals are blacks and ethnic minorities?" or, "Why do women play subservient roles?" The humanist's opinion that literary classics cultivate virtue is based upon faith; the empiricist's conclusion that violence in television cultivates fear is based on replicable, verifiable, and testable observations. The need for a pluralistic, holistic approach to the study of television thus becomes justified.

This book's first chapter elucidates the five currently popular critical approaches to television. Literary critics evaluate television fiction and drama through historical context or development, as when a hero epitomizes the contending forces of an age; through generic and archetypal criticism which categorizes programs and makes a comparative study of generic formulas; and through the author-auteur approach, in which critics study the growth and development of a creator-producer generically or chronologically. The psychoanalytic model treats TV creations as dreams and applies Freudian methods of analysis. The Marxists approach television as a cultural arm of the dominant classes trying to perpetuate their hegemony. The semiologist studies the signs of the television text to go beyond the manifest meaning and probe the latent meaning. Sociologists ask how a program serves the needs of viewers, how it gratifies them. Of several social science methods only one approach, content analysis, is discussed here as an example of empirical mode.

Chapter two picks up the refrain that television as a cultural force serves the ethos of the society embodied in free enterprise and free speech. Television assumes a dramatic mode of communication which exposes reality in the process of happening, annihilating past and future as if the

Introduction xv

existing moment were the only reality. The dialectical tension between the spoken word and the flow of audiovisual images creates heightened suspense in the news, sports, and serial drama, and makes television amusing and erotic, metaphorically speaking. Television simultaneously engages both the verbal-logical-sequential half and the pictorial-holistic half of the brain and therefore has an advantage over reading, which is linear and sequential.

Chapter three explains the developing television and communication technologies which are slowly changing our viewing habits. The TV set is assuming many more functions than it was initially designed to do. It is being used as a terminal for data processing, a monitor for VCRs and videodiscs, and a backgrounder. With a remote control in hand, the abundance of channel choices, and the options of cable, the viewer has become sovereign. This chapter sanguinely looks forward to the enhancing of the plurality and multiplicity of opinions which is the source of strength for American democracy.

Chapter four discusses the form and structure of television drama as defying the Aristotelian tenet that drama should have a single climax. That drama could exist without denouement and could flourish in spite of commercial-punctuated action is a marvelous achievement of television.

Chapter five analyzes some of the most widely watched prime time and daytime serials and explains their aesthetic and emotional appeals. It examines the segmental and episodic nature of the serials and how they build up audience loyalty as reflected in Nielsen's ratings. Chapter six discusses the half-hour situation comedy which, with its roots partly in Italian Commedia and partly in domestic comedy, has been displaying progressively increasing social content--abused children, sexual mores, ethnic prejudices, single parents, etc. The situation comedy, some have argued, uses laughter as a social corrective and therapy.

Chapter seven digs deep into the creative process of dramatic programs, which is partly individualistic and partly collective: a creative leader enmeshed in a creative team. It explores and compares the creative endeavors of Grant Tinker and Norman Lear. Chapter eight takes the reader into the mighty and glamorous domain of Dan Rather, Peter

Jennings, Tom Brokaw, and Walter Cronkite and compares their philosophies of news and newscasting. Chapter nine discusses the role of documentaries in the words of Siegfried Kracauer--"from detached pictorial to glowing social messages." It examines the question of whether the networks use serialization of news, called mini-documentaries, as cliffhangers to maintain audience loyalty.

In chapter ten the problem of reality is in focus again. In docudrama reality is condensed, manipulated, and artistically structured to create enhanced dramatic effect. Does poetic beauty falsify historical truth? Some well-known docudramas of recent times are analyzed for historical accuracy and dramatic truth.

Chapter eleven deals with mini-series and novels for television--a fascinating phenomenon because it takes audiences into serious literature. The sale of a novel increases after it has been serialized on television. Television, instead of turning viewers into idiots, sends them back to the reading of books!

Chapter twelve asks the question, "Shouldn't we be demanding more from our television critics than the present heaps of cliches and inanities?" The chapter aims at the training and education of a role model as a social prophet.

Chapter thirteen discusses what ratings measure and measure not. It explains the methods used by the world's largest market research company, A.C. Nielsen, in estimating audiences and the role the ratings play in determining the fate of programs. The chapter defines audiences as delocalized taste collectivities not given to crowd mentality. It also highlights the pressure of vested interests on programming.

The concluding chapter argues that television can't be as dense and difficult as James Joyce is, but it can be very profound and comic as clowns and fools are, sometimes. It also reaffirms the thesis that television redefines the traditional genres, dramatic and nondramatic, and creates them anew.

This book is written with three readers in mind. One is the teacher who might assign this book in classes dealing

Introduction xvii

with television criticism. The second is the enlightened common reader who watches television critically. The third is the foreign reader who would find it a window to American civilization.

NOTES

1. Learned Hand, The Spirit of Liberty, quoted in John D. Steven, Shaping the First Amendment (Beverly Hills: Sage, 1982), p. 18.
2. Clifford G. Christian and James W. Carey, "The Logic and Aims of Qualitative Research" in Guido H. Stempel III and Bruce H. Westly, eds., Research Methods in Mass Communication (Englewood Cliffs, NJ: Prentice-Hall, 1981), pp. 342-362.
3. Thomas Kuhn, The Structure of Scientific Revolution, 2nd ed. (Chicago: University of Chicago Press, 1970), p. 202.

Chapter One

CRITICAL APPROACHES TO TELEVISION

* Literary Criticism Approach
* Semiological-Structural Approach
* Marxist Approach
* Psychoanalytical Model
* Sociological Analysis

With television viewed as the most popular art and a means of utilizing a vast marketplace, the medium has accommodated critical approaches of various kinds. The profusion and fecundity of television programs and their myriad alternative uses--from education to pornography, information to entertainment to evangelism--have invited all kinds of pundits to try out theoretical assumptions about the medium. Because the medium has created a near total dependency in audiences and has become a decisive ecological factor in the growth and decay of the society, it has induced widespread anxiety and apprehensions in the minds of parents, feminists, religious leaders, politicians, educators, criminologists, minorities, or anyone whose niche in society is presumably threatened. This multiplicity of constituencies with interlocking interests has given rise to different perspectives on televisual products, motivating a search for a means to influence the medium and the makers of its products. The assumption appears to be that by controlling Dan Rather, Peter Jennings, or Tom Brokaw, you can reorder and control reality.

The following discussion provides a synopsis of some

critical approaches which critics, as guardians of public taste and social morality, use in evaluating television entertainment, news, and informative programs. Each approach needs a volume to do it full justice, but the purpose here is to give only a journeyman's account of the methods; those who want to delve more deeply into the philosophical aspects can search elsewhere, making use of the bibliography.

LITERARY CRITICISM APPROACH

Television critics trained in literary traditions and criticism have ignored television media-specifics, and have applied the same tenets to television fiction and drama that they use to evaluate imaginative literature. Following Aristotle's Poetics, they have approached TV from the stance of historical criticism, theory of genres, archetypal criticism, and authorial development and growth. Historical criticism studies epochs, movements, and social changes as a context for the study of imaginative literature or media creations. The hero or protagonist becomes a representative voice of the era and an arena for contending forces. Northrop Frye in Anatomy of Criticism[1] has distinguished five types of heroes corresponding with the five epochs of Western literature. Each kind of protagonist can be found in television fiction and drama today:

    A. If the protagonist is "superior in kind both to other men and to the environment of other men, the hero is a divine being, and the story about him will be a myth in the common sense of a story about a god." This type of hero could be seen in the television mini-series "A.D."

    B. If the protagonist is superior in degree to other men and to his environment, he is the typical hero of romance whose actions are marvelous but who is himself identified as a human being. "Incredible Hulk," "E.T.," "Superman," "The Greatest American Hero" are some examples from television. As Frye suggests, the laws of nature are suspended, and we enter a world of enchanted environment where men and beasts exchange roles. Children's Saturday morning cartoon shows belong to this category.

    C. The hero of the "high mimetic mode" is "superior

in degree to other men but not to his natural environment." He is the leader of men. The heroes of Shakespearean tragedy and Milton's epic belong to this category. Television soap opera, because of its serial nature and the necessity of quick bursts of orgasms, is not capable of the high mimetic art; but television films and mini-series do have a place for heroes of the high mimetic art. For instance, the protagonist in "Adam," the film about a missing child, does rise to a tragic level. But Aristotle defined tragedy in such exclusive and idealized rhetoric that critics cannot rest content unless they pronounce the death of tragedy in modern times. Stuart M. Kaminsky has suggested that the equivalent of a hero in this category would be a celebrity, a person with "superior poise," an "ability to perform and make jokes under pressure."[2] This working definition helps us to include in this category protagonists like J.R., Blake Carrington, Adam Chandler, etc., who create ambivalent feelings in us.

D. The protagonist of the "low mimetic mode" is the comic fool or the realistic hero who lives in the same world of probability as we do. We feel superior to the protagonist or sympathize with him, depending upon the circumstances. All television comic characters--for instance, in "Three's Company," "Three's a Crowd," "Alice," etc.--belong to this category. They make us laugh, and we feel superior. The characters in "Hill Street Blues" also belong to this category.

E. The fifth kind of protagonist belongs to the ironic mode, according to Frye. From a superior stance we look down upon this position of "bondage, frustration and absurdity," and probably feel queasy and uneasy. This ironic mode is found in many television mini-series like "Roots."

Generic Approach

The human mind imposes order upon the phenomenal world by creating categories and sets, and by pigeonholing expectations and experiences in a familiar rhythm. Each mode of ordering reality remains stable over a period of time; but within each mode there is a great possibility for innovation and change, as objects may differ from each other yet share common traits. This circumstance is the origin of the term "genre." Genre gives us experiences of novelty and familiarity, and the pleasure of the rhythm of recurrence and association. It gives us a sense of security, a feeling of shared values. As Stuart M. Kaminsky has stated:

> We order things to make sense out of the phenomena of our experiences and senses. Things happen to us. We are bombarded by experiences. We want to and must make sense out of these things, so we start putting them in order. The order may be shared or may be individual. However, people are often considered insane when their sense of order does not conform to a cultural norm. The insane person may employ unshared genres almost exclusively, having lost track of commonality and existing totality in a personal order.[3]

Since television deals with shared experiences that can be categorized according to some story line or formula, genre approach to the understanding of television arts has assumed popularity. A television program like "Three's Company" can be categorized as a situation comedy because of the common traits it shares with similar programs. All soap operas have common generic codes and so are different from police stories, adventure stories, and romances, which are built on different formulaic foundations or codes.

John G. Cawelti suggests that "one basic cultural impact of formulaic literature is toward the maintenance of conventional patterns of imaginative expression."[4] These repeated patterns give cultural stability and are also capable of assimilating "new interests and values." Cawelti, however, makes an intriguing observation which does not bear scrutiny when one considers homogeneous Oriental societies like those of China and Japan where formulaic literature has flourished in the past. He states:

> This process is probably of particular importance in a discontinuous, pluralistic culture like those of modern industrial societies. Therefore, literary formulas tend to flourish in such a society.[5]

There is insufficient evidence to support the argument that an industrial society like France achieved cultural stability because of formulaic literature or formulaic television. One should look to some other center of gravity for formulaic appeal.

Authorial Approach

One popular form of literary criticism has been to study an author's complete works and trace his or her growth and development either chronologically or according to various genres. For instance, critics have studied Shakespeare's tragedies, romantic comedies, tragi-comedies, and historical plays, and have passed their judgments according to some accepted generic ideals; they have turned his works into standards of evaluation or touchstones of literary achievement. A similar approach has been applied to television arts. Horace Newcomb and Robert S. Alley's The Producer's Medium is an attempt to look at the process of television creation as an individual's effort, even though numerous individuals are involved in the creative process from a story idea to editing and programming. While Sophocles, Shakespeare, T.S. Eliot, and other artists may have stood alone in their creations, one hesitates to say the same about Norman Lear, Garry Marshall, Earl Hamner, and other producers. It is difficult to share the gusto with which Newcomb and Alley say:

> Television depends on their creative vision, on their ability to gather and marshal the talents of others who contribute to the television process. These persons of vision and control are the creative producers. They are the television makers, and television will be their medium.[6]

"Hill Street Blues" was the progeny of NBC's Fred Silverman, who hired two producers, Steven Bochco and Michael Kozoll, to execute his vision of a down-to-earth, rough, realistic police show in the tradition of low mimetic art. Who is the real creator of "Hill Street Blues" is not an easy question to answer, as is probably true of all other television shows.

A television critic, bred in the tradition of the literary arts, may compare each season with "The Golden Age of Television," consider the protagonist according to Frye's five categories, classify serials and series according to genres as suggested by Cawleti, or look for some creator-writer-producer whose vision is being executed as drama.

SEMIOLOGICAL-STRUCTURAL APPROACH

Semiology, or semiotics, is the science of signs, sign systems, and signification. Its central concern is how meanings are created and communicated in a culture. In semiology culture could be perceived as a system of "texts" and structures creating a discrete way of life for the members, and seeking their allegiance.

If, instead of being satisfied with the "how" of meaning, we ask who creates "texts" and structures and consequently who controls meanings in a culture, we find semiological-structural analysis reaching out and building bridges with the Marxist-critical theory. This connection, as discussed in the next section, explains hegemony, class domination, and culture as reflexes of the material base.

The Swiss linguist Ferdinand de Saussure, like the American philosopher Charles Peirce (semiotics), suggested that a sign is combination of signifier and signified, and the two are inseparable.[7] It is the relationship between the signifier and the signified, varying from total arbitrariness (the word "God") to [iconic] reality (a photograph), which constitutes the sign.

Interpretation of the meaning of a "text" in a cultural system thus depends upon the degree of arbitrariness of the signifier-signified relationship and the conventions which govern that relationship. Arbitrariness creates mystery and motivates a search for meaning, or it results in loss of meaning and a sign's oblivion. Thus the life of a sign depends upon accepted conventions. Television deals with signs that have iconic actualities whose meanings require few conventions for interpretation. They are less taxing to the audience and are easily accepted. The less conventionalized the sign system, the greater its popularity and use. Or, the greater our familiarity with the conventions of a sign system in a culture, the more quickly we grasp its meaning. For instance, when television shows shelves full of skulls, marching soldiers with swastikas, and the hysterical utterances of Adolf Hitler, we are reminded of a particular era of European history; but when we see similar scenes of neatly packed skulls in an Asian milieu we understand that the fate of the European Jews was only recently re-enacted by a Cambodian Hitler, Pol Pot. And so the iconic reality of European pogrom becomes a convention to understand the meaning of the Kampuchean tragedy.

A sign which originates in an iconic particularity, say the General Motors' Citation automobile, may become generalized to a traffic sign, much as a generalized structure of two children becomes a traffic sign when the photographic reality is blurred. The meaning of a sign would depend upon not only the conventions governing the signifier and signified, but also the context, or the sign's relation with other signs in a system. A tall building alone has its own meaning, but in conjunction with hosts of similar skyscrapers it may become a symbol of New York.

A symbol is different from a sign because the signifier's relations with the signified as symbol are not totally arbitrary. As Saussure says:

> One characteristic of the symbol is that it is never wholly arbitrary; it is not empty, for there is a rudiment of a natural bond between the signifier and the signified. The symbol of justice, a pair of scales, could not be replaced by just another symbol, such as a chariot.[8]

But there is another property of the symbol which differentiates it from the sign. The symbol has emotional dimensions for its users--the Statue of Liberty, the scythe and sickle, for instance.

Contrary to what Saussure has suggested, the relation of the signifier with the signified could be totally arbitrary and yet carry emotional significance. The swastika as a symbol of the Nazi party is a case in point. Its shape has no relationship with the racial superiority it represents. It is an Aryan symbol of good luck. In Nazi Germany it became a symbol of terror for the Jews and dominance for the Nazis. A symbol, therefore, is an emotionalized sign.

Paradigm and Syntagm

A sign system works through paradigms and syntagms. The discrete units of a paradigm exist in similarity as well as in binary opposition. A network of character relationships in a daytime soap opera exhibiting mutual attraction as well as hostility would constitute a paradigmatic structure of the soap opera. Jonathan Culler has suggested that the binary opposition is a "fundamental operation of the human mind basic to the production of meanings."[9] Thus the search for meaning in a "text" involves paradigmatic analysis of the hidden oppositions which generate meaning. In the television movie "A.D.," for instance, it was the ascetic purity of the Christians which constituted a binary opposition to the Romans' massive cruelty and decay. The Romans' cruelty made the Christians' love and gentleness meaningful.

A paradigmatic unit combined with other paradigmatic units in a meaningful sequence constitutes a syntagm. A syntagm could exist in time, as in a narrative, or it could exist simultaneously in space, as in pictures. The paradigmatic chain constituting a narrative (syntagm) depends upon "function," which, according to Russian folklorist Vladimir Propp, is "understood as an act of a character, defined from the point of view of its significance for the course of action."[10]

Thus the syntagmatic analysis of a television program gives us the manifest structure of how events develop in time, whereas the paradigmatic analysis would freeze the unit to understand its subtext or latent meaning. In order to understand the total significance of a cultural text, both paradigmatic and syntagmatic analysis are required. Thus semiotics is an approach which helps to reveal both the latent and the manifest meaning of a cultural text, be it a television drama or a football game.

Two rhetorical terms, metaphor and metonymy, help us further to understand how signs function in television and how latent and manifest meanings are created and transmitted. Metaphor is a figure of speech in which the relationship between the signifier and the signified is asserted through analogy. For instance, "He is a snake" and "His brain is a computer" are metaphors which sum up the essentials of the person. One can extend the notion of a verbal

Critical Approaches to Television

metaphor to a visual metaphor. A television shot of the Big Apple's subway might show a mugging scene which becomes a visual metaphor for the city's social health.

In metonymy a part stands for the whole, a small detail suggests the total concept. A crown stands for a king. A hillbilly suggests the rural way of life of the Appalachian mountains. Both visual metaphors and metonymic communication are used extensively in the television mode. Their use enables an advertiser to say so much in a thirty-second commercial because the audience carries the codes and conventions which produce metaphoric and metonymic communication. (Video rock music is another example of metonymic communication.) Thus the way we associate signs into paradigms and combine paradigms into syntagms depends upon codes and conventions which have been implicitly agreed upon by the society.

In order to limit the meanings created by a sign system the codes must be absolutely constrained, as happens in mathematics. If the codes are less constrained by conventions the meanings rise to many connotative levels, as happens in literature. Extending Jonathan Culler's argument that aesthetic codes "question, parody, generally undermine the code while exploring its possible mutations and extention,"[11] we can say that the artistic attempt at modification of codes sometimes internalizes the meaning, making it private --something the television mode cannot afford because of the need to reach a mass audience. The codes of the television mode are close to real life codes, and the pleasures of watching television cannot be the same as those of reading a novel or an epic.

John Fiske and John Hartley have discussed television programs in <u>Reading Television</u> from the semiotics point of view. In <u>Speaking of Soap Operas</u>, Robert C. Allen approaches television serial drama from a "reader-oriented poetics," or, one might say, through semiotics. Semiotics or semiology has been a model for film criticism for a long time, but its application to the "endless" form of American soap opera produces interesting conclusions.

Allen states three specific problems while considering soap opera as an aesthetic object. First, "as the only narrative form (with the possible exception of the comic strip) predicated upon the impossibility of the closure, the soap opera resists specification as an aesthetic object." Secondly, though traditional criticism, particularly since the Romantics, is obsessed with the "twin notions of artist-as-genius and art-work-as-expression," television soap opera is manufactured on an assembly line, as it were. One cannot talk of an author-auteur but only of a team of writers, producers, and technicians coordinating creation of a collective popular art form.

The third problem in considering soap opera as an art form is that "appreciating true art requires work on the part of the receiver." Television soap opera does not need serious engagement because action moves "glacially slow," and each episode melts into another as a wave into a wave. With these three problems in mind, Allen examines American soap opera "as narrative form, cultural product, advertising vehicle, and a source of aesthetic pleasure for tens of millions of persons"; and he applies insights derived from structural linguistics and the related fields of semiotics, reader-centered critical theory, etc.

Allen makes a beautiful point when he says that the soap opera's narrative (syntagmatic) openness and slowness have been compensated by its associative (paradigmatic) richness of texture, a "complexity that makes the soap opera unique among visual narrative and unmatched in literary narrative except for the most elaborate of epic novels." The source of this complexity is the network of character relationships which exists despite the absence of an apparent center of gravity or a chief protagonist. Because of the movement of the story line through a vast network of contrapuntal relationships, the soap opera becomes "an endless string of excruciatingly retarded subplots related in episodes whose redundancy gives them an almost sisyphean tiresomeness." It is the constant rhythm, periodicity, and expectation of multiple orgasm, apart from the complexity of social, romantic, and kinship relationships, which probably makes soap opera so popular with women.

A principle of uncertainty seems to rule soap opera because of the narrative indeterminacy and paradigmatic complexity of character relationships. Characters in soap opera come and go, disappear, die, and come back mysteriously. This narrative uncertainty, combined with constantly threatened family relationships, creates an ever changing horizon of expectations for soap opera viewers.

There are other reasons for the soap opera's continuous and prosperous existence. As Allen says, "The soap opera's longevity and remarkable resilience derives from its ability to serve the same economic function today that it first served nearly a half century ago: it provides access to a huge audience of heavy consumers (women eighteen to forty-nine years of age) in a cost-effective manner." Robert C. Allen has given us a richly textured account of television serial drama by using the semiotic-structural and reader-centered approach.

MARXIST APPROACH

Marxism is more than communism. Some intellectuals believe that true Marxists live outside the communist countries. Marxism is a powerful tool of cultural analysis for television arts and products. It has great appeal for those critics who have a messianic faith in social justice. One would have thought that they flourished only in the Third World: but they practice their criticism in the affluent establishments of the West also.

Marx propounded that the material base of a society-- the modes of production and ownership--determines the consciousness of individuals, not the other way around. To quote him, "It is not the consciousness of men that determines their being, but on the contrary, their social being determines their consciousness."[12]

Ideas, concepts, consciousness, art, literature, religion, morality, laws, politics, and other symbolic forms are products of material forces. In order to understand television drama, for instance, we must ask questions about the social, political, and economic structure of the society; the ownership, control, and functions of television; and the role of the creators and auteurs. In other words, the television arts, along with other symbolic cultural products like paintings, poems, novels, and architecture, constitute, like laws and governmental forms, the superstructure.

This superstructure rests on an economic base. Whoever

controls the base controls the superstructure. According to
this argument, since the economic base in America is controlled by a relatively few capitalists, they also control the
superstructure--laws, government, art, music, television,
drama, newspapers, etc. The people's consciousness of
their existence depends upon what they read and watch in
the mass media. Their consciousness therefore is a prisoner
of the controllers of the economic base. To free consciousness we must free the economic base, say the Marxists. Here
is what Marx himself said:

> The ideas of the ruling class are, in every age, the
> ruling ideas: i.e., the class which is the dominant
> material force in society is at the same time its dom-
> inant intellectual force. The class which has the
> means of material production at its disposal has con-
> trol at the same time over the means of mental pro-
> duction, so that in consequence the ideas of those
> who lack the means of mental production are, in
> general, subject to it.[13]

The ruling classes, in order to maintain their ownership and control of the economic base, exploit the common
people by controlling their minds and their consciousness
through the superstructure. "Dallas" and "Dynasty," according to this argument, are the tools of American capitalists to keep the economic base as it is. Since men own economic power, soap operas are meant to keep women in serf-
dom. American business, through its cultural products, has
colonized the minds of not only 250 million Americans, but
also the rest of the free world, argue Marxist analysts.
Thus the capitalist media create false consciousness and
seem to be saying, "You never had it so good."

This false consciousness creates alienation of the individual from work and society. Alienation leads to ideology,
cults, religion, drugs, or some form of gratification through
media products and consumerism. In such a society advertising, according to Marxists, becomes a controlling force,
impelling all of us to work more to consume more. Though
Marshall McLuhan was not a Marxist, he made interesting
observations about how advertising colonizes our minds:

> So Hollywood is like the ad agencies in constant
> striving to enter and control the unconscious minds

> of a vast public, not in order to understand it or
> to present these minds as the serious novelist does,
> but in order to exploit them for profit.... The ad
> agencies and Hollywood, in their different ways,
> are always trying to get inside the public mind in
> order to impose their collective dreams on that inner
> stage.[14]

In what ways the minds of people in capitalist societies in America, Britain, France, etc., are more thoroughly colonized than those of people in Russia and China would be an interesting topic for empirical research. One may speculate that human imagination is autonomous and resists colonization, whether through advertising or coercion or hero worship.

A very important concept in Marxist analysis is hegemony, which posits that patterns of subordination and domination exist in any given culture. Hegemonic analysis includes both culture and ideology. Culture is the way of life, and ideology represents the ideas of the dominant classes of the society. Culture and ideology create meanings and values which in turn establish patterns of domination and subordination as something natural, something given. As Raymond Williams states:

> It [hegemony] is a whole body of practices and expectations, over the whole of living: our senses and assignments of energy, our shaping perceptions of ourselves and our world. It is a lived system of meanings and values--constitutive and constituting--which as they are experienced as practices appear as reciprocally confirming. It thus constitutes a sense of reality for most people in the society, a sense of absolute because [sic] experienced reality beyond which it is very difficult for most members of the society to move, in most areas of their lives.[15]

When looking at a mini-series like "Space" we should look at the ideological content, such as whose ultimate interest would the colonization of space serve or why should John Pope say, "I traded my wife to go into space"? Who created such a value in his mind?

Marxist analysts work through such concepts as the material base controlling the superstructure, false consciousness, alienation, consumerism, false heroes, and hegemony. Their analysis is very illuminating, particularly when applied to the flow of information from the industrialized societies of the West and Japan to the Third World. From this point of view the ruling classes in both the West and Russia are trying to establish their hegemony over the Third World societies and over their own people through books, films, television arts, and news flow. The unanswered question is why and how societies change if the ruling classes continue to exercise their hegemony by controlling consciousness-producing superstructures.

THE PSYCHOANALYTICAL MODEL

The ethos of modern times was built on the seminal thinking of Charles Darwin, Karl Marx, Albert Einstein, and Sigmund Freud. Freud conceptualized those urges and demiurges in man which make him human and beast. One of Freud's basic concepts which has passed into international currency is the unconscious. What an individual is aware of is not the same as what his unconscious harbors, and that reality makes him not necessarily a rational person, who bases his acts on logic and reason. In spite of fine intellects capable of the highest philosophical thoughts, humans indulge in irrational acts because of the pressure of the unconscious--a repository of forbidden desires, animal urges, and murderous thought which the conscious self refuses to face and represses.

Human sexuality is a controlling force in the Freudian psychoanalytic model. The sensual-sexual gratification called libido passes through four stages: oral (sucking), in infancy and childhood; anal, connected with excreta; phallic, when the penis or clitoris becomes an object of intense interest, creating an Oedipus complex or an Electra complex; and the genital stage at puberty.

The Oedipus complex is one of Freud's key concepts. All of us in childhood have an unconscious desire to possess our mothers or fathers sexually. When the Greeks saw their own oedipal myth enacted before them, they were fascinated with horror--as if the unconscious had succeeded in defying the conscious without producing any guilt. Control of oedipal desire comes through castration anxiety in boys and penis envy in girls. We repress and turn ourselves into Hamlets, "so conscience doth make cowards of us all."

The unconscious self, the seething cauldron of carnal desires and gory instincts, is what Freud later called the id. The conscious self--the conscience, the moral sense--is the super ego. Between the id and the super ego there is a mediator, the ego. One might say that the nonbiological growth of a child is a process of differentiation among the id, the ego, and the super ego. How does the ego make peace between the id and the super ego and save a person from being torn apart? The anxiety created by the warring id and super ego are warded off by the ego through what psychoanalytical theory calls a defense mechanism. This defense mechanism may consist of repression, whereby the unconscious is barred from communicating with the conscious self; or suppression, when the unwanted material is thrown out of the conscious mind but could be recalled later on. There are hosts of other defense mechanisms--fixation, identification, projection, reaction formation, regression, etc.-- which the ego uses to deal with anxiety-producing situations.

The defense mechanism, however might collapse during dreams. As Erich Fromm says:

> Dreams are understood to be the hallucinatory fulfillment of irrational wishes and particularly sexual wishes which have originated in our early childhood and have not been fully transformed into reaction formations or sublimations. These wishes are expressed as being fulfilled when our conscious control is weakened, as is the case in sleep.[16]

Interpreting dreams is difficult because a latent dream, in order to become a manifest dream, has to pass through symbolism, condensation, displacement, and elaboration. This process is called dream work. The reverse process of going from manifest dream to latent dream is called dream interpretation.

A symbol is a sign, an object or a thing which stands for something else. It has an emotional dimension. The sexual and the aggressive impulses find symbolic representation and thus escape the guilt-producing attention of the super ego. But symbols are not easy to interpret because of their ambivalence. Long pointed objects, for instance, are said to be symbols of the phallus, which may be true in some cases but not in all. Apart from the difficulty of symbols, the fragments of different elements of a dream get combined and condensed together. Sometimes an important element is displaced or substituted by something else. This process of symbolization, condensation, and displacement in dreams is given coherence through elaboration, by which inconsistencies get smoothed and dreams become plausible.

If man is nothing but a bundle of irrational energies, barely controlled by his ego, and since each individual seeks pleasure and power at the cost of others, how can a society be established? If man does not succeed in plucking out his neighbor's eyes or running away with his best friend's wife, it is because of the restraints society creates through religion. According to Freud, "eye for eye and tooth for tooth" is more instinctual than is turning the other cheek. This instinctual aggressiveness is controlled through guilt, which is aggression turned against itself. As Freud says in Civilization and Its Discontents:

> Civilization, therefore, obtains mastery of the individual's dangerous desire for aggression by weakening and disarming it and by setting up an agency within him to watch over it, like a garrison in a conquered city.[17]

The society accepts displacement of aggression through such group activities as sports and religious cults and through organized killings called wars. Collectively a group might surrender its ego and super ego to a leader, a substitute father figure, a führer. Even humor could be a substitute for aggression, as Freud suggested in Jokes and Their Relation to the Unconscious.

Some critics have applied psychoanalytic concepts and insights to the study of literature with interesting results. After all, the great writers of fiction, drama, and poetry have delved deeply into the human psyche, the irrational and emotional forces which play upon our destiny. Freud conceptualized and systematized the psychology found in Sophocles, Shakespeare, Tolstoy, Dostoevsky, and others.

Critical Approaches to Television

Since television fiction and drama are made of the same stuff as traditional drama and fiction, the critic has been irresistibly tempted to apply the same psychoanalytical approach to them.

Another kind of psychoanalytic critic argues that television criticism would be better served if the techniques of dream interpretation were applied to television. There are some superficial similarities between dreams and television. Peter H. Wood[18] has suggested such congruities as the visual quality, symbolic nature, wish fulfillment, and topicality of both television and dreams. The comparison makes television "a vivid projection of our collective subconscious." As Susan Sontag has stated, "All observable phenomena are bracketed, in Freud's phrase, as manifest content. This manifest content must be probed and pushed aside to find the true meaning--latent content--beneath."[19]

This view brings us close to the goals of semiotists who probe the manifest content to reach the latent meaning. Susan Sontag's approach, as an extension of Freud's theory of psychoanalysis, turns all human acts into blinds to be torn to see the reality. Thus all television programming constitutes the manifest content of the collective dream of the society under analysis, and probing it deeply for latent content becomes imperative to diagnose the sickness from which the society suffers.

SOCIOLOGICAL ANALYSIS

Sociologists approach the public arts, literature, music, and television through the conceptual framework of social functions and relations. Risking a generalization, one might venture to say that sociologists concern themselves with change and integration in society and empirically observe these phenomena in all societal functions. Cultural expression, in any form and media, has therefore some functions based upon some values. The values may derive their strength from class, race, role, and status, and may produce stereotypes, alienation, anomie, and particular life styles that tolerate homosexuality, unwed motherhood, etc.

For sociologists television is a kind of mapping or seismic device to observe and record the stabilizing and destabilizing forces in society. Aesthetics is not the sociologists' chief concern. Their argument is simple: since audiences have needs to gratify and since television serves this function very well, television would reveal its audiences' changing tastes, values, and modes of behavior affecting the society. Sociological analysis studies effects empirically, in a measurable, verifiable, and replicable form.

Both Arthur Asa Berger[20] and Denis McQuail[21] have given a comprehensive summary of the uses and gratifications which television provides audiences. The four broad categories of audience uses of television are:[22]

I. Information
    a. Monitoring environmental and social changes and conditions in the world
    b. Finding tips on personal and practical affairs
    c. Self-improvement
    d. Gaining knowledge to bolster one's self-confidence
    e. Fulfilling one's curiosity

II. Personal Identity
    a. Strengthening personal values
    b. Finding role models
    c. Identifying with superiors and valued others
    d. Self-knowledge

III. Social Integration
    a. Understanding others
    b. A sense of togetherness and belonging through identification
    c. A source of conversation and social exchange
    d. Learning social roles
    e. Integration with family and friends
    f. Imaginary companionship

IV. Entertainment
    a. Diversion, relaxation, and passing time
    b. Enjoying beauty and culture
    c. Catharsis or emotional release
    d. Sexual titillation

Since the gratification needs of each individual television viewer differ from time to time, their choices and motives for watching a particular television program would be reflected in ratings and other empirical observations. One such empirical mode of observing television program variability is through Content Analysis.

Content Analysis

Berelson gave content analysis research respectability and defined it as a "research technique for the objective, systematic and quantitative description of the manifest content of communication."[23] The emphasis is upon what is on the screen, obvious and measurable according to some categorical system related to the research purpose. Krippendorff defined content analysis as a research technique for making replicable and valid references between data and their context.[24] Both definitions exclude subjectivity, latent content, and individual interpretations. The meaning depends on the frequency of occurrence of a particular variable, say aggressiveness or violence, in television drama. If a variable is not measurable it cannot be studied in content analysis. Therefore content analysis requires an operational definition of constructs (concepts). Operational definition asks the question, How do you measure it? The measurement of a variable could be by a scale of one to five or by a yes/no binary. The simplest example of operational definition is the Miss America beauty contest, where what matters is how each factor, such as a contestant's appearance in an evening gown, in a swim suit, etc., gets measured on a scale. It is simply the highest average that counts. If there were a contest to select the most virtuous woman, then virtue would have to be defined operationally so that different judges could measure it independently.

This popular method of analysis is used for various purposes. Katzman[25] studied characters, events, and problems in a week's showing of soap operas; Gerbner[26] compared the world of television violence with violence in real life--a kind of reality check. Content analysis could be used as a license renewal argument to the effect that a station was unfair to a certain group; or to study cultivation analysis, i.e., how the dominant ideas presented in television were correlated with similar ideas cultivated by the people.

The essential steps for using content analysis methods are these:

1. Define the universe (population) and select a representative sample of the content, much as we do with human population. For example, women characters in prime time television from May 1985 to October 1985 would constitute a population.

2. Establish a category system relevant to the research problem. As Berelson pointed out, categories should be clearly formulated, mutually exclusive, exhaustive, and reliable. Categories are like pigeonholes into which units of analysis are placed. For example, sitcoms, children's shows, docudramas, police dramas, etc., could constitute categories.

3. Define the units of analysis which are actually to be counted and placed into each category--for example, characters, sequences, aggressive acts, violence, etc.

4. Establish a quantification system for the measurement of units of analysis in each category. We may count the frequency of occurrence of a particular unit and compare it with the frequencies of units in other categories, and also with overall content. If the frequency of appearance of blacks, for instance, in a prime time program is 2 percent while their actual population is 12 percent, we could draw an inference about the position of blacks in the society and how adequately they are represented in television.

Content analysis is a very widely used method of television research. It is systematic, objective, and quantifiable and therefore replicable. There is, however, a serious problem of reliability, which is being attacked by using computers for the purpose of coding content. The problem of validity is also serious. How far do the categories actually exist in the text? Is the researcher imposing his own category system and thus creating meanings which do not exist in the text? Content analysis ignores the subtext and does not lead to the latent meaning, the deeper significance of the text, and the question of beauty. As Sartre put it:

> Every investigation implies the idea of a nudity

which one brings out into the open by clearing away the obstacles which cover it, just as Actaeon clears away the branches so that he can have a better view of Diana at her bath. More than this, knowledge is a hunt. Bacon called it the hunt of Pan. The scientist is the hunter who surprises a white nudity and violates by looking at it.[27]

Social and behavioral science methods depend upon observation and experience, which are transformed into empirical data that meet the conventional norms of reliability and validity. But observation and experience are grounded in theory. Theory gives rise to hypothesis--a statement of relationship between two variables, say television violence and children's behavior--which must be verified by observation and experience through measurement. What Sartre said is true, and the nature of reality changes when you look at it from the paradigm of a social scientist. Violence can be very beautiful; it can also be very destructive.

When a phenomenon like television overwhelms us and has a decisive effect upon every facet of life, a single method or a paradigm tends to distort our vision rather than help us in exploring the nature of reality. Instead of being satisfied with a partial view of reality, we must shift perspectives, philosophical stance, and paradigms to understand and comprehend the totality. Instead of showing a contemptuous disregard for empirical research by calling its practitioners "number-crunchers" or condemning qualitative-critical research as wooly-headed, we should test the conclusions of each method by the methods of the others.

As our first task we must explore the nature of the television medium and its effects on our view of the phenomenal world, to see how television as a part of the larger totality conditions other structures and is conditioned by them. Not only television text and context, but also the audience's mode of consciousness (network of assumptions) and the centralizing and organizing symbol of society are important in understanding television in American culture. Hence the need for a pluralistic, multi-model approach.

NOTES

1. Northrop Frye, Anatomy of Criticism (Princeton: Princeton University Press, 1975), pp. 33-34.
2. Stuart M. Kaminsky and Jeffrey H. Mahan, American Television Genre (Chicago: Nelson-Hall, 1985), pp. 43-52.
3. Ibid., p. 20.
4. John G. Cawelti, Adventure, Mystery and Romance (Chicago: The University of Chicago Press, 1976), p. 35.
5. Ibid., p. 35.
6. Horace Newcomb and Robert S. Alley, The Producer's Medium (New York: Oxford University Press, 1983), p. xvii.
7. Ferdinand de Saussure, Course in General Linguistics (New York: McGraw-Hill, 1966), p. 67.
8. Ibid., p. 68.
9. Jonathan Culler, Structuralist Poetics: Structuralism, Linguistics and the Study of Literature (Ithaca: Cornell University Press, 1976), p. 56.
10. Vladimir Propp, Morphology of Folk Tales (Austin: University of Texas Press, 1968), p. 21.
11. Jonathan Culler, p. 100.
12. T.B. Bottomore and Maximilien Rubel, eds. Karl Marx: Selected Writings in Sociology and Social Philosophy (New York: McGraw-Hill, 1963), p. 51.
13. Ibid., p. 78.
14. Marshall McLuhan, The Mechanical Bride (Boston: Beacon, 1978), p. 97.
15. Raymond Williams, Marxism and Literature (New York: Oxford University Press, 1977), p. 110.
16. Erich Fromm, The Forgotten Language: An Introduction to the Understanding of Dreams, Fairy Tales and Myths (New York: Grove Press, 1957), p. 67.
17. Sigmund Freud, Civilization and Its Discontents (New York: W.W. Norton, 1962), p. 71.
18. Peter H. Wood, "Television as Dream," in Understanding Television, Richard Adler ed. (New York: Praeger, 1981), pp. 55-72.
19. Susan Sontag, Against Interpretation, quoted in Understanding Television, Richard Adler ed. (New York: Praeger, 1981), p. 63.
20. Arthur Asa Berger, Media Analysis Technique (Beverly Hills: Sage Publications, 1982), pp. 98-107.

21. Denis McQuail, *Mass Communication Theory* (Beverly Hills: Sage Publication, 1983), pp. 78-84.
22. Ibid., pp. 82-83.
23. B. Berelson, *Content Analysis in Communication Research* (Glencoe: Free Press, 1952), p. 18.
24. K. Krippendorff, *Content Analysis: An Introduction to Its Methodology* (Beverly Hills: Sage, 1980), p. 21.
25. N. Katzman, "Television Soap Operas," *Public Opinion Quarterly* (36: 1972), pp. 200-12.
26. G. Gerbner, "The Television World of Violence," in *Mass Media and Violence*, D. Lang, R. Baker, and S. Ball, eds. (Washington, DC: U.S. Government Printing Office, 1969), pp. 311-339.
27. Jean-Paul Sartre, *Being and Nothingness*, H.B., trans. (New York: Pocket Books, 1966), p. 738.

Chapter Two

THE TELEVISION MODE

* The Dramatic Mode
* Television as Erotica
* News That Entertains
* Why Is Television So Amusing?
* Psychology of TV Watching

Television communication is a process of signifying, perpetuating, and propagating our culture and our civilization. From the daybreak news about the dollar's rise and fall in the world market, through the betrayals and confirmations of domestic life in daytime serials, to the masterly demonstrative and dramatic narratives of world events anchored by Dan Rather, Peter Jennings, and Tom Brokaw, and then to the prime time dramas of J.R.s and Blakes, Sue Ellens and Alexis Colbys, capped by Carsonian nocturnal satires, we live in perpetuity, understanding and partially understanding ourselves and America's place in the world. To comprehend the significance of the television mode requires understanding the dominant and controlling symbol in American culture: the free marketplace of goods and ideas. Without the centrality of the free marketplace the television mode would not seek out larger and larger audiences, giving Nielsen ratings a delphic-oracular or predictive role.

The free marketplace demands pollsters and opinion polls, market research and obsession with measurement, decision under uncertainty and quantification. It confirms its respect for facts and distrust of opinions. Its currency is exchange, mutuality, consensus, and survival. It bargains for buyers and measures itself on stock exchanges. Television, as a reflex of this centralizing and preponderating force in American life, perpetuates the present mode of consciousness. This statement has serious implications. It means the televisual mode in America differs from the mode in such closed societies as China and Russia, because television is culture-bound to a great extent. Similarly, in a semisocialist country like Britain, where the pressure of ratings (and advertising) is not as fierce and brutal as in the United States, cultural products and information processing in the form of news stories are also different. The same television mode cannot sustain a capitalist society, a semisocialist class-ridden society, and a communist society. In American culture the free marketplace of goods and ideas and the televisual mode exist in a dynamic interrelationship of great force. The soap operas, sitcoms, bloopers, trivia games, and evening news ritualize the free marketplace of goods and ideas through which we see the Japanese cars, the weakening pound, the antinuclear demonstration in Frankfurt, and the American dream in the making and unmaking. Blake Carrington, Tina Turner, Dan Rather, and the rest must serve the purpose of the marketplace. As Davis Marc has said:

> Television's greatest power ... is its ability to select and legitimate the "normal." The importance of normalcy cannot be over-estimated in the modern political state. It is the principle that regulates the charcter of all mass-produced consumer goods and services.[1]

The "normal" in every society is controlled by its centralizing symbol: class in Britain, party in Russia, Islamic orthodoxy in Khomeini's Iran, the free marketplace of goods and ideas in America. As an ally of the free marketplace of goods and ideas television offers a dual mode of perception--diegetic and dramatic. Among the several possibilities of the television mode (recording of life's randomness and society "red in tooth and claw"; rehearsed and reconstructed realities, as in docudrama; highly imaginative filmic creations or televised literature) the free market chooses several permutations and combinations to capture the largest audience encompassing the normal distribution curve.

The free marketplace of goods and ideas is not a self-conscious monolithic organization imposing its will upon the audience through coercive persuasion or indoctrination; rather, it is a conglomeration of competing interests wanting to exploit the demographics reflected in Nielsen's mirror. It is important to understand the concept of the audience's mode of consciousness, as discussed earlier. Only when the television microcosm corresponds with the audience's mode of consciousness is a large audience drawn out of the normal distribution. This fact explains an audience of 100 million for an event like "The Day After" or a Super Bowl. Television, unlike any other popular art, has both explanatory and predictive capabilities. It not only expounds the complexities of modern American society, but also shows the realm of alternative probabilities: it has both "choric-bardic"[2] and delphic-oracular functions.

> In our terms, this central cultural function is best described by the "choric" nature of television. We take the term from the role of the chorus in Greek drama. The chorus expressed the ideas and emotions of the group, as opposed to those of individuals. Its focus is on the widely shared, the remembered, the conventional responses that take into account the notion of socially approved--because socially tested--notions of heroism, epic event, and collective memory. Dependent on widely recognized "types" rather than on the unique, the choric forms render for their audiences patterns of experience within which to couch new problems and issues. They aid in the maintenance of society, but also in the repair and renovation of that society.[3]

The choric-bardic function of television perpetuates the centrality of the free marketplace of goods and ideas and has accentuated the medium's predilection for a dramatic mode of presenting reality. The delphic-oracular function of television (see chapter 13) necessitates its adopting an empirical mode of interpreting reality and projecting it into the future as an arc of probability. Thus television is like a two-headed snake. It dramatizes and validates reality, making television the most powerful surrogate of the central and controlling force in American culture: the free marketplace of goods and ideas, the free-enterprise-free-speech continuum, the grand alliance between the First Amendment and capitalism.

THE DRAMATIC MODE

Dramatic perception and empirical perception, as a kind of double seeing, are not necessarily at loggerheads with each other. As Sergei Eisenstein put it, "At this late date no one needs really be reminded that quantity and quality are not two different properties of a phenomenon but only different aspects of the same phenomenon."[4] The empirical mode--observation, verification, and replication--uses the redemptive power of television to investigate those covered and concealed facts of the Vietnam War, for instance, which the generals thought were buried with the bones of America's youth. The dramatic mode of television reconstructs the historical reality into an enveloping and shocking 1982 documentary, "The Uncounted Enemy: A Vietnam Deception." As Mike Wallace, the narrator of the CBS documentary, said:

> We Americans were misinformed about the nature and size of the enemy we were facing, and tonight we're going to present evidence of what we have come to believe was a conscious effort--indeed, a conspiracy--at the highest levels of American military intelligence to suppress and alter critical intelligence on the enemy in the year leading up to the Tet Offensive.[5]

Wallace's statement might normally have gone unnoticed because it was too overwhelming or too mundane for us to cope with, but when its abstractness was dramatically reconstructed as a documentary, the audience felt that tragedy on their pulses. The empirical mode and the dramatic mode blended to redeem truth from the dustbin of history. Keats once remarked that truth is not truth unless we feel it on our pulses. Truth for television does not exist unless it can be demonstrated and dramatized--a view derived from the culturally central and dominant position of the free-speech-free-market continuum in American society.

The imperatives of the free and competitive marketplace of goods and ideas have transformed television time into a highly prized marketplace commodity to be sold in units of seconds. Since the commercial value of segmented time depends upon the audience size picked up from the normal curve, television programming has assumed the dramatic mode of communication as being the most engaging, entertaining, involving mode--history bears witness to man's interest in drama in all climes and cultures. No doubt television could adopt a linear and discursive mode of communication: all news and commercials could be presented as in newspapers or as in those countries where the free marketplace of goods and ideas does not have a controlling and centralizing role. But American television's dramatic mode of communication in newscasting, sportscasting, talkshows, game shows, and commercials is necessarily a product of the free market's centrality, which demands maximum audience exposure or the biggest chunk of the normal curve. The optimum alignment of television, audience, and free market necessitates a dramatic mode of communication.

In the process of maximum alignment between the free market and the audience, the television mode has liberated humans from the tyranny of the written word, discursive thought, and hair-splitting rationalization. It has restored to us our natural mode of thought. As Martin Esslin has observed:

> ... whatever else it might present to its viewers, television as such displays the basic characteristics of the dramatic mode of communication--and <u>thought</u>, for drama is also a method of thinking, of experiencing the world and reasoning about it. After all, much of our thinking consists in devising scenarios for different situations and decisions--which is using drama as a form of thought.[6]

The dramatic mode is not necessarily plotting of action to create suspense or to suspend disbelief; but it consists, so far as televisual communication is concerned, in using spoken-discursive language to frame sequentially arranged audiovisual events theatrically in order to enable the audience to experience reality in the "process of becoming."[7] The television camera redeems the reality of Lebanon, Love Canal, Andy Rooney's problems with gadgets; but it is the framing and sequencing, partial staging and partial rehearsing, which thrills, involves, and envelops the audience in the multidimensional reality. It is in this sense that the television mode is dramatic. Televisual discourse is dialogical and confrontational, nonlinear and processional. The logical exposition of the spoken word in television exists in

The Television Mode

dialectical tension with the montage flow of audiovisual images, creating suspense but not diminishing television's redemptive empirical function.

Consider sportscasting of a Super Bowl. Many cameras are carefully planted in positions where the most dramatic aspects of an action can be visualized. The sportscaster-commentator selects the same action in different frames and monitors these to the audience from different perspectives--from multiple live-action shot to slow-motion replay--simultaneously recording multidimensional reality and giving it dramatic intensity. Events are being observed, verified, replicated, and dramatized as they are linguistically framed.

We understand with compassion when we see Ethiopians dying of famine; but when Peter Jennings says America is hungry and then shows the camera dwelling upon a ragged man searching a waste heap for food, the reality of hunger in America is not only empirically rendered but also dramatized. Not fictionalization of reality, but reality's redemption through confrontation is an aspect of the dramatic mode of communication. According to Martin Esslin, "in drama the complex multilayered image predominates over the spoken word."[8] In television, however, the spoken word and multilayered imagery exist in dialectical tension--each is a partial commentary upon the other, complementing and supplementing an aspect of reality and making it more engaging, with greater emotional impact. This quality of television--its capacity to present abstract ideas in a discursive manner and its need to dramatize them--makes it superior to any other existing mode of mass communication. Since television deals with personalities who in turn handle ideas and events, it becomes very important for networks and TV stations to select their newscasters and anchormen for personality and looks. If Dan Rather's personal charms, coupled with his journalistic abilites, could carve out a substantial share of the audience and over a year gross the network $50 million more in advertising revenues, then he is worth his millions in annual compensation. But his world news and views, seen as a procession of framed and partially staged events, do not detract from verifiable reality; rather the reality is enchanced, multiplexed.

TELEVISION AS EROTICA

Motives for turning to television depend upon the time of day. Since news is limited to certain hours of the day (despite CNN), people turn to television for other reasons than to keep abreast of political and economic events. Television is a great source of diversion and entertainment, ranging from the voyeuristic delights of peeping into bedrooms of glamorous soap opera stars to the masochistic and bloody fights in a boxing arena. Since the market has an insatiable thirst for demographics, television provides volumes of exciting programs in order to keep audiences glued to their sets. "Don't go away, we'll be back," is a repetitive, urgent appeal often heard on television. Because television offers an abundance of fantasy but lacks that sense of special occasion associated with movies and legitimate theater, the station's fear that the audience might not be there is genuine. This fear has been aggravated by the increasing availability of cable and the profusion of channels. The solution to the problem of audience fickleness has been to soak viewers with the fantasia of a dream world in a structured, habit-forming pattern. Serials and minidocumentaries are among the devices used to hook the audience and create viewer loyalty.

Daytime serials provide the audience an opportunity for being on a slow-moving commuter train, where the same characters act out their adulteries, murders, betrayals, subterfuges, and fleeting moments of happiness. Each segment gives viewers a different episodic content and yet assures them of the same people and places returning at the same time next day. Housewives plan their days according to scheduling of their favorite soaps, as families anchor their activities around prime time weekly serials. The recurring characters in course of time become as familiar as members of a family. Our world is as much inhabited by Jack Tripper, J.R., Blake, Erica, Adam, and Bob Hart, as it is by Tip O'Neill, Kennedy, Reagan, and Jesse Helms. For a common man all these characters inhabiting a fantasy world provide cozy familiarity. In fact, audiences see their own problems and aspirations reflected in them, confirming television's bardic function. It is like the collective psyche being projected on the screen. As Martin Esslin says:

   The pantheon of archetypal characters in ever

The Television Mode

recurring situations on present-day American television does, I believe, accurately reflect the collective psyche, the collective fears and aspirations, neuroses and nightmares of the average American, as distinct from the factual reality of the state of the nation. Does not the prominence of hospitals and disease in story lines indicate a national preoccupation with health, even a certain hypochondria? Do not the sex kittens of the evening series accurately represent current ideals of beauty? Are not the mix-ups and grotesqueries of family situation comedies an accurate, if exaggerated, scenario of the family life, real or fantasized? These problems may present caricatures of real situations, but like all good caricatures and all myth, they merely intensify and enlarge the true features of the daydreams from which they spring.[9]

The networks thus capture the audience by creating erotic, segmental, and episodic dramas which, like daydreams, recur day after, season after season.

Since the audience has developed a cultural taste for this recurrent pattern of serial episodes, the popularity of miniseries and serialized novels on television is not difficult to appreciate. The audience has developed a new taste for delayed denouements, partial denouements, even multiple orgasms. Each television season brings hosts of bizarre cliffhangers which entice audience members to look deep into the precipices of their psyches.

The increasing appetite for series-serials has spilled over to newscasting, and consequently television stations are doing more investigative reporting in the form of mini-documentaries. Through its crack investigative news team a station reaches a larger audience, creates a new audience, and holds it in expectation till the mini-documentary is completed. Mini-documentaries deal with drug abuse, mental health, institutions, slum conditions, used cars, and child abuse. Serial programming, from the erotic daydream world of soaps to serialized television news, keeps the audience coming back.

NEWS THAT ENTERTAINS

Scholars and researchers have been asserting for a long time that television entertainment in the form of fictional drama and music has cast its shadow on the presentation of news and has blurred the boundaries between fiction and reality. The maddening race for the demographics of the normal curve forces an entertainment format on the actualities of life. What is true of the televisual mode, however, is equally true of any other mode of communication. In print journalism the value of headlines, the placement of stories, the reverse pyramidal mode of story presentation, and various other stylistic tricks of the trade entertain and distort reality. It is impossible to separate the cognitive and affective attributes of a communicative act, be it in a televisual or discursive mode.

Recall a scene from an episode of "Dynasty" when Steven confronts his father Blake Carrington: "I love Claudia very much. I also love Luke...." The agony of confession and its resigned acceptance in a moment of suspended silence could never be expressed factually. Only a dramatic enactment could have redeemed Steven's reality, just as only a television camera could have brought to us the reality of the futility, waste, and horror of the Vietnam War--the so-called living room war.[10]

All forms of communication partly rest on information and partly on entertainment for their success. Communication is a cognitive-affective continuum. The strategy of successful communication as measured in Nielsen's ratings lies in striking a judicious balance between the drama and the actuality--harnessing drama to redeem reality. Credibility does not depend upon delineation of facts, but upon enactment of facts. Journalist Harry Ashmore has commented:

> The journalist who attempts to do no more than simply record what he and others saw and heard at the site of the news will not only have an unreadable report but a hopelessly incomplete one; selecting and ordering the available facts and placing them in context is a subjective process, and if he is dealing with any human event that really matters his own values will color his judgement.[11]

The Television Mode 33

In The Newscasters, Frank Magid, a media consultant famed for his philosophy of action news, is quoted as saying: "Ratings rise when the broadcaster is successful in exposing the listener to what he wants to hear, in the very personal way he wants to hear it. In terms of news, this means ratings are improved not when listeners are told what they should know, but what they want to hear."[12]

There is neither empirical nor historical evidence to substantiate Frank Magid's observations. In his intuitive way Magid has suggested that the dramatization of news would net a larger audience by bringing viewers to the ringside and making them watch as witnesses to life's events. If, as he claims, the networks and local stations are offering only those stories which audiences want to hear, then there would be no news about the murder of nuns in El Salvador, the killing of American troops in Lebanon, crime in New York, the collapse of banks, the pollution of lakes and rivers, and the cyanide lacing of Tylenol. The networks would be saying, "God's in his heaven, All's right with the world!" and there would be no audience. The television stations are increasingly resorting to a mini-documentary format to delve deeply into important problems and to incite political action. As Leo Bogart has said, "The form in which we perceive reality has been transformed by the evolution of communication technology, of which television is the most recent example, and further important changes are on the way."[13] The emerging communication technologies, the merging of television and computer, will enhance man's reach for reality, rather than confuse reality with illusion, as Leo Bogart fears.

WHY IS TELEVISION SO AMUSING?

From an artist's point of view art is a serious act of imaginative creation, but from the viewer/audience's subjective stance it is entertainment. Unless a person is a student of literature, the only reason why he or she would read James Joyce's Ulysses is to seek pleasure, to have a feeling of expansiveness and euphoria which comes after a long struggle. Art exists for the artist and the critic, but for most of us Beethoven's Fifth Symphony and Shakespeare's King Lear are great entertainment. Students of aesthetics and literary criticism are familiar with the concept of vicarious experience provided by works of art, including popular art. Though television watching does not involve as serious an engagement as reading an epic, it does help viewers to extend themselves and to intensify their experiences by providing vicarious existence. Did we not experience vicariously the pain and sorrow of Adam's parents when we watched the docudrama of the missing child? The experience was rewarding through expansion of our sympathies for a family we never met. Television does not help people to escape, but it helps them to expand to unknown dimensions of emotional and imaginative experiences even when they are watching news--say, Sadat going to Jerusalem or the Pope meeting his would-be assassin.

"Calm of mind and all passion spent," the state of mind induced by various fictional drama, is not a common fare on television. But an audience does feel entertained by tearjerkers, horror movies, and suspense drama because such programs exhaust the emotions. A viewer achieves a different kind of calmness, the kind one feels after getting over a nightmare. Such shows, like a roller coaster, show the viewer not a way to escape from life's problems, but how to see new dimensions of reality. Intrinsically, all human beings know the limitations imposed by the senses and the immense possibilities offered by imagination. Television, in a manner of speaking, conspires with imagination to overcome the limits of our physical senses. Imagine the breathtaking view of the earth from space, an astronaut floating in dark immensity, the birth of a baby as revealed by slow motion, time-lapse television photography, the blossoming of a bud into a flower, a caterpillar becoming a butterfly. Television has not only freed man from the tyranny of the written word, but also from the limitations of the five senses; it tends to be coextensive with man's imagination.

Not only sports but all artistic activities correlated with motion, like ballet, dance, opera, and theater, have become enjoyable because of the mobile, floating, hop-jumping perspective of multi-locus and multi-focus camera shots. Television has enhanced our capacities for enjoyment in all fields of human activity--art, science, news, sports--because it recovers those dimensions of reality which ordinarily are not accessible to our senses. Most of the time when viewers turn on their tubes they expect to see the unexpected, not the unreal but the real as enacted drama, the real which they could not see or hear, something like the black hole in space, the music of the spheres, the fall of a president, the beating of a mechanical heart--stuff of drama as reality. Hence the perpetual fascination with television, the redeemer of the lost dimensions of reality.

PSYCHOLOGY OF TV WATCHING

Human beings are environment dependent, and as psychologists and educators such as Jean Piaget have told us, environmental enhancement or deprivation influences a person's innate capacities for learning and information processing as well as his or her emotional state. The way we make sense of the world depends upon the interaction of two environments:

1. The internal environment, consisting of immediate concerns, like personal worries, fears, phobias, and fantasies, and of cultural archetypal images like the savior on the cross, a witch-hunting McCarthy, E.T., etc. This internal environment is constantly changing and is yet the same. It is collective as well as individual and exists in an everflowing stream of consciousness.

2. The external environment, consisting of the corporate world, government, technology, international events, etc.

It is the interaction of these two environments which enables an individual to process information and establish emotional homeostasis. The process of living consists in how much and how soon we convert the external environment into the internal environment and how we use this augmented internal environment to further process the changing external environment. Deprived of the external environment, we feed on our internal stream of consciousness, daydreams, fantasies, and nightmares.

This interior landscape articulated as silent interior monologue constitutes what we earlier called mode of consciousness. This mode of consciousness determines how much information and learning will take place in a given case. A child would be confused and frightened while watching a live broadcast of a heart transplant or Othello smothering beautiful Desdemona in her bed. A child's cognitive-affective terrain, or mode of consciousness, is not so well integrated as to withstand and understand such outrages as the violence done to a human body to save a life or for reasons of honor and jealousy.

The mode of consciousness, which varies from individual to individual, also creates differentiated anticipation and expectations and therefore different capacities and motivations for information processing, learning, and deriving entertainment from the environment. This mode of consciousness is not only individual but also collective in nature. For instance, Khomeini's Iranian society as a whole has a collective mode of consciousness which regards America as a stereotypic external environment, although individual Iranians--students who have lived in the U.S. or those who have relatives here--may have different individual expectations and anticipations.

This individual mode of consciousness turns off and on external environmental stimuli and gives each individual selectivity in dealing with wanted or unwanted information or entertainment. Jerome L. Singer talks of such deliberate volition on the part of each human being:

> ... our ongoing thought and our daydreaming play a rather important role in how we organize information and in how we begin to set up new plans and anticipations for our future behaviors. In the course of such continuous mental activity, we are clearly also laying the groundwork for carrying forward our major motives and values. We are creating intentions that have decision making and action implication.[14]

Humans are not passive receivers of information or entertainment available from the external environment, but rather they exercise choices dictated by their cognitive-affective terrain or mode of consciousness.

The question, therefore, is which of the external environmental factors--the linear discursive mode, as in reading, or the multi-dimensional television mode--would activate the internal cognitive-affective terrain or mode of consciousness so that a person is motivated to learn, to seek information, or to amuse himself? Before we attempt to marshal evidence to answer this question, it is imperative to explicate the widely accepted two-hemisphere brain theory. M.S. Gazzaniga has stated in The Bisected Brain[15] that the human brain is divided into two subsystems. The left side of the brain is correlated with right-handed persons and has evolved to process information which requires logic, mathematical formulas, grammar, and all those human activities which need abstraction, sequential ordering, deductive and inductive reasoning. For a left-handed person, the right side of the brain would perform these activities.

The right side of the brain processes whole scenes, images, emotional states, or totalities. Its function is holistic, intuitive, and creative. Some psychologists have suggested that in girls the right hemisphere is more developed than the left, which explains why they do not do as well in mathematics and hard sciences as boys do. There is also sufficient evidence that culture discourages girls at very early ages from excelling in subjects like math, accounting, etc., and consequently their left hemispheres are not allowed to develop fully. It is also certain that the degree of development of both hemispheres varies from individual to individual. Since the information-processing methods of the two hemispheres are different, each individual makes different uses of both hemispheres. The left hemisphere's information processing method is sequential, like that of a computer, while the right part of the brain registers information wholly and simultaneously, as an audiovisual camera does--patterns of meaningful sound synchronized with corresponding pictures. Briefly, information can be handled by the left brain in a verbal-logical-sequential system or by the right brain in an audiovisual system. Obviously, the most efficient method of information processing and learning is when the left brain records sequentially what the right brain has acquired audiovisually and holistically.

Reading demands more effort than television watching because the language has to be decoded by the left brain into meanings which in turn provoke and kindle the audiovisual imagery that creates fantasies and daydreams and all the pleasures we associate with reading. The meaning of the text is largely a function of our interior landscape, mode of consciousness, or cognitive-affective terrain. For instance, reading Hamlet gives us a different kind of aesthetic enjoyment than seeing Laurence Olivier acting as Hamlet on the screen. Similarly, no amount of reading will tell us as much about the behavior of whales as a National Geographic documentary showing us that whales seek man's friendship; thus our mode of consciousness is qualitatively changed. From Moby Dick to whales as man's friends is a great stride--a reality redeemed by television since reading is an autonomous activity, self-paced and lonely.

The great advantage of the televisual mode, and hence its immense popularity, is that it engages the whole brain, both the verbal-logical-sequential and the pictorial-holistic parts of the brain. If the spoken words or voiceover contradict what the video-shows, then probably information overload becomes a total noise and viewers will turn off the television. But the evidence is that spoken language has become more refined because of the necessity of its interaction with visual images. The play-by-play and blow-by-blow description of sports events is an example of the visual and the verbal working together to supplement and complement each other. Plays and novels have found television to be their natural mode of expression. Thus Shakespeare's plays are well rendered on television, as the BBC and Time-Life ventures show. Television has rehabilitated the spoken word which was lost by theater and cinema.

In television the verbal and the visual exist in dialectical relationship, both appealing to the whole mind, a function which reading cannot perform. Television redeems reality in a way no other mode of communication can do because, due to its capacity for multi-focus and multi-locus visualization, it can present multi-dimensional reality simultaneously. The myriad possibilities of the television mode have just begun to be explored.

NOTES

1. David Marc, Demographic Vistas (Philadelphia: University of Pennsylvania Press, 1984), p. 134.
2. John Fiske and John Hartley, Reading Television (London: Methuen, 1978), p. 85.
3. Horace Newcomb and Robert S. Alley, The Producer's Medium (New York: Oxford University Press, 1983), p. 31.

4. Sergei Eisenstein, The Film Sense, trans. and ed. by Jay Leyda (New York: Harcourt Brace Jovanovich, 1975), p. 8.
5. Don Kowet and Sally Bedell, "How CBS News Broke the Rules and Got General Westmoreland," TV Guide (May 29, 1982), p. 44.
6. Martin Esslin, The Age of Television (San Francisco: W.H. Freeman and Company, 1982), p. 8.
7. Roland Barthes, Image--Music--Text, trans. Stephen Heath (New York: Hill and Wang, 1977), p. 124.
8. Martin Esslin, p. 22.
9. Martin Esslin, p. 44.
10. Michael Arlen, The Living Room War (New York: The Viking Press, 1969).
11. H.S. Ashmore, "Uncertain Oracles," Center Magazine (November/December 1970), p. 17.
12. R. Powers, The Newscasters (New York: St. Martin's Press, 1977), p. 78.
13. Leo Bogart, "Television News as Entertainment," in The Entertainment Functions of Television, P.H. Tannenbaum, ed. (Hillsdale: Lawrence Erebaum Associates, 1980), p. 209.
14. Jerome L. Singer, "The Power & Limitations of Television: A Cognitive-Affective Analysis." The Entertainment Functions of Television, P.H. Tannenbaum, ed. (Hillsdale: Lawrence Erebaum Associates, 1980), p. 36.
15. M.S. Gazzaniga, The Bisected Brain (New York: Appleton-Century-Croft, 1970).

Chapter Three

EMERGING TELEVISION TECHNOLOGIES AND THE CULTURAL LAG

* Satellites

* Cable TV

* Subscription TV

* MDS and SMATV

* Direct Broadcast Satellite

* Translators, LPTV, etc.

* Videocassettes/disks

* Teletext, Videotex

* Cultural Lag

* Privacy

* Free Speech and the Fairness Doctrine

The burgeoning television technologies--satellite broadcast, cable television, videocassettes/disks, videotex, fiber optics, digital television, to name a few--constitute, along with computers, the core of the communications revolution. This revolution aims to effect fundamental changes in the socioeconomic, political, and cultural environment, and in the process threatens to upset the existing applecart of social arrangements. The change is so fast-paced that even the resources of a rich language like English/American cannot contain its demand for new terminology; the language seems to be brutalized by terms generated by the emerging and converging electronic technologies: videodisc, video-disk, vid disk, videotext, videotex, music-video, video-music, for example. We are at that clumsy stage of a toddler taking his first step. As Ithiel de Sola Pool observes:

> Each new advance in the technology of communication disturbs a status quo. It meets resistance from those whose dominance it threatens, but if useful it begins to be adopted. Initially, because it is new and a full scientific mastery of the options is not yet at hand, the invention comes into use in a rather clumsy form. Technical laymen, such as judges, perceive the new technology in that early, clumsy form, which then becomes their image of its nature, possibilities, and use. This perception is an incubus for later understanding.[1]

The explosive proliferation of communications technologies and their headlong convergence is creating legitimate concerns about lagging policies concerning personal liberty, centralization of power, illegal surveillance, access to information, and free speech.[2] Some have raised the specter of a "Big Brother" in the Orwellian tradition, while others are worried about the quality, substance, and content of television programs. Abundance of communication may itself be a form of subversion if the quality of programming does not keep pace with the diversification and profusion of channels. Consider the innumerable studies of the effects of television violence and the inconclusive reports about their findings; this inconclusiveness itself creates diffused anxiety among the people.

Broadly speaking, this chapter attempts to explore three major issues: cultural lag, privacy and the American Dream, and the First Amendment and television technologies. To discuss these issues it is imperative first to give thumbnail sketches of the major television technologies struggling for the marketplace and necessitating new policies and social vigilance.

SATELLITES

Satellite technology has revolutionized television, and transmitting information has become inexpensive and plentiful. The alliance of cable and satellite creates a greatest promise of abundance, which raises questions about the assumptions behind the Fairness Doctrine, a concept originally based upon the scarcity principle.

Satellites launched by a space shuttle or a rocket are positioned geosynchronously about 22,300 miles above the equator. Since they move with the same speed and in the same direction as the earth, they are virtually stationary for receiving and sending signals. Once they are in orbit, the sun energizes the satellites. A network of such strategically placed satellites covers the earth and makes the transmission of television signals possible from one end of the world to the other. Communication satellites are nothing but highly efficient relay stations which receive signals from uplinks, or ground station dishes, and retransmit them to earth receiving dishes, or downlinks. In comparison with coaxial cables which require the stringing of wires from point to point and the microwave form of signal transmission which requires the placement of line-of-sight dishes, satellite communication is unencumbered and accessible.

A communication satellite has twenty-four transponders which receive different program signals from the earth transmitting station. Normally, eighteen to twenty-two transponders are functional. The transponders communicate their signals to downlinks, which distribute them via cable to subscribers, or they may be received directly by backyard antenna dishes. Satellite transmitted communication can be received by many receivers without degradation of signal quality--an advantage over coaxial or microwave distribution systems. Two kinds of earth stations, a parabolic reflector and a conical horn, are used today. The conical horn is used to avoid interference from microwave sources.

Satellites are positioned four degrees apart from each other and transmit on the same frequency in the four to six gigahertz range (C band) and twelve to fourteen gigahertz range (K band).[3] Most of the ground stations (downlinks or receiving stations) can receive the channels from only one satellite, though more expensive dishes enable reception from several satellites. Further technological improvements would enable the placement of satellites at a shorter distance from each other without causing interference. The technology would also improve the antenna dishes so that a single multiple-beam satellite antenna could receive signals efficiently and from more than one satellite.

Satellites at present are being placed in orbits by NASA's shuttles or by launch rockets, but in keeping with free enterprise ideology and profit motives, private companies have also been developing launching facilities. Corporations like RCA, Western Union, and AT&T operate satellites either for their own uses or to rent transponder time to smaller companies. A company like the Robert World Company might lease large blocks of satellite time and then sublease them to several other companies. The Robert World Company pioneered the concept of video-conferencing or teleconferencing via satellite.[4] Various organizations can rent satellite time and equipment from a satellite operating or leasing company in the teleconferencing business and hold a conference between various groups of people gathered, for instance, in Los Angeles, New York, and Chicago. The major networks use tele-interviewing and tele-discussion with people at far-off places. Teleconferencing is an extension of that practice. Besides saving time and money it can turn a convention, for instance, into an international event. But it has some serious social consequences which are being slowly recognized. For instance, conventions and conferences are occasions and excuses for people to have informal exchanges and to negotiate privately behind the apparent din of meetings and public rhetoric. Awareness of the cameras, dishes, and satellite may create posturing, gesturing, and heroics which inhibit human communication. In addition, the hotel and airline industries will experience severe economic effects.

Just as the advent of the automobile profoundly transformed social life in America, similarly, the satellite is emerging as such a dominant technology that no aspect of life will remain untouched for long. It is dominating television now and will soon dominate computer technology; consequently, in course of time existing ideologies will come under attack and begin to crumble since technology determines ideology, as is being demonstrated in China today. Ideology, defined as a network of widely-held assumptions creating patterns of dominance in a society,[5] subsequently asserts its control over technology to stabilize social structure. For instance, the Fairness Doctrine was intended to provide ideological management of problems created by broadcasting technology; now satellite technology, in alliance with cable TV, is deconstructing the Fairness Doctrine's assumptions based on scarcity of information outlets. Daily newspapers like <u>U.S.A. Today</u>, the <u>Wall Street Journal</u>, and <u>The New York Times</u> are transmitted via satellite for facsimile printing, thus confusing the concept of public ownership of airwaves. The distribution of newspapers as videotex further confuses the ideological assumptions behind the Fairness Doctrine. Thus technology creates new problems which existing ideologies must either solve or give way to and be displaced by new ideologies.

CABLE TV

One legend has it that a television appliance shop owner in Pennsylvania found that one half of the town was not buying his sets because a hill was obstructing the signals. Motivated by profits, he installed cables at the houses of prospective television set buyers and connected them with a hilltop antenna. Another legend gives the credit to a "ham" radio operator in Oregon who converted his interest in the field to a $100 hook-up for fees.[6] Cable television beginnings were halting and uncertain, but once the possibilities of the satellite connection became a technological fact, the gold rush began. Today, to have a cable franchise is the realization of the American Dream. A cable franchise gives the operator a virtual monopoly in a society where monopoly is supposed to be anathema.

Cable television is different from broadcast television in many ways. Unlike broadcast television, cable TV does not depend upon line-of-sight antennas. It may receive signals from satellites or broadcast antennas and then transmit them via cable to subscribers. While an over-the-air broadcast network can give only one channel, cable television now can deliver up to 108 channels because, whereas broadcasting depends upon electromagnetic frequencies which are scarce and cause mutual interference, cable television does not depend upon the air waves. The satellite cable connection has created an abundance of channels, but due to cultural lag no worthwhile programming is available,

Emerging Television Technologies

though the whole of mankind's imaginative literature and drama are available for adaptation and the field of education could benefit immensely from this television technology.

It was the Ali-Frazier heavyweight championship from Manila in 1975 which prompted Home Box Office (HBO) to experiment with satellite transmission, and its successful experiment brought the two technologies together. Cablecasting since then has assumed new meaning. HBO became a nationwide TV programming service, marketing its programs to cable systems. HBO's satellite connection was soon followed by a little-known station (WTBS) in Atlanta, owned by Ted Turner, which used the same satellite to beam its programs nationwide, giving birth to the concept of a superstation. WTBS has grown into a giant, and today, in spite of a setback in attempting to take over CBS, Ted Turner has taken over MGM-United Artists, thus enriching his station's cultural resources for programming.

There are four different kinds of cable television programming: Pay-cable, basic cable, local programming, and auxiliary services. Pay-cables like HBO, Showtime, and Movie Channels show mostly movies, though occasionally they broadcast sports, documentaries, informational series, interviews, and children's programs. Some pay-cables, like Playboy Channel, Penthouse Entertainment Television, Private Screenings, and Eros, show explicit sex movies during the late night and early morning hours. Still other pay-cables, like the Entertainment Channel and Disney have growing subscriber lists.

For basic cable television services, subscribers are charged a small amount over and above their initial montly fee. These advertisement-supported services are aimed at special interests, giving rise to the concept of "narrowcasting," as opposed to broadcasting. Examples of such narrowcasting cable television services are ESPN, providing around-the-clock sportcasting; USA Network, which gives not only sports but children's programming, drama, etc.; Weather Channel; Financial Newsnetwork; Dow Jones Cable News; CBN; Spanish International Network (SIN) and C-SPAN; MTV, with twenty-four-hour-a-day video music; Nashville Network, featuring country music; and Nickelodeon. Narrowcasting of basic service cultural programs has not been financially successful, and many such services, like CBS's ARTS, have folded.

An essential part of cable television programming is called local programming, which originates locally and offers local access. Local origination programming is produced and controlled by the cable stations. Local access programming is produced by nonprofit local organizations using facilities provided by the station; such programming is incorporated into franchise agreements which differ from community to community and is considered by most stations to be an unavoidable nuisance.

The fourth area of cable television, auxiliary services, which will explode into significance in the coming decade, results from the two-way communication capability of the cable system. These services include videotex, videogames, computer shopping, and home security. A television receiver becomes a watchman, a monitor, and a shopping guide. How viewers will use these technologies depends upon many variables, one being a standardized regulatory policy, which is not yet forthcoming. It seems, however, that satellite-delivered cable programs will break the dominance of the networks.

SUBSCRIPTION TV

Subscription television (STV) uses airwaves to transmit its scrambled programs to paid subscribers who use decoders to unscramble the programs. Unlike cable television, which uses satellites, microwave dishes, and coaxial cables, STV is a local signal distribution system. Its customers receive specialized programs, mostly on a per-channel basis. Improved technology might enable STV operators to charge per program, much as the long-distance telephone system does. STV, unlike cable TV, does not operate nationally. The problem for STV operators is to scramble and unscramble signals so efficiently that piracy is prevented and the subscribers do not complain about program reception. STV operates on a UHF band on a single channel and its signals are broadcast locally. Most programming consists of movies which have already been shown in theaters; some of the movies are adult films or special feature films or 3-D movies which are not available on other circuits. Special attractions for subscribers are such events as major league baseball, football, or basketball games. STV is a costly system to operate, and to break even a station needs from

Emerging Television Technologies

35,000 to 75,000 subscribers.[7] Eventually, like pay-cable, STV will flourish when it provides services which are not available elsewhere. The FCC's deregulation policies have helped STV, and it is becoming competitive in the marketplace. It is feared that the FCC's encouragement of STV could adversely affect movie theaters because movie producers might make movies only for STV. Similarly, major sporting events could be coopted by STV, threatening people's free access to viewing sports.

Since STV and cable TV compete for the same viewers (and in fact most viewers do not know the difference) and since there is a paucity of new theater movies, most of the time what the viewers get is trash. How many new, good movies could be available for twenty-four-hour transmission? The deregulation policy lifting all restrictions from STV will not ease the shortage of cultural programming. Maybe the marketplace will suggest new ideas to enable survival and profitability.

MDS AND SMATV

Multipoint Distribution Service (MDS) and Satellite Master Antenna TV (SMATV) are other technical services which present a symbolic challenge to existing services and keep the marketplace free from monopoly. Economically these systems do not amount to much, but in keeping with the ideology of the free marketplace of goods and ideas they have symbolic significance.

MDS is a conventional over-the-air broadcast system which uses frequencies (2500-2690 megahertz) that are far beyond the normal TV signals (45-890 megahertz), and hence need down-converters. Unlike VHF and UHF, the MDS signals have a range of only fifteen to twenty miles. MDS is only a carrier service and cannot originate its own programming. The system is primarily used for supplying pay movies to hotels and apartments, and thus directly competes with STV and cable TV.

SMATV is a multi-channel system which is similar to cable TV and is used by large apartment complexes, condominiums, mobile home parks, and other residential complexes. It is a miniature cable television system but does not come under FCC regulations so long as the number of subscribers remains less than fifty or the system serves residential complexes under common ownership. The source of program supply is the same as that for cable TV, but since SMATV is free from public regulations and scrutiny, it could distribute programming of its members' choice. The SMATV medium is making cable TV owners nervous,[8] because it can receive signals via satellite and thus compete with cable.

The rationale behind the FCC's support of MDS and SMATV is to offer viewers alternatives so that cable TV does not gain monopolistic control over any area. Cable TV owners want MDS to limit its services to rural and farm areas and not enter the lucrative top fifty markets. MDS is a common carrier and unlike cable TV it cannot originate its programming; but, at the same time, it is free from the restrictions of cross-ownership or multiple ownership.

Similarly, SMATV is presenting a serious challenge to cable by entering into exclusive arrangements with large residential facilities, hotels, and condominiums. Because it is free from the FCC's regulatory constraints, it can provide programs and services which cable may not. The FCC as a watchdog of the free marketplace encourages competitiveness, so that viewers could benefit.

DIRECT BROADCAST SATELLITE

A direct broadcast satellite (DBS) system transmits TV signals directly to the general public without the intervention of cable companies. DBS technology requires the transmission of high-powered and concentrated signals that can be received by a small one-meter dish. Smaller dishes are cheaper and within the reach of customers. At present Communication Satellite Corporation (COMSAT) is the forerunner for the commercial exploitation of DBS.

The main difference between a cable satellite and a Direct Broadcast Satellite is that the latter is much larger and more powerful. Instead of twenty-four transponders using the available energy, DBS will have only three transponders using the same energy, thus giving each transponder much greater power than the transponder of a traditional satellite. As technology develops, more energy for trans-

Emerging Television Technologies

ponders and hence more availability of channels will become possible. The transponders retransmit signals back to earth to one-meter dishes located on housetops; the down converter and the decoder transform the signals to conventional signals for the TV receivers. The chief aim of DBS is to bypass the traditional retailing intermediaries, such as cable TV and broadcast stations, and serve viewers directly. COMSAT will provide subscription programming of commercial-free movies, sports, games, data, and text transmissions. Programming will be geared to markets of taste rather than geographical areas. DBS's chief competitor would be cable television.

TRANSLATORS, LOW-POWER TV, AND OTHER TECHNOLOGIES

Translators and Low-power TV (LPTV) are limited in scale and power. A translator retransmits the programs and signals of a primary television broadcast station without changing the content and characteristics of the original signals. LPTV uses the same low-power technology as does a translator station but could originate programs and may be used for commercial purposes. The service area of LPTV is limited by power--10 watts in the case of VHFs and 1,000 watts for UHFs--and can reach only fifteen to twenty-five miles in any direction. The original purpose in authorizing LPTVs was to provide participation in broadcast opportunities for minorities and other deprived groups. LPTV stations are regulated by the FCC but with less stringency than the regular stations. They are to observe the Fairness Doctrine, community standards about obscenity and indecency, copyright regulations, etc., but they can raise funds in any manner they choose.

Because their reach is small, the FCC has given them greater freedom than it does to conventional TV stations. The original intention was to encourage small investors to operate LPTVs, but all sizes and kinds of organizations have begun to apply for licenses to corner the technologies.

VIDEOCASSETTES/DISKS

The challenge of the videocassette recorder (VCR) to broadcast and cable television is unfathomable at present, but it is certainly changing our viewing habits and tastes. The two videocassette formats, VHS and Beta, use different tape threading methods and are incompatible with each other --that is, the software for one cannot be used on the other. The features VCRs offer are numerous. For instance, a viewer may clock a particular program to be taped automatically during his or her absence. Programs on different channels and different days and at different times can be recorded in the absence of the owner. Other features include recording time of up to eight hours, still frame, frame-by-frame advance, slow motion, and fast motion. Using a built-in tuner, a VCR can record one program while another is being viewed. People are using video recorders and cameras, instead of 8mm home movie cameras, to tape their own materials and make home movies.

Increasing use of VCRs is diverting audiences from network programming. A tape-recorded program can be purged of all commercials, defeating the purpose of advertisers. The old adage, "programs deliver audiences to the advertisers," is being challenged. Even the rating system is being challenged because the audimeter cannot record whether a program is being watched or taped. A program taped on Monday becomes irrelevant for the rating system if it is watched on Wednesday. Prerecorded videocassettes have increased the autonomy of viewers, who can selectively pick the best available programs in the market.

Videodisks have not made as much mark on the market as VCRs because they cannot be used for taping programs. As in videocassette systems, videodisk formats vary but are incompatible with each other, though they display their pictures through videodisk players connected with TV sets. The two systems on the market at present are the reflective laser optic disk and the capacitance electronic disk. The laser system involves no physical contact with a disk and it can access any of the 54,000 frames on one side of a disk speedily and efficiently. Because they provide random access, laser disks constitute excellent information retrieval systems for educational, medical, and library purposes. The potential for laser videodisk technology is immense. The capacitance electronic system, which uses a diamond stylus, is much less sophisticated and resembles a phonograph. It lacks the capacity for random access, still frame, or interfacing with computers.

TELETEXT AND VIDEOTEX

Teletext and videotex are methods of transmitting textual materials, numbers, and graphics on the television screen. Teletext is an over-the-air transmission system which uses a vertical blanking interval for signal transmission. A blanking interval is the signal-free time span when a scanning beam moves vertically from the bottom to the top of the screen. This signal-free interval, traveling vertically and appearing in a cycle, is used for textual transmission. Thus there are two simultaneous transmission systems: one the regular televisual program using normal signals; the other the teletext signal, which uses the blanking interval and requires a decoder for viewing. A decoder can shut out the regular television signals and allow the teletext to appear on the screen, or both the regular television and the teletext information can appear simultaneously, as happens in "closed caption" service to the deaf. When the vertical blanking interval is programmed, the same information appears in cycles--that is, it is repeated again and again. Some teletext systems offer viewers choices in the form of a menu, or tree, and only that information appears on the screen which viewers want--the only interactive possibility with the teletext system. A maximum of two hundred pages of text is possible with the teletext system at present.

Three major systems are used today: the British, called Ceefax and Oracle; the French, called Antiope; and the Canadian, called Telidon. The Americans, who are behind the Europeans, are using PLDS, a system developed by AT&T. The various systems are incompatible with each other. At present Southern Satellite Systems uses teletext for news services. Advertisers could also use this service, and the teletext system could become financially viable.

Videotex is transmitted over cable or telephone wires and has a two-way interactive capability, a feature not available in teletext. Videotex has far-reaching sociological implications because of its two-way (upstream and downstream) capabilities. At the center of a videotex system is a large computer which sends information to a modem that encodes the information for the phone lines. Another modem decodes the information as text for the television screen. The reverse process--a TV-modem-central computer--enables information to be transmitted upstream. Instead of using phone wires, the system could use cable for the same purpose. This computer-TV interaction technology is changing how people think about their television sets and themselves --from being passive consumers of information and entertainment to being active seekers and choice makers. The sophisticated viewdata system promises banking, paying bills, credit checks, home shopping, adult education, public opinion polls, delivery of newspaper when a printer is attached, library services, mail delivery, telephone directory service, etc. Of course, every time a viewer interacts with the central computer, he or she discloses a bit of information about his or her lifestyle, and bit by bit privacy is lost. Privacy is basic to the American way of life and will continue either to exist or perish together with the American Dream.

CULTURAL LAG

The abundance of electronic modes of communication, from traditional over-the-air broadcasting to satellite, cable and microwave and their various permutations and combinations, have created a serious cultural problem: what to program in those 108 channels available twenty-four hours a day? Imagine that the President issues an executive order that every village, town, and city in America must have a legitimate theater building, and the task of building the new theaters must be completed within a year's time. If this is done, then each village, city, and town will need at least one director, actors, and support staff to stage plays --presuming that suitable plays meeting community standards are available. People are ready for theater productions, which they have eagerly awaited; but because of a lack of theater artists, the citizens find that auctioneers and political demagogues are occupying the stages and are using all kinds of gimmicks to hold their audiences while proclaiming, "We give you what you ask for." This metaphor probably reveals what is happening in television today. There is not enough cultural programming available to transmit over so many channels, and consequently most of the new telecommunication technologies are dipping into the Hollywood reservoir of old and new films. But Hollywood cannot make movies on an assembly line; even the soap opera producers are slow in making new programs, despite the networks' spending $50 million every year on program development. There is a cultural lag in America because, while technologies have grown exponentially and scarcity has been transformed into plenty, entertainment is not keeping pace with expectations. This cultural lag is not intrinsic to America but is a function of the growth of the means of communication. Englishmen do not feel this cultural lag because the number of channels and the programming hours are limited, and their creative people can give audiences high-quality programming to fill these limited opportunities. In America the cultural and artistic resources are thinly spread to fill time and channels with cloned and recombinant progenies. Even if we plunder or plagiarize the cultural resources of the entire world, the problem of emptiness, in a metaphorical sense, will be obsessive.

A very perceptive American social scientist, William F. Ogburn, propounded the theory of cultural lag, which has become a part of international currency. He said, "A cultural lag occurs when one of two parts of culture which are correlated changes before or in greater degree than the other part does, thereby causing less adjustment between the two parts than existed previously."[9] Ogburn used the term "culture" in the anthropological sense, which of course includes artistic activities. Explaining his theory further, Ogburn added that delay in understanding of ideas is not cultural lag. Cultural lag involves two variables: one of them changes too quickly to continue the old dependency relationship. The theory of cultural lag, according to Ogburn, calls for the following four steps: the identification of at least two variables; the demonstration that these two variables were in adjustment; the determination by dates that one variable has changed while the other has not or that one has changed in greater degree than the other; and the realization that when one variable has changed earlier or more greatly than the other, less satisfactory adjustment exists than before.[10]

As we have observed, the rate of change and growth of communications technology is much higher than the rate of growth in cultural programming, which depends upon individual talents and creativity and is naturally a slow process. Also, in a larger sense of the concept of culture, privacy and free speech are under strain because new interpretations of the First Amendment reflecting communications developments are not forthcoming. Law and policy making processes are slow, but can we slow down technology?

PRIVACY

The struggle for freedom of expression, to print and speak without prior restraint, lasted in different countries for half a millennium; it found its supreme embodiment in the First Amendment of the U.S. Constitution. For two hundred years Americans have built their material and spiritual prosperity around the First Amendment. But Americans have also enjoyed another right without which free speech is meaningless, the right to privacy. Free speech and the right to privacy constitute important components of the American Dream: the right to make your fortune through the system of free enterprise, retreat to the privacy of your hearth, and exercise your free speech. In fact, the American Dream is a universal dream: a Chinese or a Russian also wants privacy and freedom with the right to live a rich life.

Will the emerging and converging television technologies protect and enhance our freedom? Or, in Ogburn's language, will the correlation continue? Or would the new technologies bring about new forms of slavery? Alexis de Tocqueville wrote in <u>Democracy in America</u>: "It would seem that if despotism were to be established among the democratic nations of our days ... it would be more extensive and more mild; it would degrade men without tormenting them."[11] In a recent survey, Neil Vidmar and David H. Flaherty found an increasing concern about personal privacy in North America and concluded that "concern for privacy is a latent social and political issue that needs only some particularly outstanding incidents to foster its emergence."[12]

One might ask, what is television doing in our living rooms and bedrooms? Is it there to inform and entertain us or to monitor us through cable television's addressability? Viewdata and videotex give us immense opportunities for interaction with central computers, banks, and other institutions, but they also strip us of privacy. What is true of the individuals' loss of privacy is equally true of business organizations which use two-way interactive systems. Former FCC chairman Charles Ferris said:

> The history of repression has been interwoven with the history of technology. There was wire tapping almost as soon as there were telephones to be tapped.

But in the future, significant facts about every American could be available by gaining access to just one or two giant computers.

Should our right to be let alone be entrusted solely to the marketplace? Or should we rely on government to set and enforce standards--to preserve the spirit of the Bill of Rights during an era when our privacy could fall victim to our inventive genius? These questions demand the very best of our imagination.[13]

The invasion of privacy can occur in two ways: intrusion of unwanted information and unauthorized access to information.[14] The unwanted information via cable may be cultist propaganda aimed at the young, pornographic material, political canvassing, etc. The cable operators will have to develop their own code of conduct, on the model of the broadcasters' code, and exercise their judgment and good taste. Instead of relying on government "to set and enforce standards," the industry should regulate itself, as a way of making up the cultural lag.

While unauthorized intrusion of information or electronic "junk" mail could be ignored as a nuisance, unauthorized access to information collected through the videodata system is a grave danger. Those who may wish to collect information about users include direct-mail marketing companies that seek information about peoples' television viewing habits; police interested in gathering information about the suspected individuals; governments wanting to seek information about individuals' incomes and expenses for tax purposes; or the cable company itself, which may want to sell information. The two-way communication system provides easy access to intruders who can tap a cable television wire at any point of transmission.

Thomas F. Baldwin and D. Steven McVoy argue that encrypting data with a frequent change of code, though expensive, might make unauthorized access difficult.[15] Along with technical steps for the protection of privacy, legal measures resembling the Privacy Act of 1974 are essential to cover proper use of data banks formed by cable television and videotex services. Baldwin and McVoy suggest that a universal code of privacy modelled on Warner Amex's "Code of Privacy"[16] may initiate awareness of the problem. That code states the following:

The company will explain its information gathering function to subscribers;

maintain physical security and confidentiality;

use individual viewing records only for billing of service purposes;

aggregate data never identifying individuals;

deny requests for individual subscriber data unless legally required;

allow subscribers to review and copy data about themselves;

correct inaccurate information about subscribers;

keep information only as long as necessary;

make subscriber mailing lists available only with the permission of subscribers;

comply with all federal, state, local and industry privacy codes;

and require adherence to the Code of Privacy by third parties involved in the provision of service

Such a code, which is a form of self-regulation, along with the administrative and judicial remedies available, may stem the rising tide of fear of a medium whose entertainment and education benefits are immense. Government intervention and enforcement of the rules become inevitable when the industry does not police itself and the free marketplace is threatened.

FREE SPEECH AND THE FAIRNESS DOCTRINE

The major dilemma before policy makers is that, like the print medium, broadcast-cable television has become a big business. Big business has been entrusted with the responsibility of running the free marketplace of goods and ideas. What is the big business interest in ensuring the freedom of thought and expression enshrined in the First Amendment? The First Amendment states: "Congress shall make no law respecting an establishment of religion, or prohibiting the free exercise thereof; or abridging the freedom of speech, or of the press; or the right of the people peaceably to assemble, and to petition the government for a redress of grievances."

For 200 years the tradition of free speech and free press has endured all vicissitudes, though interpretation of

Emerging Television Technologies

the clause's meaning has changed from time to time. In essence, freedom of expression means freedom from prior restraint, and American courts have always upheld the rights of editors, writers, and speakers, even though the nation has changed from a nation of pamphleteers, small magazine owners, and small newspaper proprietors to one of giant corporation-owned newspapers. Troublesome ideas began to creep in and the intellectual climate of the country began to change when a new broadcasting medium arose in the twenties, governed by the Federal Radio Act of 1927. The act required that no one could operate a radio station without a federal license. This licensing procedure became necessary because of the scarcity of radio frequencies. Besides, the airwaves belong to the public and their use must be fair and in the public interest.

The Communication Act of 1934 extended the same argument to television. In 1949 the Federal Communications Commission established its famous Fairness Doctrine, which states:

> This requires that licensees devote a reasonable percentage of their broadcasting time to the discussion of public issues of interest in the community served by their stations and that such programs be designed so that the public has a reasonable opportunity to hear different opposing positions on the public issues of interest and importance in the community.[17]

What we see is the emergence of the listener's right to know as a necessary corollary to the speaker's right of self-expression. A new interpretation was given to the First Amendment: free speech for what purpose?

The answer to this question was provided by the philosopher Alexander Meiklejohn, whose book <u>Free Speech and Its Relation to Self Government</u> has played a significant part in shaping post-World War II thought on political freedom and the role of mass communication. He said, "We listen, not because they desire to speak, but because we need to hear.... It is the program of self-government."[18]

The rationale for free speech is that it helps people to make up their minds about political and social issues.

Indirectly, Meiklejohn was arguing for the listener's right to know all sides of an issue. "What is essential is not that everyone shall speak ... the point of ultimate interest is not the words of the speakers, but the minds of the hearers. The final aim of the meeting is the voting of wise decision ..." and for communication to be "the thinking process of the community."[19]

The background for Meiklejohn's philosophical lectures in the 1940s was the rise of Nazism in Europe. If the Germans, an enlightened people famed for their philosophy, arts, and science, could lose their mental balance and become enslaved by the Führer's hypnotic speeches, what about the Americans? In a similar vein, Zechariah Chafee, Jr., said, "We have found that we cannot depend on unmanaged processes, whether in economics or in communications."[20]

The decade of the 1940s was a period of intellectual turmoil for Americans who wanted to protect themselves from the dangers of Nazism. This turmoil led to reinterpretation of the First Amendment. The new exegesis highlighted the centrality of the right of the listeners, their right to know, which became the basis and justification for the 1949 Fairness Doctrine confirmed by the Supreme Court in the landmark case of Red Lion Broadcasting Co. vs. FCC. As Justice White said:

> But the people as a whole retain their interest in free speech by radio and their collective right to have the medium function consistently with the ends and purposes of the First Amendment. It is the right of the viewers and listeners, not the right of the broadcasters, which is paramount.... Nor can we say that it is inconsistent with the First Amendment goal of producing an informed public capable of conducting its own affairs to require a broadcaster to permit answers to personal attacks occurring in the course of discussing controversial issues or to require that the political opponents of those endorsed by the station be given chance to communicate with the public. Otherwise, station owners and a few networks would have unfettered power to make time available only to the highest bidders, and to communicate only their own views on public issues, people and candidates, and to

> permit on the air only those with whom they agreed.
> There is no sanctuary in the First Amendment for
> unlimited private censorship operating in a medium
> not to open to all [emphasis added]. Freedom of
> the press from governmental interference under the
> First Amendment does not sanction repression of
> that freedom by private interest. [Associated Press
> vs. United States, 326 U.S. 1, 20 (1945)].[21]

Because the broadcast spectrum is limited, a licensee has only a "temporary privilege" of using his or her station for public interest; he or she is to act only as "a proxy or fiduciary" for the community, to which the broadcaster is obliged to present all sides of controversial issues. Of course, the print medium has been treated by the courts on a different footing, as was established in the Supreme Court's 1964 decision in New York Times vs. Sullivan,[22] because the scarcity principle does not apply to the print medium. Theoretically, anyone can start a newspaper or use a copier machine to print and distribute materials, something which cannot be said about the broadcast medium, which uses the limited resources of the spectrum.

It has been argued that cable television does not use the airwaves and therefore should be treated like the print medium. Moreover, the convergence of various media has blurred the distinction between print and broadcast media, and therefore the latter should be freed from the burden of the Fairness Doctrine or the government will have no choice but to regulate the print medium as well. CBS chairman William S. Paley (now retired) said:

> Broadcasters and print people have been so busy
> improving and defining their own turf that it has
> escaped some of us how much we are being drawn
> together by the vast revolution in "electronification"
> that is changing the face of the media today....
> Convergence of a delivery mechanism for news and
> information raises anew critical First Amendment
> questions.... Once the print media come into the
> homes through the television set, or an attachment,
> with an impact and basic content similar to that
> which the broadcasters now deliver, then the ques-
> tion of government regulation becomes paramount
> for print as well.[23]

It seems that the communications revolution which has created an abundance of delivery systems has created confusion about the role of the First Amendment. The speaker today is not an individual writer, a streetcorner preacher, or a pamphleteer, but a giant multinational corporation or the head of a powerful conglomerate like Ted Turner or Rupert Murdoch who buys cable/broadcast stations and newspapers as a housewife buys groceries. The central issue raised by the emerging technologies and merging media is not whether the Fairness Doctrine is fair but whether speech can be free if the rights of listeners, viewers, and readers are not recognized. The courts, in behalf of the people, have rightfully started looking into the newsgathering processes, as recently occurred in the cases of <u>Time vs. Sharon</u>, and <u>CBS vs. General Westmoreland</u>. A healthy rivalry between print and nonprint media may serve the people's right to know.

What is the uppermost interest of giant companies which own newspaper, cable, and broadcast industries: to speak the truth, or to earn profits at any cost? The free marketplace of goods and the free marketplace of ideas are not necessarily compatible. Some form of the Fairness Doctrine for all media may help in creating plurality and diversity of opinions and saving America from the scourge of singlemindedness that characterizes totalitarian societies.

NOTES

1. Ithiel de Sola Pool, <u>Technologies of Freedom</u> (Cambridge: The Belknap Press of Harvard University Press, 1983), p. 7.
2. Louis Harris and Associates and A.F. Westin, <u>The Dimensions of Privacy: A National Opinion Research Survey of Attitudes Towards Privacy</u> (New York: McBain and Small, 1979).
3. "Communication Satellite: The Birds Are in Full Flight," <u>Broadcasting</u> (November 19, 1979), p. 89; "Satellite Spacing: Multifaceted Debate," <u>Broadcasting</u> (March 15, 1982), pp. 136-138.
4. Lynn Schafer Gross, <u>The New Television Technologies</u> (Dubuque: Wm C. Brown Company Publishers, 1983), p. 21.
5. Stuart Hall, "Signification, Representation, Ideology:

Althusser and the Post-Structuralist Debates," CSMS, 2:2 (June 1985), p. 103.
6. Thomas F. Baldwin and D. Stevens McVoy, Cable Communication (Englewood Cliffs, NJ: Prentice-Hall, 1983), p. 8; David L. Jaffe, "CATV: History and Law," Educational Broadcasting (July/August 1974), pp. 15-16.
7. "STV: Scratching Out Its Place in the New Video Universe," Broadcasting (April 7, 1980), p. 58.
8. "SMATV: The Medium That's Making Cable Nervous," Broadcasting (June 21, 1982), pp. 33-46.
9. William F. Ogburn, On Cultural and Social Change, Otis Dudley Duncan, ed. (Chicago: The University of Chicago Press, 1964), p. 86.
10. Ibid., p. 89.
11. Alexis de Tocqueville, Democracy in America (New York: Knopf, 1945), pp. 316-318.
12. Neil Vidmar and David H. Flaherty, "Concern for Personal Privacy in an Electronic Age," Journal of Communication, 35:2 (Spring 1985), pp. 95-103.
13. "New Technologies and the Merging Media: A Time for Imagination," a Speech to the Audit Bureau of Circulation's Annual Meeting, New Orleans, LA, November 7, 1979. Quoted by Dougles R. Watts in "A Major Issue of the 1980s: New Communication Tools," Chamberlin & Brown, eds., The First Amendment Reconsidered (n.p.: Longman, 1982), p. 193.
14. Thomas F. Baldwin, etc., pp. 181-184.
15. Ibid., p. 182.
16. Ibid., p. 183.
17. Frank J. Kahn, ed., Documents of American Broadcasting, 4th ed. (Englewood Cliffs, NJ: Prentice-Hall, 1984), p. 177.
18. Alexander Meiklejohn, Free Speech and Its Relation to Self-Government, reprinted in Political Freedom (New York: Harper & Row, 1960), p. 57.
19. Ibid., pp. 26-27.
20. Zachariah Chaffe, Jr., Government and Mass Communication, 2 vols. (Chicago: University of Chicago Press, 1947), p. 27.
21. Frank J. Kahn, pp. 287-288.
22. 376 U.S. at 256.
23. The New York Times (July 7, 1980), sec. B, p. 3.

Chapter Four

FORM AND STRUCTURE OF
TELEVISION DRAMA

* Screen Realism

* Formulaic Conventions of Television Series Drama

* Plot and Characterization

* Cliffhangers

* Topicality

* Commercial-Punctuated Action

* "Hill Street Blues": The Case of Recombinant Progeny

Great drama of the past transcended its time because it presented life in mythic dimensions, negating the actual and the natural to comprehend the mystic depth of reality. Its gestic grandeur, sublime action, and thundering declamation evoked ecstasy or grief never felt by audiences in their daily lives. It created contemplative awe. It should be remembered, says Tyrone Guthrie, that

> ... the drama which has survived from past ages has done so, not because it presented a modest slice of everyday life, but because, on the contrary, it offers an enormous helping of something larger, louder, and more high-colored than most of us are ever likely to experience. Also, great acting has never been known as such because it imitates the behavior of everyday ordinary decent

people. Great acting has always been outrageous. Let television actors aim to be human, life sized and natural; great actors never have been and never will be that. They aim to be superhuman--twice as large as life and three times as natural. The theatre must go back to Greek and Elizabethan ideas of drama, a re-enactment of great stories in such a way they do not resemble life but rather ennoble and illuminate it.[1]

SCREEN REALISM

If at present television drama has not touched the "impossible probability" of classical dramatic art, it is because it is limited by the screen realism and the formulaic conventions of the popular arts. Television has an affinity for concreteness and photographic reality and tends to transform all events, even when staged, into documentary status. It reduces the super-natural to the natural and manifests it in photographic particularity to achieve greater authenticity. The television camera, for instance, captures the details of the environment of a ramshackle New York habitat or the vastness of a sprawling ocean island, Honolulu. Its affinity for physical details and its capacity for redeeming physical reality relieve spoken language of its burden of description and free it for probing character relationships. If television creators have not taken advantage of the opportunity, it is because of other constraints. Television works through a closeup and two-shot mode which gives the viewers a sense of intimacy and character relationships and exposes those human acts which are normally concealed by moral taboo or physical remoteness. That so far the medium's potential has been exploited only for sexual explicitness and physical romance is regrettable. The dramatic possibilities of the camera in exploring the agony and ecstasy of a human soul have been shown particularly in the television versions of Shakespeare's plays (BBC's <u>King Lear</u>, for instance).

Television realism involves viewers in the immediacy and spontaneity of life's seemingly haphazard occurrences and steaming confusion, as one finds in "Hill Street Blues." This documentary narrative form, borrowed from cinema technique which records happenings in a direct and unobtrusive manner, is being increasingly adopted in television drama, making it part of our daily life experience.

Viewers begin to discover and order details to make sense and in the process become deeply involved. Skillful camerawork, rapid shifts of attention through editing, and other controls place viewers in the steampit of reality the dramatic personae are experiencing. Luis Buñuel called it "an integral vision of reality,"[2] beyond the capability of newspaper or other linear modes of communication. While the best theater gives the audience a vision of "impossible probability," television rejoices in a sense of discovery by providing viewers multiple vantage points from which to watch and experience reality as if they were omniscient.

Richard L. Stromgren and Martin F. Norden remind us that "television has become a conditioner of visual perception that has affected and will doubtless continue to affect the way we see images ..." because television programs and commercials have "developed a style in visual design and pacing that is direct, streamlined, fast and free of the encumbrances of transitional links and details in composition."[3] Fast-paced commercials, rock music, MTV, video music, etc., have raised viewers' expectations and are changing the very mode of consciousness; in time they will affect television dramaturgy, taking it still further away from the legitimate theater.

THE FORMULAIC CONVENTIONS OF TELEVISION SERIES DRAMA

At the core of television series drama is a secularized version of the savior who arises at critical times to rid the world of an evil and restore harmony. The evil may be a fatal disease or life threatening accident, or a drug-mafia chief or other crook threatening an innocent individual or a society; the savior may be a highly trained surgeon (Trapper John, M.D.), a professionally trained and dedicated police officer (T.J. Hooker), a macho-romantic detective (Magnum P.I.), or a fumbling fool, but he will certainly come and fight the evil, save the innocent, and restore peace, order, and sanity. Though the idea of some kind of divine savior is prevalent in the ancient cultures of China, India, and Israel, its secular version as a human agent of the life force began to take shape with the progressive loss of faith in formal religion. What persists is the collective fantasy that there is order and justice in the world, that in the long run evil will be destroyed. The television series drama--centered on a police officer, doctor, or detective--is a variation on the same theme because deep within each episode is the eternal promise of the savior: "I shall be there." The savior is never crucified or martyred; he is ultimately triumphant. Just as the miracle plays of the medieval ages represented episodes from the life of a miracle-working saint or martyr, the television series drama plays out the miracles of such human saviors as doctors, police officers, or detectives distinguished by their essential goodness, professionally dedicated to their duties, and overflowing with human kindness. What springs them to action are life-threatening forces, which they overcome through their superior knowledge, logical deductions, sheer physical stamina, moral courage, and organizational power. Each television series episode is a celebration of life, an audiovisual and secular hallelujah.

This celebration of life as a secular miracle play uses formulas for thematic variation. According to John G. Cawelti, "formulas are ways in which specific cultural themes and stereotypes become embodied in more universal story archetypes."[4] What interests the audience is the particular way the stereotypes and cultural themes are motivated and ordered to present a probable world. Take the case of "Kojak," a now defunct but once highly popular prime-time series. Theo Kojak, a police lieutenant, rose from episode to episode to immense human possibilities and tended to shatter the stereotype of an inept policeman. The callous policeman became a moral force to satisfy the fantasy of perpetually harassed and beleaguered New Yorkers that there is an order after all.

PLOT AND CHARACTERIZATION

Each episode of a television series drama is a self-contained, closed-end narrative with dramatic unity, having a beginning, a middle, and an end. Sitcoms, police dramas like "Miami Vice," medical stories like "Trapper John, M.D.," etc., fall into this category. Serials are never ending narratives like "Dallas," "Capitol," etc.

John G. Cawelti has listed two characteristics of formulaic literature that are exemplified in such prime-time series: their essential standardization and their goals of escape and entertainment. Standardization is the essence of mass production of goods with only utilitarian value. It is associated with quality control and taste fixation. The product is based upon certain specifications, and the process of production is predetermined to exclude any possibility of innovation or deviation. In art this standardization process constitutes conventions which both the artist and the audience accept as givens for artistic communication. Within these conventions the artist is free to create and give form and shape to his vision. When the artist breaks the conventions, as Beckett did in <u>Waiting for Godot</u>, the audience might fail to see the art; but when the new conventions become part of the network of artistic assumptions, the artist-audience rapport is reestablished. In short, art is a convention-invention continuum, and the degree to which an artist follows conventions will determine his or her status as an artist. High art plays a cat-and-mouse game with the received conventions, threatens to subvert them, and creates a suspense of form rather than of plot. The aesthetic pleasure for audiences lies in their recognizing how far the artist would stretch the conventions to create a new form.

In popular arts like television series dramas there is greater adherence to conventions, and innovations are introduced only for the intensification of "expected experience without fundamentally altering it."[5] Each time we watch "Dukes of Hazzard," for instance, we know its field of reference and expect nothing new except to reawaken the form which we experienced before. The pleasurable experience of a nighttime series is awakened in us again and again by reassurance and intensification, but using a thematic variation which "is clearly one of the fundamental modes of expression in popular culture."[6]

Since the television series drama works within rigid formulaic conventions, it does not have the freedom to develop character or to invent totally new plot situations; instead, it prospers on stereotypes which consist of a "standardized mental picture that is held in common by members of a group and that represents an oversimplified opinion, affective attitude, or uncritical judgement."[7]

Since audiences are familiar with the stereotypes of policemen, doctors, and detectives, as well as with the stock situations in which they operate, the pleasure lies in watching how each stereotypic character breaks out of the mold or conforms to the expectations created by the particular stereotype. Kojak remained a policeman but occasionally broke out of the mold to speak out his denunciation like a saint. "Lou Grant" had all the stereotypical characteristics of the journalistic world, but it was the crusading spirit which shook the formula and created the thrill of a rollercoaster. Each episode of a television series is unique because of the new problems the characters have to face, requiring that they show some untypical qualities, even though solutions are to be found only in the rigid framework of the formula. Great art uses conventions as a point of departure to create forms and characters with universal appeal which transcend a time and a culture's mode of consciousness. On the other hand, the creators of television series dramas seem to be filling in the blanks, most of the time. A series program like "Cover Up," for instance, has two undercover agents, a lady photographer and a male model, who in every episode work in a foreign country to protect American citizens. Stock situations consist of photographic sessions and semi-clad people, fights, shoot-outs, and chases. The thematic variation lies with the particular person to be protected--perhaps a scientist, a corporation executive, or a politician. The intensification of experience is proportionate to the degree of importance the audience attaches to the character who must be protected. In light of the political reality of murder and kidnapping of American citizens in Lebanon and elsewhere, "Cover Up" comes as an assurance that Uncle Sam's arms are long and strong and that there are saints to protect us, at least in television fiction.

CLIFFHANGERS

What kind of pleasure does a formulaic television series provide? Broadly speaking, all art, literature, drama, music, and popular arts help us escape from whatever conditions we are placed in. The escape may be from ennui, boredom, insecurity, loneliness, or some physical or mental pain. If escapism is a necessary concomitant of both high and low art, then there must be something else that distinguishes the escapist experience one enjoys on the dreary heath with King Lear from that of the barbecue at Southfork. It is the quality of the imaginatively reconstructed world to which we escape that makes the difference. Television series art gives us a world infused with moral fantasy where the good prevails in the end, which is only an hour away; and even this hour-long wait is full of the intense excitement of chases, fistfights, shoot-outs, and sex kittens in a guilt-free atmosphere.

According to John G. Cawelti,

> In reading or viewing a formulaic work, we confront the ultimate excitement of love and death, but in such a way that our basic sense of security and order is intensified rather than disrupted, because, first of all, we know that this is an imaginary rather than a real experience, and second, because the excitement and uncertainty are ultimately controlled and limited by the familiar world of formulaic structure.[8]

Of course, while reading Romeo and Juliet we know that the experience is unreal, though probable. What high art does is to invite participation through confrontation but not through identification, though identification in the beginning is necessary for sympathetic engagement. We do not identify with Macbeth but confront his problems and his nightmares and are confirmed in our humanity at the end. The television series drama is comparable to a rollercoaster which hurtles you from the peak of one suspenseful excitement to another--short periods of explosive excitement and then quiet again. It is a beautifully ordered world full of guilt-free enjoyment where, unlike tragedy or epic, no questions are asked because the secular saints take care of them. The television serial gives us a free, thrilling ride from one season's cliffhanger to another season's cliffhanger, from Friday's unresolved crisis to Monday's unanswered question, from one commercial's solution to another's problem. Think of the last episode of the 1985 season of "Dynasty." The wedding party was mowed down by the Moldavian rebels. We had the certainty of knowing that the Carrington dynasty would survive, but which members would live? Similarly, who would survive after Bobby in "Dallas"? Or would Reva return to her old husband H.B. in "Guiding Light"? Television drama depends on suspense of plot, whereas serious literature develops characterization and motivation through suspense of form. Plot suspense simply creates temporary fear and uncertainty about a conflict.

Suspense of form and suspense of story plot are both indispensable to narrative art--what matters is the degree of emphasis; it is a zero-sum situation. One might say narrative art, literary or audiovisual, is born out of the interaction between paradigmatic (associative) and syntagmatic (combinatory) elements, a compromise between the network of character relations and the need for the story to progress through suspense. The serial television drama, such as the soap opera, displays rich associations of character relationships and dwells leisurely on human emotions which slow down its narrative pace, yet contains enough suspense to hold the daytime audience's interest five days a week. Soap operas, with their open-end narrative structure, do share melodramatic elements with the other forms of television drama but are not formulaic in nature,[9] because formula by its very definition is predicated upon closure, the final resting point of the narrative. Therefore, it is difficult to agree with John G. Cawelti when he includes soap opera among formulaic narrative literature, because soap operas, including the nighttime serials, are not dependent upon closure.

TOPICALITY

The fantasy world of television drama, which breathlessly hurtles us from one segmental suspense to another and functions according to our desires and dreams, predicates its appeal upon the issues of the day. Though drama reduces all actions to the present, television drama deals with the present moment only. Television drama, unlike movies, has no memory or history. Suspense, triumph over evil, and topicality inform its structural principles. Its emotive power is derived from the process of the world being recast before our eyes--rid of its grossness, sickness, crime, deceit, injustice.

If all television series embody moral fantasy, wish fulfillment, and topicality and are soaked in violence and sex, how do we explain the decline in the popularity of a genre, say, the Western? How do we account for the fact that certain programs like "Mary Tyler Moore Show," "Kojak," and "Lou Grant" are no longer enjoyed by audiences?

It could be said that when a particular narrative or dramatic pattern has exhausted all the possibilities of exploration in a certain domain, the series begins to create audience fatigue. When we have indulged in all the combinations and recombinations that fantasizing can allow, the mind begins to withdraw its allegiance. Maybe the original creativity and innovativeness of the series has dried up, and what we see are remakes of the residue. This is a problem with the closed-end narrative or the dramatic series but not so much with open-end structures like soap operas because of their capacity for assimilation and improvisation. The very predictability of T.J. Hooker, Trapper John, Magnum, et al., which gave a sense of security earlier, begins to get on one's nerves. Saints and formulas make life secure and safe but also create boredom, and the audience looks for alternative sources of enjoyment and gratification.

Probably a more important cause for the death of a formula, genre, or program is the slow and imperceptible change in the mode of consciousness. The way we fantasize about life's possibilities is a consequence of the basic set of values of the society and its topical concerns, problems, anxieties, fears, hopes, and dreams. Though basic values remain unchanged over a long period of time, obsessive concerns and moods change, thus altering the mode of consciousness. Such change necessitates new conventions, new structures, and different ways of ordering our imaginative and real life experiences. Therefore, the key to understanding the longevity of a formulaic program does not depend on audience suspense, interest, and excitement or identification with a protagonist, but the correspondence between moral fantasy embodied in the program and the mode of consciousness of the audience. If a mode of consciousness were empirically observable (quantifiable), one could predict the life of a program or whether a new program would succeed with the audience, thus obviating much of the guesswork in programming. But at present we are prisoners of a circular argument: since "The Cosby Show" is a hit, it must articulate the audience's mode of consciousness, and vice versa.

COMMERCIAL-PUNCTUATED ACTION

In the traditional narrative the progress of the storyline, action, and character has only one aim: to shape the vision which would give the work of art unity and wholeness.

Form and Structure of TV Drama

To complete this unformed vision, or form-in-suspense, all narrative threads, scenes, and acts are joined. Control of narrative is a function of artistic creation.

But television programming is also a merchandiser, and its narrative flow is not determined by the imperatives of artistic vision but by the utilization of television time for commercial interruptions. For millennia humans expected and enjoyed uninterrupted narrative discourse, but since the advent of commercial broadcasting the sanctity of non-interruption has been questioned and found almost unnecessary to the enjoyment of narrative. It was presumed that undivided attention and a contemplative mind were essential requirements for the fullest enjoyment of the narrative, oral, written, or performed. Television has called forth the human's ability to enjoy interrupted narrative discourse without loss of meaning through the mind's capacity for what Gestalt psychologists call "closure." Mind perceives the configurated whole rather than the individual units. In fact, commercials whet the appetite and prepare us for more to come. They serve as a background beat that heightens the audience's expectation of the narrative.

How have commercials shaped the structure of television drama? They have become conventions of the television drama, as the five-act division of a play, the fourteen lines of a sonnet, or the invocation to a goddess in epic were conventions of former times. The important point is how the television creator orders dramatic narrative to bridge over commercials and impose a unity of impression upon segmented action.

Each segment of an episode has several storylines developing simultaneously but at different stages of crisis. The camera cuts from one storyline to another, so that before the commercial break at least one subplot reaches a crisis point to sustain the suspense. In an episode of "Guiding Light," for example, Maureen tells Claire that she knows whose child Claire is carrying. Does she really know, wonders Claire, and we have a commercial. But when we resume, Billy is talking to his father H.B. about the financial crisis the family (the Lewises) is caught in. Each segment is a complete act in itself, and it is the configuration of these vivid acts that creates the Gestalt impression of wholeness. David Thorburn says that the effect of commercials upon television drama has been,

> ... the refinement of a segmented dramatic structure peculiarly suited to a formula story whose ending is predictable--the doctor will save the patient, the cop will catch the criminal--and whose capacity to surprise or otherwise engage its audience must therefore depend largely on the localized vividness and potency of the smaller units or episodes that comprise the whole.... Good television melodramas are those in which an intricately formulaic plot conspires perfectly with the commercial interruptions to encourage a rich articulation of the separate parts of the work....[10]

Thus each segmented unit is complete within the larger unfolding completeness of the whole drama. One might look at a series drama as consisting of a number of what Brecht called Grundgestus--a composite of sound, sight, and gesture, or an emotionally charged and eloquent tableau with memorable dialogue. A television dramatic series narrative moves from one explosive, sensuous, vivid, and memorable tableau to another. Take the case of the crime drama, "Miami Vice." At the heart of each episode is a crime boss--remote, unforgiving, protected by massive walls of concrete and by guards. He controls the drug traffic, call girls, streetwalkers, nightclubs, and whatever is worthwhile. One of the episodes passes through the following six tableaux, each with an emotionally charged and memorable slogan:

a. WE HAVEN'T TRIED A TRICK WHICH WE CAN'T HANDLE
The words are uttered by Gina, one of the two vice squad girls who volunteers to trap the crime boss. Will she sleep with the boss?

b. DON'T YOU WANT TO SEE YOUR WIFE AGAIN?
Crockett of the vice squad tells the drug warehouse boy (Bob) to inform on the criminals. The boy is between the devil and the deep blue sea. He is history, with a young widow, if he does not squeal.

c. CROCKETT, YOU ARE JAILED FOR CONTEMPT
The judge asks Crockett to name the accuser so that the defense attorney can ask him questions. The judge seems to be thwarting justice, but

common law says everyone is innocent until proven otherwise.

d. CROCKETT DIDN'T LET DOWN HIS INFORMANT
The whole town talks about Crockett. Two street bums inform the squad that Alverado is not the real boss but only an operator.

e. POLICE TAKE CARE OF PEOPLE WHO DON'T PAY THEIR DUES
Alverado is arrested in his sanctuary, the club.

f. ARE YOU GIRL SCOUTS?
The crime boss meets his destiny at the hands of Gina, whom he had violated the previous night, and Trudy.

Each episode of a series drama consists of a flow of spectacles with enchanting music, titillating females, breathtaking scenery, and fireworks culminating in the victory of law and order over chaos, health over sickness, life over death.

Each series episode is a drama of reassurance which is reinforced by several thirty-second commercials in dramatic format, assuring audiences that life would be happy if they ate at Wendy's or used spray that makes the hair bounce or tried kiss-kiss Closeup. Thus the melodramatic structure of the television series drama is supported by the persuasive little dramas of the commercials--which explains why commercials are not perceived as interruptions but rather are accepted as reinforcements of the miracles of saints. One could argue the opposite as well: that the melodramatic structure of the nighttime series drama conditions the audience to an unquestioned acceptance of the commercial messages (this assertion would, however, need empirical evidence to support). As Martin Esslin says:

> ... the TV commercial, exactly as the oldest known types of theatre, is essentially a religious form of drama which shows us human beings as living in a world controlled by a multitude of powerful forces that shape our lives. We have free will, we can choose whether we follow their precepts or not, but woe betide those who make the wrong choice.[11]

The wrong choice in the nighttime drama would be to side with the forces of destruction; in the case of commercials, it would be to not use the product being advertised. Since the commercial and the series drama both use melodramatic formulas consisting of problem-solution narrative, music-dance, slogans, and spectacles, each is supported in its emotional impact. Not much research has been done on the interaction between the melodramatic structure of nighttime series and commercials; the field is virgin and fertile.

Television drama, instead of succumbing to the impossible limitations imposed by the medium, is emerging as victorious, creative, and vital. Its vitality comes from its topicality; its capacity to use literatures of the past as living museum of ideas and episodes; its unabashed and unhesitating tendency to borrow, adopt, and innovate, and to reject what does not correspond with the audiences' perceptual network and mode of consciousness. According to David Thorburn:

> Like the Renaissance sonnet or Racine's theatre, television melodrama is always successful when it most fully embraces that which confines it, when all the limitations imposed upon it--including such requirements as the 60 or 90 minute time slot, the commercial interruptions, the small dimensions of the screen, even the consequences of low-budget filming--become instruments of use, conventions whose combined workings create unpretentious and spirited dramatic entertainments, works or popular art that are engrossing, serious, and imaginative.[12]

The virility of television drama comes from the fact that it has redefined the received dramatic traditions and wedded them to the specifics of media technology and the demands of the marketplace.

"HILL STREET BLUES": THE CASE OF RECOMBINANT PROGENY

When on January 15, 1981, an unusually rough-grained cop show went on the air, audiences received a cultural shock because they had become indoctrinated with the notion that good television came only from the banks of the Thames.

Form and Structure of TV Drama

Of course the audiences were familiar with the rapidity of video music images, the melodramatic narratives of the series and serials, "M*A*S*H," "Barney Miller," and "Fort Apache, The Bronx." But they never thought that NBC would dare to break out of the security of formulaic concoctions, risk profits, and stake its reputation.

"Hill Street Blues" once again raises questions about television creativity. Who was the real creator of the show: NBC's Fred Silverman or Steven Bochco and Michael Kozoll? Or was it MTM, which owned the show? One might escape the question by citing several combined factors, like two particular writer-producers at their creative best; the right company; the proper choice of directors, line producers, and cast; etc. Probably the truth is that the urban audience's mode of consciousness and network of assumptions were changing and needed articulation; Fred Silverman intuitively grasped the groundswell and had the creative inspiration and courage to want a new kind of police drama. The rest is the story of organization and executed vision.[13]

Narrative Structure and Atmospherics

"Hill Street Blues" plunges viewers into a disturbed beehive, in contradistinction to a traditional crime drama's presentation of a problem predicating heroics, resolution, and restoration of order with hallelujah to the secular saints. The junkies and the Blues (police) of the Hill Street are caught in the same moral web, which is not of their making, and there are no clear distinctions between good and evil, "ours" and "theirs." What is the difference between a cop whose personal life drives him to alcoholism and a teenager whose unsupportive home life drives her to prostitution? The cop visits Alcoholics Anonymous and makes promises; the teenage prostitute visits the precinct station and makes promises. The Blues and the junkies shoot at each other and sometimes shed tears for each other. Hill Street is a multidimensional world where the planes of compassion, futility, and cruelty crisscross to create a helter-skelter sense of reality.

Thus there is the absence of clearcut conflict in "Hill Street Blues" necessitating any climax or resolution. At best each situation demands a compromise, a patch-up solution, a dissipation. Though a television series, as distinguished from a serial, consists of self-contained episodes, "Hill Street Blues" episodes do not contain closures as resolution. Each episode seems to say, "This is the solution for the time being. For a final solution don't come to Hill Street." According to J. Ellis:

> The TV series repeats a problematic. It therefore provides no resolutions of the problematic at the end of each episode, nor, often, even at the end of the run of the series.... Fundamentally, the series implies the form of the dilemma rather than that of resolution and closure. This perhaps is the central contribution that broadcast TV has made to the long history of narrative forms and narrativised perception of the world.[14]

What Ellis says is true of "Hill Street Blues" but not of other nighttime series like "Trapper John M.D.," "Matt Houston," etc., because each of their episodes does have a closure and resolution. What Ellis has in mind is a television serial like "Guiding Light," for instance, which has an open-end narrative structure where every solution is a problem. The open-endedness of "Hill Street Blues" is of a different kind. It is a self-conscious refusal to provide answers because there are none in a society which is crumbling and disintegrating and needs socio-politico-economic action rather than mere police action. Instead of restoring order to a chaotic world, "Hill Street Blues" ricochets society's sickness on its face, thus redefining the ethos of melodrama. It has the trappings of melodrama yet does not have its spirit. At the end of each episode we are left with drug busts, broken vending machines, child shoplifters, teenage prostitutes, grand but empty gestures, heightened but hollow dramatic utterances ("I shall not allow you to violate the Constitution," says Judge Wachtel), with more to come at the next episode's roll call. "Hill Street Blues" mocks the vision of melodrama but borrows its thunder and glory. It is a mock-melodrama.

"Hill Street Blues" multilinear plot structure is soap-operatic. As in soap opera, there are three or four stories simultaneously struggling for closure, thrusting themselves forward for narrative attention. Some situations get involved, others continue and dissipate, which makes the

Form and Structure of TV Drama   77

show coterminus with life's happenings and explains to an extent its attraction for urban intelligentsia. While the soap opera's multilinear plot moves excruciatingly slowly, the multiplane action of "Hill Street Blues" moves quickly to nowhere, thus mocking the soap opera's promise of resolution.

    Consider how a typical episode solves its problem. In an episode coinciding with the Thanksgiving weekend, four situations call for our attention:

>   A. A teenaged parolee on trial for murder, Floyd Green, has threatened to kill the witnesses who will testify against him. Hill Street Precinct captain Frank Furillo requests Judge Wachtel to grant a restraining order, but the judge (who reminds viewers of Brecht's Judge Azdak in the <u>Caucasian Chalk Circle</u>) refuses to oblige the police and orders the Blues to keep at least one hundred yards away from Floyd Green.
>
>   B. Officer Bobby Hill struggles with a tax audit and makes a grandiloquent statement heard since the days of the prophets: "This government makes people into thieves."
>
>   C. Detective Johnny LaRue has wrangled six airplane tickets for Las Vegas for the Thanksgiving weekend and plans to make a profit by inviting his colleagues.
>
>   D. Sergeant Lucy Bates is called to solve a shoplifting problem caused by a black teenager, Fabian.

The four stories are enacted with traditional melodramatic noise and chaos, shoot-outs and chases, and there is lot of intermeshing of the personal tales of the officers, but what stands out loud and clear in this episode are two tableaux which for the emotionalism and dramatic distillation are remarkable, yet they are equally silly in the solutions they propose.

    Floyd Green is suspected of killing again; when closeted with Public Defender Joyce Davenport, the suspect turns out to be not Floyd but his brother Bernard Green, who is only sixteen and believes himself beyond the pale of

law. Bernard erupts violently when the public defender
tells him that the law has changed. He is brought before
the court, and Judge Wachtel asks the question we all ask
about assassins: "Are you evil or a case of pathology?"
With one question the judge turns television into a political
and moral forum. Then another criminal whose bail was
raised from $2,000 to $5,000 yells out and threatens to shoot.
There ensues a remarkable scene. Everyone, including Judge
Wachtel, draws his gun and assumes the ready-to-shoot posture of a stereotypical policeman show. The judge upturns
the scale of justice and shoots like a cop. Does this mean
that the best way to deal with criminals is to shoot them?

In the second story, Sgt. Lucy Bates offers a personal solution to Fabian's problem. She persuades the street
urchin to stay with her. He refuses; she cries. Imagine a
police officer crying! She gets legal custody of him, confronts him again, and says, "I can't be your mamma--one
look would make it obvious--but I want to help you." The
boy, in spite of his objections ("I might have to do school
stuff"), agrees to live with her. Lucy Bates' solution to
the problem of a homeless street urchin is compassionate but
futile, as Judge Wachtel's solution to Green's problem was
desperate but futile. This is not melodrama, where disorder
is temporary, only to be set right by heroes with the right
stuff.

Characters

"Hill Street Blues" is an overcrowded place where too
many characters are doing (or not doing) too many things,
mixing irrelevancies with the problems at hand. Complexity
and congestion, reminding one of the city's continuous crisis, are achieved by the frantic pace, quick cuts, and jerky,
handheld camera technique. Added to this is the complexity
of characterization which makes the show interesting, involving and demanding participation from the audience. Captain
Furillo (Daniel J. Travanti), who is the narrative agent,[15]
gives viewers a point of reference by which to understand
the philosophical drift of the show. The problems of a police officer who leads an organization as undisciplined as Hill
Street are many and frustrating. There are simply too many
constituencies expecting too many quick results. Captain
Furillo is a compassionate man who understands his own

frailties and those of his fellow officers. He is a recovered alcoholic, and for him heroism is conquest of self-defeat. He lives and works in a brutalized world where police officers wielding guns are tempted to go out and shoot, but he restrains them. Society can be torn apart by overenthusiastic policemen as much as by criminals. Furillo's pragmatic and compassionate temperament disciplines the raw energies of the Hill Street community.

Other characters are equally well developed and individualized and have their own ideological ways of setting the world in order. Goldblume, for instance, recoils at violence, though as a policeman he should have become desensitized to the cruelties of both the police and the goons. He is the peacemaker, the negotiator who tries to remain sane and stick to his principles in spite of many provocations. In contrast, Howard Hunter would settle most societal issues with a gun, while Chief Daniel responds to political pressures and does not mind bending the rules.

The women characters are equally fascinating. The police women are independent, sexually liberated, and tough. Lucy Bates (Betty Thomas) is a fascinating study of a woman who proves herself capable of advancing to the rank of sergeant after the death of Sergeant Esterhaus. She retains a tender heart, as we find in the episode when she cries over the street urchin's plight. In Joyce Davenport (Veronica Hamel) the audience sees not only a sexually desirable woman, but also a tough and intelligent professional who as a public defender constantly reminds her lover Furillo, even in bed, of the rights of alleged criminals. This makes her a force at the precinct station house.

"Hill Street Blues" has many fascinating characters, some drawn with the rapid strokes of a painter's brush and others in the process of developing and growing. Though each has his or her own philosophy of coping with crisis in society, they are all subservient to Furillo's dominant point of view that while the total elimination of crime is not possible, crime could be prevented and misery could be lessened; since the society is out of joint, the police can do this much and no more.

Audience

This highly acclaimed show, which received twenty-one Emmy nominations and won eight (best series, lead actor, lead actress, supporting actor, writer, director, cinematography, and film sound editing) apart from the Humanities Prize, has now succeeded in finding an audience large enough to justify its commercial existence. It is popular with urban trend-setting viewers (ages 18 to 49) who in the long run have a greater effective voice in the political and economic life of the country than their number would show. "Hill Street Blues" has now become a prestigious program for NBC and may be a trendsetter. It is maintaining viewers' loyalty in spite of the fact that it demands from the audience more attention than the usual dramatic series. The factors which combine to appeal to sophisticated, literate, and socially conscious viewers are responsible for turning away a large audience which could be satisfied with "CHiPs" or "Matt Houston," for instance. In short, "Hill Street Blues" audio-visual text demands from the audience a serious engagement in unfolding the narrative and understanding its hermeneutic codes. The text needs interpretation because characters are not stereotypes but complex, rounded personalities with their own personal problems and interlocking relationships which pass through a multilinear plot structure. The photographic style, soap-operatic intercutting, and soundtrack laced with bursts of laughter and irrelevant conversation all create a kind of estrangement, alienation, or what Brecht called "verfremdungeffekt," which deprives the audience of the candy of the eye and ear and makes them think and participate. Yet the reality of "Hill Street Blues" is not so grim as to turn the viewer away. Its world is still manageable, though ugly.

NOTES

1. Tyrone Guthrie, "Theatre and Television," in The Eighth Art (New York: Holt, Rinehart and Winston, 1982), pp. 96-98.
2. Luis Buñuel, "Cinema: An Instrument of Poetry," Theatre Arts, 46 (July 1962), p. 18.
3. Richard L. Stromgren and Martin F. Norden, Movies: A Language in Light (Englewood Cliffs, NJ: Prentice-Hall, 1984), p. 207.

4. John G. Cawelti, Adventure, Mystery, and Romance (Chicago: The University of Chicago Press, 1976), p. 6.
5. Robert Warshow, The Immediate Experience, quoted in Cawelti, p. 10.
6. Throughout the chapter I have depended on Cawelti's discussion on formulaic literature.
7. Webster's New Collegiate Dictionary.
8. Cawelti, p. 16.
9. Horace Newcomb, TV: The Most-Popular Art (Garden City, NY: Anchor Press, 1974), pp. 162-163.
10. David Thorburn, "Television Melodrama," in Understanding Television, Richard P. Adler, ed. (New York: Praeger, 1981), pp. 78-79.
11. Martin Esslin, "Aristotle and Advertiser: The Television Commercial Considered as a Form of Drama," Horace Newcomb, ed., Television: The Critical View, 3rd ed. (New York: Oxford University Press, 1982).
12. David Thorburn, p. 87.
13. Todd Gitlin, Inside Prime Time (New York: Pantheon Books, 1983), pp. 273-288.
14. J. Ellis, Visible Fictions: Cinema, Television, Video (London: Routledge & Kegan Paul, 1982), p. 54.
15. S. Rimmon-Kenan, Narrative Fiction: Contemporary Poetics (London: Methuen, 1983), pp. 71-76.

Chapter Five

DRAMATIC SERIAL: PRIME TIME AND DAYTIME

* Origin, Form, and Structure
* Structural Characteristics
* Inside Soap Opera Today
* Prime-Time Series and Serials
* "Dallas" to "Dynasty"
* "Guiding Light"

The daytime serial television drama, which is America's greatest and most puzzling contribution to world dramaturgy, has stubbornly flourished in defiance of all known tenets of drama from the Greeks to Grotowski. The billion dollars in revenue and millions of loyal viewers it holds attentive day after day are an embarrassment for the high-brow critic. Its very name, "soap opera," seems to mock the critic. Its generative mechanism--conceived in suds by toiletry manufacturer Procter and Gamble, et al.--derides the romantic notion of art as an act of inspired creation. Soap operas are manufactured by assembly-line writers, directors, and other substitutes. They serve the free marketplace and enrich popular culture.

ORIGIN, FORM, AND STRUCTURE

Soap opera rose amid the din of the market to serve commercial broadcasting and to entertain generations of homemakers in the early days of radio. Broadcast historians trace the development of commercial radio to an attempt by AT&T in 1922 to start toll broadcasting, which would have given access to commercial users to advertise their messages over AT&T telephone lines. Out of the ensuing struggle of the giants--RCA, General Electric, Westinghouse, and AT&T --two networks were born, NBC in 1926 and CBS in 1928. The Radio Act of 1927, which established the FRC, gave final shape to the structure of commercial broadcasting in America, consisting of "a nationwide system of stations linked by telephone lines, local stations on temporary licenses, revenues from advertising, and a regulatory agency that by law is to respect the rights of broadcasting under the First Amendment to practice free speech while requiring broadcasters to base their decisions on the public interest, convenience, and necessity."[1]

Though advertisers were slow to recognize the immense potential of commercial radio broadcasting, the groundwork for an advertisement-supported cultural expression for the millions had been established when America reached the threshhold of the Great Depression. Advertising agencies of the time played a crucial role in producing programs which would bring audiences back to their radio sets at the same time each day. Through many trials and errors, a radio serial called "Amos 'n' Andy" broadcast by WGN succeeded in hooking millions by 1929. "Amos 'n' Andy," a "radio programming phenomenon,"[2] which was about two uprooted southern blacks portrayed by white actors, was a prime-time serial. By the early thirties studies had established that the housewife was the real household spender, particularly for soap, food items, and toiletries, and she was home eager to be entertained. Advertising agencies developed entire programs financed by sponsors, and networks sold time to sponsors to earn profits. Because most of the sponsoring companies manufactured soap and toiletries, their sponsored serial programs came to be known as soap operas--a marriage between the sublime and the mundane.

Some scholars like Raymond W. Stedman[3] give Irna Phillips, an employee of WGN, credit for creating the first real soap, "The Painted Dreams," which premiered on October 20, 1930. The soap told the story of an Irish-American woman, Mother Moynihan, her family, and her friends. It had various intertwined plots which moved the story slowly but created interest through complications and their resolutions. It dealt with love, marriage, motherhood, and the tribulations which were every woman's destiny.

Eventually when Irna Phillips fell afoul of her employer WGN and filed a law suit, she claimed ownership not of the original story, but of the development of the story's idea through characters and the dramatic milieu, thus establishing the fact that a creative act could be split and shared by many people. And subsequent events showed that every participant in a collective creative act was replaceable. As Robert C. Allen says, "Interestingly, the basis of the suit reveals that even in this embryonic stage of the development of the soap opera form, it was viewed as a set of structural principles that motored narrative and character development."[4]

Since the court established that WGN had originated the soap opera idea and title and therefore owned the property rights, Irna Phillips transformed "Painted Dreams" into "Today's Children" for NBC. Irna Phillips continued writing and developing soap operas until her death in 1974. Her most important contribution to daytime serial drama is "Guiding Light," which premiered in 1937. Transferred to television in 1952, it was broadcast daily on CBS; it has been running for half a century. Irna Phillips, an unemployed schoolteacher who wandered into a Chicago studio in the Depression era, began a type of program which has since entertained millions of women and men and generated a lasting dramatic structure.

The contribution of Anne Hummert and her husband Frank to the development of soap opera's form and structure is of a different kind. They created an organizational prototype for the collective production of soap opera through a team of writers, dialoguers, editors, and others, more in the nature of an army commander conducting a war campaign than an artist indulging in a single act of imagination. Stedman states that through many failures the Hummerts learned that for a daily serial a slow-moving plot was advantageous. Though their first radio serial, "The Stolen Husband," did not attract much attention, "Betty and Bob," which premiered in October 1932, was a great success. It was the story of a secretary who married her boss, resulting in complications which constitute the basic theme of the domestic novel and woman's fiction. Apart from romance, "Betty and

Bob" dealt with issues like child rearing, divorce, family, infidelity, and jealousy, the staple soap ingredients even today. The Hummerts contributed to the open-end narrative of soap opera, redundancy in storytelling to encourage listeners to tune in the next day, and the concept of housewife as audience. According to Madeleine Edmondson and David Rounds, all this was done in the name of the housewife, who was "assumed to be trotting about her daily chores with mop in one hand, duster in other, cooking, tending babies, answering telephones," and the serial had to be "powerful enough to hold her interest despite all interruptions and bring her back for more."[5]

The Hummerts and Irna Phillips, along with others, created soap opera dramaturgy, which centered on radio time as commodity with the housewife as consumer. As the end of World War II ushered in a peacetime economy, radio began to lose its ascendency to television; the cosmetic and toiletry manufacturers needed television to reach out and tap the increasing commercial demands of the postwar population. Procter and Gamble pioneered the first network television soap opera serial, "The First Hundred Years," in December 1950. Despite initial conceptual doubts and production hurdles, television soap opera got a shot in the arm when, in the fall of 1951, CBS introduced three daytime serials, one of which, "Search for Tomorrow," continues even today. "Guiding Light" made the transition to television in 1952 and was simulcast on radio and television through 1956. In the autumn of 1960, CBS cancelled its last four radio soaps, and since then television soap opera has not only prospered but has "survived changes in network programming strategy, regulatory upheavals, innumerable network management regimes, cyclic economic fluctuations, and the entry of millions of American women into the paid work force."[6]

From the very beginning soap operas have served the marketplace as well as the cultural needs of the housewife. Their open-end narrative form can be adapted to changing times and modes of consciousness. American soap opera binds the symbolic with the real.

STRUCTURAL CHARACTERISTICS OF
THE SERIAL

The television serial adopted from the radio soap opera its openness of serial narrative, contemporary issues, didacticism, and ethos of the domestic novel. One might visualize a serial drama as an unending succession of waves in the vast ocean of life. Serial drama promises to last forever. "The most obvious structural feature of daytime serials is that they never begin and never end," observe Muriel G. Cantor and Suzanne Pingree.[7] Serials are slow-paced operatic dramas with several miniclimaxes and without progress in the sense of change or new order, though there may be change and progress in the sense of assembly-line operations. Calling serial drama antiprogressive, Tania Modleski comments that "just as Sarraute's work is opposed to the traditional novel form, soap opera is opposed to the classic [male] film narrative, which with maximum action, always pertinent dialogue, speeds its way to the restoration of order."[8] What attracts viewers to the slow-paced serial without progress? According to Allen it is the richness of its texture, the intermingling and intermeshing of characters and the complex web of destiny they weave--"a complexity that makes the soap opera unique among visual narratives and unmatched in literary narrative except for the most elaborate of epics."[9]

In the traditional novel or drama the action revolves around a protagonist and an antagonist, with the minor characters acting out their destinies either as victims or as spectators. A single action motivated by the protagonist or antagonist fuels the narrative on relentlessly. There is no such relentless inevitability in soap operas. A soap opera is a vast community of characters whose actions crystallize into many intertwining subplots of nearly equal importance. The camera as narrator, built on closeups and two-shots, moves from one subplot to another as a question is posed or an emotion bursts forth. Soap opera dramaturgy has done away with indispensability of characterization because although individual characters may disappear, return or suffer many adversities or vicissitudes, the soap opera community goes on. As Allen states:

> The soap opera community is a self-perpetuating, self-preserving system little affected by the turbulence experienced by its individual members or

the fate of any one character. The naive might attend only to the constant state of crisis experiences by individual characters but the experienced viewer is watchful for the paradigmatic strands that bind the community of characters together and the sometimes glacially slow but far more significant alterations in the network. "Who a character is" is as much a function of his or her place in this paradigmatic system as what he or she "does" in a syntagmatic sense.[10]

This network of character relationship, which Allen calls "paradigmatic complexity" in semiotic terms, explains the soap opera's heritage of redundancy from the days of the radio serial. Each day's episode begins with developments of the previous day, which enables irregular viewers to keep posted on the narrative's progress. This repetitiveness also acts as a patterning device which characters use to echo and re-echo their relationships to the maze of characters in the community. The result is richness of texture and depth of feeling which the soap opera invokes in its viewers, partly explaining its continuing attraction. For example, in "Guiding Light" at one moment Claire is pregnant with Ed's child, though she thought her boy friend Fletcher, whom she was going to marry, was the real father. Claire refuses to live a life of lies with Fletcher and declines to marry him. For several episodes her pregnancy becomes the topic of conversation until viewers begin to feel the throbbing of new life, as Claire herself does when she says, "I feel it kicking now." Ed cannot escape the consequences, nor can his wife Maureen. They are all caught in a web of intricate relationships, unable to break away. In soap opera there is no escape, no forgetfulness, though there may be temporary amnesia. This constant refrain, or mnemonic device, deepens emotional content for the viewers and at the same time makes the soap opera "an endless string of excruciatingly retarded subplot, related in episodes whose redundance gives them an almost Sisyphean tiresomeness."[11] But soap opera viewers are ready to exchange fast-paced story development for prolonged moments of intimacy and harmony; however, the dramatic conflict is the staple.

Instead of having a controlling center, soap opera gives us a floating center, a moving point of view from one network of character relationships to another. The total effect is the grandeur of a slow-moving juggernaut. The moving point of view leaves each strand or segment of the story at some critical juncture to be picked up again later, thus maintaining viewers' interest. The interrupted narrative from episode to episode holds viewers' interest by partially fulfilling their expectations of closure, or orgasm, as it were. Soap opera viewers are tantalized and teased along the episodic and segmented structure through the promise of tomorrow and tomorrow and tomorrow.

INSIDE SOAP OPERA TODAY

Soap opera's world is mostly confined to indoor locations representing fictional towns, valleys, hospitals, or even big cities like Washington, D.C., or New York. Whatever the locale, the thickening of the plot, with its interweaving of destinies, loves, jealousies, marital infidelities, and deceptions, is acted out in bedrooms, bars, restaurants, or living rooms. In this world action is dialogue,[12] a gesture, a twinkle, a wink, a tear. People dwell upon their emotions more than upon their thoughts.

America has undergone a change in sexual morality which finds faithful reflection in soapland. A pure woman is not a virgin. Adultery is not frowned upon. Premarital and extramarital sex are common, but sexual intercourse is not shown explicitly--rather it is suggested through conversation, fades, or other devices. Simply because a character is married does not mean he will not sleep with his friend's wife. Most of the characters sexually bait each other, yet deep down everyone strives for a lasting interpersonal relationship. This tremendous urge and need for love and for power over others is the driving force in the paradigmatic intricacies of character relationships, and it results in slow-moving action. People in the soap world pause over an emotion, linger on a kiss, turn their glances into eternities, as it were, to nullify the perpetual threat of impermanence and the transitoriness of human relations. Thus sexual immorality in soap opera has become a means of searching for deeper values and lasting emotions. An unwed pregnant girl might say, "This life is precious to me. I shall not abort it." By rejecting institutional marriage and all other traditional props which keep man and woman together, the characters in the

Dramatic Serial 89

daytime serials nakedly face existential truth: can humans be good without marriage, love, God? In such a world there are no heroes or villains, although there may be detestable creatures like Zach Grayson in "All My Children" or Debujak in "Ryan's Hope."

When this fictional world is grafted upon our real world day after day through the years, its subtle impact can only be surmised. As Dorothy Hobson says in <u>Cross Roads: The Drama of a Soap Opera</u>:

> The power of soap opera is immense and it is not normally recognized by the broadcasting industry as a whole. Many of the most socially aware and committed people in television are working in the area of documentary programme making and are often attempting to get over the exact message which Jack Barton achieves successfully in "Cross Roads." The clue to the success is certainly in the comment which he makes that the issues are grafted on to some of their characters, and the fact that the viewers care about these characters. It is potentially a very powerful form and implications for its misuse could be considerable, but the possibilities for its use are equally considerable.... One of the criticisms which is leveled at the programme is its simplicity, but there is a great strength in communicating a message in an accessible way, without trivializing the viewer.... [P]ushing back the boundaries or arousing political awareness is the business of the single play, or a current affairs or documentary programme.... However, there are areas of social concern which are a recognized part of soap opera, and "Cross Roads" in particular has intertwined social comment with its fictional form.[13]

American soap opera has been always characterized by its didactic spirit, and today the creators talk of their personal vision infusing their whole work.

PRIME-TIME DRAMA SERIES AND SERIALS

The series are made of exclusive and self-contained

episodes with the same principal characters and similar situations. They lack continuous narrative and revolve around some easily recognized formula. Since they are not sequenced in any order, they could be syndicated and run in any order; and they are very profitable to industry. Examples of drama series are situation comedies like "Three's a Crowd" and "E/R" and action, adventure, detective, and police dramas like "Miami Vice," "Simon and Simon," "Magnum, P.I.," etc. Mini-series have a continuous narrative which comes to an end. They are television versions of traditional novels. Prime-time serial drama, like daytime soap opera, is characterized by an opened-end structural flow of narrative from one segment to the next, destined to no inevitable conclusion or closure. "Dallas," "Dynasty," "Falcon Crest," and "Knots Landing" are some of the widely watched prime-time serial dramas, or nighttime soap operas.

Cantor and Pingree would not call prime-time serial dramas "soap operas" because they are not shown daily and are not meant exclusively for women, but Dorothy Hobson warns us that this narrow view would exclude British twice-weekly drama serials like "Cross Roads" and "Coronation Street" from this category.[14] There are, however, some structural and formalistic differences between daytime serials and prime-time serials. A season of a prime-time serial has 26 weekly episodes, as against 260 episodes for the daytime soap opera serial shown Monday through Friday throughout the year. A daytime soap is more like a mass transit system: commuters come and go, it is always there creating the illusion of perpetuity--life goes on. Because of its once-a-week occurrence, nighttime serial drama predicates a different structure. It is comparatively quick-paced, has lots of outdoor location shooting, dwells upon the star system, centers upon wealthy families, and is characterized by lust and power. Its lineage is traced to both movies and radio serials.

Although it has been observed by many critics that serials do not have a closure, they do have the distinctive characteristic of a season finale. As the season ends the mass media reverberate with cliffhangers: "Who shot J.R.?", "Who Shot Bobby?" The 1985 season finale of "Dynasty" showed a coup d'etat in the kingdom of Moldavia, where the whole wedding party at a gala dance was massacred. The viewers did not know whether or not the Carrington dynasty would survive. In "Dallas" Bobby was shot by the sister of his ex-wife Pam. Does that leave J.R. an uncontested heir to the Ewing family fortune? Cliffhangers do not have the inevitability of a developing crisis but are implanted as a deus ex machina in reverse, not to cut a knot but to create a sustained, lingering suspense-in-form. This dramatic illusion keeps the audience hoping. A daytime soap serial cannot afford to use this structural device, although ABC's "All My Children" created a puzzle to engage viewer loyalty by asking a public question: "What were you doing the night Zach Grayson was killed?"

Prime-time television serials have become identified with stars. J.R., Blake Carrington, Krystal, Alexis Colby are the most talked about television characters, and the actors and actresses who play them have negotiated their contracts on the basis of their popularity. A commercial cult is being created around them. Even a fashion industry is rising on their popularity. Nightime soap operas are on the whole marked by grandeur, display of wealth, elegance, and style. Lust for power and economic control is the motivating force that impels men and women into action in these prime-time series. In daytime soap operas prolific sex is a search for interpersonal relations, but in prime-time soaps sex is lust and domination.

While the daytime soap opera is community centered, the nightime serial is family centered. The number of characters in a prime-time serial is comparatively small and there is less time for paradigmatic complexity in the network of character relationships. The narrator camera does not cut from one strand to another as swiftly as in the daytime soap, and consequently the action is fast-paced. A viewer gets the impression of stable family structures in prime-time soap operas. One reason Cliff Barnes cannot stand against the Ewings is that he does not have a family name--he is an upstart attempting to take over from the Ewings. Alexis Colby is a breakaway bent upon revenge against her former husband Blake Carrington. And the families are associated with vast, romantic establishments--La Mirage, Falcon Crest, Southfork.

There is another marked distinction between the daytime and prime-time serials. In spite of the infidelities, adulteries, and treacheries, a strong sense of morality acts as a backdrop for the daytime community; consequently, guilt and remorse are its ruling emotions. In contrast, the nighttime serial drama is an amoral world where nothing succeeds like success. Humans use humans as fodder. The only thing that matters is personal power, family, dynasty. There is nothing good or evil in this world, but life is very exciting.

"DALLAS" TO "DYNASTY"

"Dallas" unfolds a society which never developed strong traditions of institutional morality, church, art, music, literature, or other trappings of culture. Nothing softens its relentless drive for power and lust for flesh--the forces which fuel the narrative. "Dallas" gives a shock of discovery that humans can live without morals and manners and still be happy. Sue Ellen and J.R., for instance, have matrimonial relations which are not based upon any kind of fidelity, emotional or sexual; they both cheat each other and know it. They have a son whose paternity was in doubt and was the subject of media gossip until at a cocktail party for the Dallas elite Miss Ellie dramatically announced the result of a blood test which conclusively proved that J.R. was indeed the father. This is the emerging mode of consciousness in American society today: what matters is not who is married to whom or who sleeps with whom but whose genetic code the child is carrying, which forms the basis of a custody battle, division of property, and the continuation of a family line. In a recent episode, when John Ross Ewing was rushed to the hospital for an emergency operation, Sue Ellen, the boy's mother, happened to be away on a shopping spree. J.R., who was having another affair, used this opportunity to press a feeling of guilt on Sue Ellen and drive her back to alcoholism. But the whole Ewing clan was mobilized and concerned about John Ross' life. John Ross is important because, as a probable heir to Ewing Oil, he is the future. Sue Ellen, Pam, Jenna--the mistresses and wives--come and go; in a male-dominated society every woman is a fleshpot unless she has the virtues of Miss Ellie and assumes the role of benevolent matriarch. Even if she is a doubting intellectual like Donna Ray, she survives only as a milch cow on Southfork.

The life force on "Dallas" as audiovisual narrative is Ewing Oil, built by the redoubtable Jock Ewing, who embodied the perpetual pioneering spirit which lurks in every American heart and of which dreams are made. Jock's original will enjoined his two sons, Bobby and J.R., to compete for control of Ewing Oil, but Miss Ellie, sensing that beastly competitiveness was tearing the boys apart, modified the will and asked them to manage Ewing Oil as a team. "Dallas" as a dramatic narrative is structured around the challenges to the Ewings' control of Ewing Oil, and no morality, law, or tradition is too sacred if it clashes with the goal of controlling Ewing Oil. So the dramatic conflict in "Dallas" is very clear: you are either a preserver or a destroyer of Ewing Oil. If you are not with J.R., you are against him, and he would go to any extent to destroy you.

Of the two brothers, Bobby is confused and soft. He is not J.R.'s conscience because he too would throw morality to the wind when Ewing Oil's future is in jeopardy, as happened in episodes when Cliff-Jamie made a takeover bid for the oil company. In fact, Cliff-Jamie's challenge was the severest ever faced by the Ewings, and even the worst critic of J.R., Ray, the illegitimate son of Jock who is the Ewings' ranch manager, forgot his differences and joined with the family to fight for Jock's honest name. He even separated from his wife Donna to help his half-brothers, who normally keep him on the fringes of Southfork.

In a dog-eat-dog world, the Ewing boys would tread any devious path to save Ewing oil. They reluctantly agree to part with 10 percent of Ewing Oil and give it to their hostile cousin Jack, who leads them to information which finally establishes the legality of Ewing Oil. J.R. would blackmail, bribe, threaten, cajole, and sleep with any woman to have his way. In a crisis he regards every human as a tool to be used to meet his ends. Is he a monster? He is redeemed not by his Southern charm, idiosyncratic gait, accent, or sexual prowess (at an age when men look for therapy), but by his capacity to get things done and attain his goal, an overvaulting ambition to establish his dynasty, and his faithfulness to Jock's memory. He enjoys his victories, sexual and financial, and is beyond the pale of law. His iconoclastic, lawless, and irreverent nature, steeled in ruthless determination and answerable to only one imperative--to hold on to Ewing Oil for John Ross--make his actions seem legitimate, his trespasses forgivable. We forgive the trespasses of a hero of melodrama because his actions restore order and peace, but J.R. escapes our contempt and wins our admiration because he stands for family, for dynasty, for continuity --aspects of the network of assumptions which audiences hold at present. Actor Larry Hagman's characterization of J.R., with his twitching smile, mannerisms, and cynicism, has made him into a star. It is not that he has no morals, but moral posture without material base is an empty threat particularly when the world is full of Cliff Barneses.

"Dallas" in many ways has a narrative structure similar to daytime soap operas with their endless intermeshing story lines. Like the soaps, it has all the trappings of melodrama --violence, sex, outdoor scenes rife with sensuality--and its plot does not obey any formula, apart from the end-of-season cliffhangers. "Dallas" represents an America untouched by international crisis, radical politics, racism, or other modern sickness of a super power. It represents a collective fantasy, a memory of a past which never existed yet is beautiful and desirable. It is a male fantasy of an America which is being lost daily to feminism, Jerry Falwell, Japan, terrorism. It is captivating in its pristine glory.

With "Dynasty" we move to a contemporaneous America of multinationals, foreign alliances, international terrorism, homosexuals, and liberated women on the prowl for sex or inheritance. From "Dallas" to "Dynasty" represents not only loss of accent but also loss of America's isolationist innocence. It is still a world of oil, but America through free enterprise is embroiled in all the major theaters of the world. Through the glitter and glamour of "Dynasty's" beautiful women and handsome men, with their mixed accents, viewers see America extending its tentacles to South America, the South China Sea, the Middle East, and some mythic kingdom for investment today, bases tomorrow. "Dynasty" is imperial America at its regal best.

Blake Carrington (John Forsythe), a handsome, debonair tycoon who controls Denver Carrington, is patriarch of a big family: two sons, one of whom cannot make up his mind between his wife and his gay lover, and the other a rapist who acts as his father's trouble-shooter; two daughters, one neurologically disturbed, who is in and out of marriage, has mysteriously vanished at the time of her remarriage, and has staged a comeback, and another, Amanda, who has an English accent and is to be married to the

Moldavian prince Michael. A third daughter, Kristina, was born to Krystal, the ravishing beauty and Carrington's former secretary, who stole his heart and drove his former wife Alexis Colby into perpetual hostility and business rivalry.

Blake Carrington and Alexis Colby share four children and a rich past. Alexis Colby's maneuvers to regain control over her grown-up sons and daughters and over Denver Carrington is the source of conflict that motivates the dramatic narrative. Blake versus Alexis, like J.R. versus Cliff Barnes in "Dallas," constitutes the main axis around which the narrative structure pivots; but what makes "Dynasty" so richly textured is the way it deals with tributary problems which flow into the mainstream and make it rich, colorful, and contemporary. Dominique, for instance, is black America symbolically fighting for her fair share, and at least at the level of popular art the problem is solved. Dominique is accepted by Blake Carrington as his half-sister, and when she is suddenly taken ill and is rushed into the emergency room, Blake's compassionate self pours out, "She is my sister. Please do everything you can." The white man accepts his black sister at least at the level of narrative fiction. Blake shows the same broad acceptance of life's realities when his son Steven's marriage breaks up because of his gay tendencies. He tells his son with stoic magnanimity that he would accept Steven as he is, though he would prefer that the marriage should continue for the sake of Steven's son: dynasty is very important to Blake Carrington.

Blake Carrington, as a patriarch concerned with the destiny of his children and with dynasty, would adopt all decent means to protect and enhance his fortune, but he would not hesitate to fight ruthlessly if driven to the wall. It was not his intention to have the Arab oil adventurer Rashid killed, but Rashid's written confession re-established Blake's political financial reputation. For his wife Krystal he went to the end of the world to fight his rival Daniel Reece. "My wife is not up for grabs," he warned Reece. Like J.R., Blake Carrington holds on and fights, but he is like a man who went to Oxford or Cambridge, as it were, and can converse with kings and queens.

Alexis Colby is no Miss Ellie. She is one of those females who never grow old, have a lover in every country, are connoisseurs of culinary delicacies, and believe that the world is made for them. She is feminism in full blossom. Alexis is the female version of J.R., combined with the graces of European culture. She is fascinating--call her vixen, if you are a male chauvinist.

In several respects "Dynasty" is closer to daytime soap opera than it is to "Dallas," but its reach is much greater than that of either. In "Dynasty" struggle for power is intricately complicated with love and romance. The undying love of Jeff for Fallon, Blake Carrington's passionate attachment to Krystal, Alexis' spasmodic cries of motherhood, Amanda's search for her true father, Sammy Jo's claim to Daniel Reece's fortune to establish her legitimacy, Dominique's struggle for legitimacy and respectability in an all-white family, the wildcat adventures of Lady Ashley, Steven's homosexual dilemma, King Galen's romance with Alexis, Dexter and Daniel Reece's involvement in a South American revolution, and the latter's rescue mission in Libya where he is killed in action are some of the romantic and adventurous stories which constitute the woof and warp of the rich paradigmatic structure which makes the narrative action flow majestically. The 1985 season finale brought viewers to the shocking world of terrorism, which ended in bloody carnage and sent them into a wild guessing game: who will survive the Beirut-style terrorist massacre of the Carringtons?

Although "Dynasty" shares its narrative structure with both "Dallas" and daytime soap operas, it orchestrates different and much wider concerns and values. Its mode of consciousness is not of sunbelt America, isolated and sheltered, but of contemporary American society facing growing concerns with life styles, multinational operations, international political imbroglios, racial integration, and the changing role of the family. Of course, like "Hill Street Blues," it too gives only a partial view of reality.

"GUIDING LIGHT":
KING OEDIPUS TO KYLE SAMPSON

A reader who has the patience to go through Lempriere's <u>Classical Dictionary</u> would have the impulse to say that probably the ancient Greeks' greatest contribution to human heritage was their mythology rather than their philosophy, tragedy, or the practice of democracy. If we secularize the intricate relationships of the gods and goddesses at Olympus, we come closer to the vast jungle of human relationships in the American soap opera, which is populated with innocent victims, secret agents, bed-hoppers, amnesia victims, lost relatives, successful sluts, waitresses turned heiresses (or is it the other way around?), the dead-come-alive, girls using pregnancies as shortcuts to marriage, characters in eternal love triangles, sweet all-sacrificing girls, people with terrible secrets, and those who would survive anything. Throughout its unprecedented narrative history, "The Guiding Light" has exhibited every kind of character, plot twist, and intrigue which the dramatic imagination can conceive. It is impossible to ignore its nearly half century of dramatic narrative, beginning with America's Depression years and extending through her humiliations in Beirut. In the July Fourth (1985) episode of "The Guiding Light," Kyle Sampson not only staged a hostile takeover of Lewis Oil from his father (H.B. Lewis), but also successfully took away his father's wife Reva. Kyle came to Springfield to find his identity, his family, his father, but when told that H.B. Lewis might be his father, thus making Reva his stepmother, he said that nothing mattered to him except Reva. From King Oedipus to Kyle Sampson, man has been freeing himself from sex as a source of guilt even when he sleeps with his stepmother, his father's wife: a woman is a woman. Greek and Roman gods and goddesses did the same; so did the Caesars. One finds the same sexual fluidity in other Springfield families--the Bauers of Cedars Hospital, the Spauldings, and everyone else.

The dilemmas characters in "The Guiding Light" face are not the same as those faced by the ancients, but they are terrible nonetheless. It is a grim world without humor,[15] yet it does not rise to a tragic level, not even to the status of domestic tragedy, because characters do not push issues to the limit of human forebearance. One might visualize the action in "The Guiding Light" as a pendulum movement--from one threatening brink to another--or as the beating of waves upon a rocky shore, which prompts Robert C. Allen to call the soap's action excruciatingly slow and Horace Newcomb to pronounce it "no action at all."[16] The dominant morality in "The Guiding Light" is acceptance of life as it comes, not survival at all costs, but acceptance of the impermanence of human relations and ties. This morality drives characters to look for deep and sincere relationships, lasting ties, final resting places for the heart, which consequently leads to paradigmatic complexities and moral and emotional conflicts.

Although the Springfield community has many events in progress at different paces and on different planes, often crisscrossing one another, two major dilemmas audiences witness are faced by the Lewises and the Bauers. A brief account shows the nature of the threatening brink and the possibility of retreat in preparation for another crisis. Kyle Sampson, son of a rich slut and a rich industrialist, comes to Springfield to be closer to his supposed family but is diverted from his pursuit by a ravishing beauty, Reva, who, unknown to herself, is his stepmother. Kyle takes control of Lewis Oil from Billy, his stepbrother, thus fueling a bloody feud. Probably the only way Kyle can identify with his father and recover him from oblivion is to take over his father's industrial empire and his young wife. Sally, Kyle's mother (an erstwhile prostitute), confronts her former lover H.B. Lewis with the question: "Why don't you tell Kyle that you are his real father and stop Billy and Kyle from killing each other? When Kyle realizes that Reva is his stepmother he will back out." This is the stuff of which tragedies are made, but the problem lacks tragic dimension because its resolution is predicated upon acceptance and survival.

A similar dilemma is faced by Claire, Maureen, Ed, and Fletcher, all staffmembers at the Cedars Hospital in Springfield. Maureen attempts to reassure her friend Claire, "I know you called off the wedding because Fletcher is not the baby's father." Maureen does not know that her own husband Ed is the father of Claire's child, and when Claire asks her if she knows who the father is, Maureen innocently says, "Yes, and I understand." The stunned Claire replies, "I thought when you found out you would hate me." Later, when Maureen and Ed go on a second honeymoon, she learns that it was Ed who impregnated her best friend. The sky seems to fall as she accuses her husband, "Why didn't you tell me? Don't ever touch me again! I am surrounded by pity and lies."

The dilemmas faced by the inhabitants of Springfield cannot be resolved by any authority because there is none in the soap opera world. The lack of resolution of these perpetually occurring problems in "The Guiding Light" and other soap operas is a source of everlasting fascination. Not suspense of plot but entanglement and disentanglement of the life of emotions is the soap's theater. In series drama every problem has a solution; even a mongrel breed like "Hill Street Blues" has a solution, however flimsy, to every problem. But "The Guiding Light" confronts the audience only with dilemmas and ends in an implied question: What would you do in such circumstances? Soaps are forever. "The Guiding Light" is light eternal.

The originator of "The Guiding Light," Irna Phillips, based the soap opera on the life of a minister, Dr. Ruthledge, and his daughters at Five Points. There his forgiveness, tolerance, charity, and self-sacrifice were tested, and he became a light of hope for the community. From its first radio broadcast in 1937, its brief interruption and reinstatement in 1941, its simulcast on radio and television in 1950, its final transfer to television in 1956, to the present time, "The Guiding Light" has changed with historical developments in America. "The Guiding Light's" females today ask for much more than "a home, a child, a man to kiss." They ask for and seek a respectable place in the business and professional world without being distracted from abiding values and topical concerns like health, children, pregnancy, etc. One thing which has not changed in "The Guiding Light" is that all dilemmas are faced with the guiding light of liberal Protestant values like tolerance, forgiveness, self-sacrifice, and charity. H.B. Lewis of 1985's open marriage is no Dr. Ruthledge of 1937's chaste widowhood, but like the latter he is a compassionate man who abhors violence and is charitable even to his wife when he knows that she is falling in love with his own son. Such brooding compassion has been the controlling ethos and the mark of distinction of "The Guiding Light" for the half century of its glorious existence. No wonder middle America constitutes its demographics.

The dramatic serial, along with the situation comedy and other forms of television programming, needs a vast demographic base to flourish as a cultural form. Since its survival depends upon the popular will as reflected in the ratings, its form and structure are a manifestation of the controlling center, the organizing symbol, in American society--the free marketplace of goods and ideas.

NOTES

1. Muriel G. Cantor and Suzanne Pingree, The Soap Opera (Beverly Hills: Sage Publications, 1983), pp. 33-34.
2. Robert C. Allen, Speaking of Soap Operas (Chapel Hill: University of North Carolina Press, 1985), p. 104.
3. Raymond William Stedman, The Serials: Suspense and Drama by Installments (Norman: University of Oklahoma Press, 1977).
4. Allen, p. 112.
5. Madeleine Edmondson and David Rounds, From Mary Noble to Mary Hartman (New York: Stein & Day, 1976), p. 46.
6. Allen, p. 126.
7. Cantor & Pingree, p. 22.
8. Tania Modleski, "Search for Tomorrow in Today's Soap Operas," in Understanding Television, Richard P. Adler, ed. (New York: Praeger, 1981), p. 192.
9. Allen, p. 69.
10. Allen, pp. 70-71.
11. Ibid.
12. Horace Newcomb, TV: The Most Popular Art (Garden City, NY: Anchor Press, 1974), pp. 168-169.
13. Dorothy Hobson, Cross Roads: The Drama of a Soap Opera (London: Methuen, 1982), p. 47.
14. Cantor & Pingree, p. 25.
15. Horace Newcomb, p. 169.
16. Ibid.

Chapter Six

SITCOM: THE HALF-HOUR COMEDY

* A Typology of Sitcom

* The Early Phase

* First Phase: Television Sitcoms of Traditional Families

* Second Phase: Back-to-Nature Sitcoms

* Third Phase: Social Problem Sitcoms

* Fourth Phase: Sitcoms Which Delight and Instruct

"It is hard to die ... but comedy's harder."

Not given to hero worship and the ritualistic formalities of feudal ages, Americans extend their hands to their fellow beings with a chuckle and a twinkle in their eyes. Informal posture and a self-deriding sense of humor are the American ways of confronting the world. Americans not only package their goods in laughter, but also mix their most sublime and profound thoughts with a sense of humor. Laughter has kept America sane. Laughter has now become a serious business in America.

American show business was born in the early nineteenth century in the burgeoning cities of the Northeast when enterprising promoters discovered that they could make a great deal of money producing inexpensive, crowd-pleasing entertainment that average city people could enjoy, understand, and afford.[1] And as the country grew, following the railroads to the West, so did the laughter, from coast to coast, inspired by the diverse comic sources and styles of Mack Sennett, Charlie Chaplin, Harold Lloyd, Buster Keaton, Laurel and Hardy, Disney's Mickey Mouse, Marx Brothers, Woody Allen, Will Rogers, Fred Allen, Jack Benny, George Burns, Gracie Allen, Milton Berle, Bob Hope, and Johnny Carson, to name a few. The comic spirit in America moved from the vaudeville stage and the circus to movies, radio, and television, thriving in each medium and enriching it in turn.

Television is the natural abode of comedy, at the heart of which is a family--traditional, nuclear, ethnic, contrived, eccentric, or social[2]--which gets into a situation precipitating complication and confusion. Laughter and optimism are the trophies of the situation comedies. Among the family members in a television situation comedy there is an emotional interdependence which creates a closely knit network of relationships. Any attempt by an outsider to get into their emotional network or by any member of the group to get out creates a problem situation. In the process of solving the problem or in resolving the conflict lies the source of laughter. Comedy, being no respecter of humans, solves problems through laughter. Every accident in comedy not only teases a laugh but also ties more knots which can be undone only through more laughter. The comic spirit says there is no evil in the world--only misunderstanding[3]--and when misunderstanding clears like the morning fog, we are drenched in an abundance of sunshine. The family is together again in "peace, love, and laughter" till next day some restlessness within the family or some outside incompatibility creates destablization, and the family members are up again like buzzing bees, crisscrossing and humming, piling confusion upon confusion.

Comedy is an unfinished business which creates conditions for perpetual optimism. A robust sense of optimism is a constituent part of the American ethos, and no wonder the comic spirit has flourished so much in the American mass media from early stage and circus clowning to Klinger's transvestite clowning in "M*A*S*H." The Europeans seem to say that to cut the Gordian knot you need an Alexander the Great or maybe a Hitler; the Americans think (at least IBM does) that Charlie Chaplin can do an equally good job, though his job will be always unfinished. Every "M*A*S*H" will have an "After-M*A*S*H"; every company tends to be a crowd: "the rigid patterns of a narrative frame involving families, problems, solutions, and specific social attitudes in a comic outline have developed in the television years into a major form of mass entertainment."[4] The comic spirit's path is that of common sense, though the magical and the fantastic may be used to create confusion and complication, as in "I Dream of Jeannie" or "Mork and Mindy."

Comedy is said to be so much tied up with local color and local humor that it is "incapable of translation." According to the <u>Oxford Companion to the Theatre</u>, "the greater its appeal to its contemporaries the less its impact on future ages, and the history of the theatre shows innumerable instances of comedies enormously successful in their own day and soon forgotten. This handicap is, of course, subject to the overriding force of genius, and the comedies of Aristophanes, Shakespeare and Molière can still be enjoyed, though they demand from the audience a certain amount of cooperation in recapturing the spirit of their time, and translation suffers a loss which it is impossible to assess."[5] The magic of the television medium is that it prevents that loss due to translation because it translates the spoken word of the stage into visuals and montages of comedy which transcend their time and local habitats. In television, time is always present time, which explains why reruns are proving moderately acceptable to audiences. Something is inevitably lost due to the passage of time and change in the audience's mode of consciousness, but the loss is much less in television than on the stage. When we watch the reruns of "I Love Lucy," "I Dream of Jeannie," or "The Honeymooners," we not only redeem the past, but also our present mode of consciousness transforms these sitcoms into, as it were, comic docudramas about the past. Much of the fun in shows like "Leave It to Beaver," "The Addams Family," "The Brady Bunch," "Barney Miller," etc., which are being shown as reruns, is due to the comic visuals rather than the scripts. Television's moving images and visuals, unlike spoken and written language, are not anchored to grammatical tense and therefore transcend time and locale. Television tends to annihilate time.

A TYPOLOGY OF SITCOM

Broadly speaking, there are two types of television situation comedies. In one type complication and confusion arise from within the family, and their resolution brings the family members back into reunion or a form of secular baptism; examples are "Amos 'n' Andy," "Father Knows Best," "Happy Days," "Sanford and Son," "All in the Family." The other type of sitcom does not concern itself with domesticity, but all its values are derived from and aim at family life, a group's togetherness, or communality among a closely knit group of people. Some well-known sitcoms which fall into this category are "Gomer Pyle, USMC," "I Dream of Jeannie," "Petticoat Junction," "Mork and Mindy," "M*A*S*H." Whether the predominant ecology is rural ("Beverly Hillbillies"), military-medicine ("M*A*S*H"), fantasia ("My Mother the Car"), racial-ethnic ("The Jeffersons"), working group ("Mary Tyler Moore"), or domestic ("All in the Family"), all sitcoms trade in stock characters such as a dumb, sexy blonde (Chrissy in "Three's Company"), smart kids (Beaver), a wise mother (Donna Reed), an all-knowing father (Jim Anderson in "Father Knows Best"), a benevolent, authoritarian boss (Colonel Potter in "M*A*S*H"), a middle-aged sex-crazy woman (Mrs. Roper in "Three's Company"), a self-disciplined and sacrificial mother (Ann Romano in "One Day at a Time"), boasters (George Jefferson; Frank in "M*A*S*H"), bigots (George Jefferson, Archie Bunker), and many others frozen into molds.[6] These characters do not change and develop. Many are automatons with limited, programmed responses to certain stock situations; "their standardization and their primary relation to needs of escape and relaxation" have enabled formulaic creators of sitcoms to become prolific producers of the genre.[7]

From Shakespeare's Shylock to "M*A*S*H's" Klinger, comedy has always flourished on racial innuendos, malapropism, mistaken identities, coincidence, irony, pie-in-the-face, pretended or real amnesia, and many other similar devices. When comedy does not go beyond formulaic situations and repeats stock humor, it begins to tire audiences, who then seek other avenues of entertainment. As cultural historian A.F. Wertheim has stated, radio[8] during the early fifties lost its audience to television not only because of the magic of the new medium, but also because radio programming had become totally stale. Most radio comedy programs used old, tired gags in predictable, formulaic situations, and the new medium came like a waft of fresh air. In a similar tone, Gilbert Seldes observed:

> Maybe a philosopher will discover deep meaning in this mania for cruelty. All I say of it is that it begins to bore me ... there's a speakeasy age staleness over it and I feel that other sources of humor must exist beyond the physical deficiencies and imputed meanness of the comedies.[9]

If television audiences today are passing through the same psychological phase as radio audiences did in the early fifties, new technologies like the videocassette recorder may draw them away from network programming. Or maybe the phenomenal success of "The Cosby Show" is a straw in the wind that a new crop of situation comedies will compete for Nielsen's demographics.

THE EARLY PHASE

During the four decades of television situation comedies, one can discover certain distinct phases in the evolution of this genre. The early phase was the time of transition from radio to television, when many comedy shows and stars were struggling for survival by trimming their sails and pruning their talents for the new medium.

Some of the sitcoms which had their roots in radio were "The Goldbergs," "I Remember Mama," and "I Love Lucy." One remarkable sitcom with some kind of story continuity was "Amos 'n' Andy." This show is also given credit as a progenitor of the soap opera serial format.[10] In radio days "Amos 'n' Andy" was played by two white actors who portrayed the antics of two black people. When the sitcom was transferred to television, it seemed very offensive and degrading to black people. The hilarious comedy of the radio days became a slur on blacks during the age of television, and because of protests from black organizations it was withdrawn in 1953. Now, when blacks are more self-confident about themselves, a re-run of "Amos 'n' Andy" might become as popular as "The Honeymooners," "Man from U.N.C.L.E.," "The Mary Tyler Moore Show," etc. "Amos 'n' Andy" is a "docudrama" about the past, history in the present tense.

FIRST PHASE: TELEVISION SITCOMS OF TRADITIONAL FAMILIES

Along with the transplanted and rehashed sitcoms of the dying radio era, there were several fresh starts in sitcoms which hit the public taste. These comedies, of which "The Adventures of Ozzie and Harriet," "Leave It to Beaver," "Father Knows Best," and "The Honeymooners" had respectable ratings, were about traditional families. Though "Leave It to Beaver" and "Father Knows Best" have been rerunning without much fanfare, "The Honeymooners" has made a splendid splashdown and is being shown on cable TV; the old sitcoms have begun to assume artistic respectability. "The Honeymooners" originally ran for fifteen seasons[11] but never won an Emmy award.

"The Honeymooners" fame rests on thirty-nine filmed episodes which Jackie Gleason, auteur, creator, producer, did live on film in the presence of a studio audience. But for these surviving filmed episodes, television history would have lost one of its most delightful creations and a primary source of evidence.

"The Honeymooners," in a manner of speaking, is a comic version of the American dream. Ralph Kramden, a bus driver on Madison Avenue, carried the burden of this dream, and like a comic Sisyphus he had to carry the burden to the top again only to fall down--in a splash of laughter. If Ralph had been alone in the execution of his harebrained schemes to get rich, he would have been a pathetic, melodramatic character, or at the most a man of courage who failed (like the protagonist in <u>The Old Man and the Sea</u>). But Ralph Kramden involved in his schemes his equally nutty friend Ed Norton, who lived only a floor above his Brooklyn ramshackle apartment. Ralph's and Norton's bloated fantasies of becoming rich were punctured by their down-to-earth wives, Alice and Trixie. Most of their schemes, as Norton said with a sense of unselfconscious humor, went by the sewer. Norton was, after all, an underground engineer. The fat bus driver and the lanky sewer man, like Laurel and Hardy of the silent era, argued and fussed and pursued their dreams, which included diet pizza, working a uranium mine, a mystery appetizer, and many other schemes. Of course a combination of a loud-mouthed husband and a witty wife with a biting tongue has been a perpetual source of comedy. When Ralph boasted about his newest scheme to get rich ("This is probably the biggest thing I ever got into"), Alice shot back, "The biggest thing you ever got into was your pants." What sustained Alice's marriage was Ralph's sincerity and love for his wife. He was a lovable fool, a Micawber, who was repeatedly told to be satisfied with his lot. Alice's good sense and sanity turned Ralph into one of the most engaging comic characters in television situation comedy. His failure to get rich and failure to assert authority over his wife were the two wellsprings of humor in "The Honeymooners."[12]

SECOND PHASE: BACK-TO-NATURE SITCOMS

The sixties, which witnessed flower children, love-ins, yoga, and civil rights protests, also gave rise to back-to-nature or rusticity sitcoms like "The Beverly Hillbillies," "Petticoat Junction," "Green Acres," "Here Comes the Bride," etc. America was passing through a phase of nonviolence, passive civil disobedience, and Nehru jackets.

The rural sitcom corresponded with that dominant mood of the audiences. The phenomenal success of "The Beverly Hillbillies" was anticipated by "The Real McCoys," which portrayed a mountain family from West Virginia that moved to the San Fernando Valley and its subsequent trial and tribulations in dealing with city life. The back-to-nature theme has persisted in every culture. Not going far back to the ancients, one could hear its strident call in Rousseau's noble savage, and Wordsworth's lament that "the world is too much with us and we have no time to stand and stare." Nearer home, Thoreau preached and practiced rural simplicity.

The modern thematic variation is to make your millions and retreat to a ranch. "The Beverly Hillbillies" offers a crazy twist to the back-to-nature theme. The Clampetts of the Ozarks who strike oil and are loaded with $25 million, move to the richest tract of land on earth to impose their own cultural hegemony on people they think have no morality except to make money. It is this stubborn sense of superiority of their mountain life style which is the source of humor in the more than 200 episodes of "The Beverly Hillbillies." The Clampetts refuse to yield an inch to the civilized world, and viewers begin to wonder in what ways the psychiatrists' prescribed tranquilizers of Beverly Hills are less harmful than granny's possum, poultices, and mountain remedies.

It does not seem that Paul Henning wanted to make a comic statement about America's march of progress from the Ozarks to Beverly Hills as one kind of absurdity to another. Nor was it a philosophical statement that moneyed people impose their own ideology on others. He simply saw great comic possibilities in a rural family, reinforced by $25 million, confronting its counterpart in a sophisticated, decadent atmosphere--one decadence confronting another decadence. Or was it rural America's last laugh, last gasp?

THIRD PHASE: SOCIAL PROBLEM SITCOMS

This era began with some widely popular and critically acclaimed sitcoms like "All in the Family, "The Mary Tyler Moore Show," "Sanford and Son," "M*A*S*H," "Barney Miller," "The Jeffersons," and many others. It was the era when President Nixon was shaking hands with Chairman Mao Tse Tung in Peking while his operatives were simulatenously breaking into Democratic National Committee Headquarters in Washington D.C. The Vietnam boys came home in sickness and humiliation. America suffered spiritual agony, and through this brooding pain were born some of the most poignant sitcoms. The laughter of the seventies is not the full-throated belly laugh of "The Honeymooners" or "Green Acres" and other sitcoms of America's age of innocence. Situation comedy in the seventies began to think emotionally, and the laughter stopped halfway as if in doubt.

"M*A*S*H"

In some ways "M*A*S*H" reminds us of Albert Camus' existentialist novel The Plague. Both present a situation of total annihilation and despair from which there is no escape except through commitment. Humans are condemned to be free, and freedom is a terrible responsibility. For the quarantined, plague-afflicted Algerian town and the war-beleaguered army hospital in Korea there is no escape, no passive resistance or withdrawal. In the long run what emerges from the tragic despair of The Plague and the comic despair of "M*A*S*H" is the realization that though we do not understand, we may overcome the vicissitudes and the consequences of war and plague.

Though hope and despair are at the heart of both The Plague and "M*A*S*H," Camus' novel is plunged in gloom, while "M*A*S*H" is smothered in laughter. The Plague cries out a thesis; "M*A*S*H," as a television series lasting a decade, does not strike a philosophic posture. It does not even condemn war, nor does it rail and rave against war's futility, though satire abounds, and comedy has a grim load to carry.

> Hawkeye: I just don't know why they are shooting at us. All we want to bring them is democracy and white bread, to transplant the American dream: freedom, achievement, hyperacidity, affluence, flatulence, technology, tension, the inalienable right to early coronary disease, sitting at your desk while plotting to stab your boss in the back.

There have been plays like George Bernard Shaw's Arms and the Man and Shakespeare's Troilus and Cressida which debunk romantic love and heroic wars, but "M*A*S*H" shows life without the inevitability of a dramatic plot. It is a great artistic achievement that a television dramatic series could keep its audience for ten seasons without the formulaic devices of a whodunnit or other traditional plot suspense formulas. Nor has "M*A*S*H" left a formula for other sitcoms to copy. Formulaic conventions create expectations in audiences, the fulfillment of which gives a feeling of limited satisfaction, and in course of time satiation, fatigue, and desire for change, leading to a temporary eclipse of the genre. "M*A*S*H" gave American audiences, intellectual or not, a unique aesthetic experience, something like that of a religious Mass. In a religious Mass there is no plot suspense; there is only form-in-suspense, whose completion gives both religious and aesthetic experience.

It was this completion of a known incompleteness of the episodes of "M*A*S*H" which gave audiences thrills and apprehensions (Korea to Vietnam) submerged in laughter. After all, the basic situation in each episode was simple: a bunch of doctors and nurses behind the enemy lines expect the wounded to arrive every day. There is no dramatic conflict because an antagonist-protagonist situation does not exist. The physicians and other hospital personnel are deeply entangled with their loved ones at home and, for some, at the camp. In the pull and push of the relationships at the camp and back home, against the backdrop of exploding bombs and torn human bodies, "M*A*S*H" gives the illusion of dramatic movement or syntagmatic advance; but in "M*A*S*H" action does not progress because there is no action. If there is action it is in the limited sense one finds in Waiting for Godot; it is ritual as action, fulfillment of the form-in-suspense.

"M*A*S*H" was originally published as the fictionalized experience of Dr. Richard Honberger, who was a surgeon in a MASH unit during the Korean War in the 1950s and had to work long hours to repair torn flesh and broken limbs. The novel, after hitting the bestseller list, was turned into a movie by Robert Altman for Twentieth Century-Fox. The movie was as popular as the book, and the cloning of it into a sitcom series was the next logical step. As an example of "the collective as creator," Gene Reynolds, Larry Gelbart, and Burt Metcalfe together raised a milestone in television creativity, displaying passion for quality without sacrificing sensitivity, compassion, and dignity for humans.

Based on the Korean War experience, "M*A*S*H" was viewed by audiences of the post-Vietnam War era as if they were looking at a distant war through their recent painful experiences. China, which had called the United States a paper tiger and had supported North Korea in the 1950s and North Vietnam in the 1960s, now was hosting a visit by President Nixon. The Asian wars seemed silly and tragic. As Colonel Potter, while operating on a small Korean girl, says:

> Colonel Potter: Somebody dropped a bomb on her building from an airplane.
> Pilot: Who did it?
> Hawkeye: He just dropped it. He did not autograph it.
> Pilot: Was it one of theirs or one of ours?
> Hawkeye: What difference does it make?
> Colonel Potter: Not to her.

"M*A*S*H's" humane comedy was played by some of the

most highly trained actors in television fiction and drama. Their interpersonal relations and their unperturbed reactions to the war created compassionate laughter, occasionally reminding the viewers of Shakespearean humor, comedy touched with sympathy.

Pivotal to the whole series was the character of chief surgeon Benjamin Franklin ("Hawkeye") Pierce, played by Alan Alda.[13] Hawkeye had a puckish sense of humor, with the dedication of a true disciple of Hippocrates. His jests ranged from innocent verbal fireworks to profound revelation. For instance:

> Radar: How can I thank you?
> Hawkeye: Well, you can give us your firstborn.
>
> Colonel Potter: By the way, what is this war about?
> Hawkeye: The latest war to end all wars.
>
> Hawkeye: While I am cutting, Frank, you give him a manicure.

Through gestures, facial expressions, and varied humor, Hawkeye would clear the mist, giving a revealing insight into the human situation. His humor had the force of a beautiful metaphor which would transport the audience out of despair to compassion and understanding.

It was Corporal Klinger, played by Jamie Farr,[14] who added endless mirth to the series. His long Roman nose and comic face forbade calling himself a conscientious objector against the war, and he looked for a Section Eight (mental instability) discharge to con his way out of the war. He dressed as a transvestite to prove his insanity. He would explain to anyone who would listen: "These are the outward trappings of my unfortunate insanity. I don't belong here. If two doctors will sign a form, I will be able to go home. And, so far, I have got all but both of them." In one episode he threatened self-immolation, but it was found that the can was full of water, not gasoline. His creativity and ingeniousness in devising ways to get out of the army were a perpetual source of fun for the beleaguered medical unit and the audience.

One of the most colorful personalities of "M*A*S*H" was

"Hot Lips" (Major Margaret Houlihan), charmingly played by Loretta Swit.[15] She was a great nurse, was rumored to sleep only with the big brass, had a long affair with buffoon officer Frank Burns, married another one (Lt. Colonel Penobscott), and later divorced him. Her toughness protected her lonely heart, as she once revealed when yelling at the nurses: "Can you imagine what it feels like to walk by a tent and know I am not welcome?" Loretta Swit's role was to turn Hot Lips' humorless character into a source of humor for others, and she did it brilliantly. The contradictions in her personality made her unforgettable.

All eleven characters, some played by different actors in different seasons, carried the series through beautiful portrayals of multifaceted personalities. The characters suffered, changed, grew wiser and more humane from episode to episode. But they never ceased to be funny and disturbingly profound.

> Frank: Unless we each conform, unless we follow our leaders blindly--there is no possibility we can remain free.

"The Mary Tyler Moore Show"

"The Mary Tyler Moore Show," its art and literariness, gave respectability to a new sensibility that arose in the 1970s when the birth control pill gave sexual freedom to women. Once sex became dissociated from love, children, and family, the pill-liberated career woman began to wonder how much of a man she needed or for how long. The man-woman relation changed from a binary yes-no possibility to a continuum from celibacy to total commitment. It was Mary Richards' acrobatic tap dance, metaphorically speaking, on that tightrope between nothing and everything in man-woman relationships that was a source of comic charm in "The Mary Tyler Moore Show," which kept adult America home on Saturday nights. If CBS had accepted the original story of Mary as a divorced woman, as the Brooks-Burns team suggested, the sitcom would have taken a different route, maybe of a camouflaged slapstick sex comedy. The CBS brass were probably in tune with the mode of consciousness and the changing structure of assumptions held by American audiences at that time, and their insistence that Mary be a single girl turned out to be a good creative hunch. It is almost a decade since the show was taken off the air, and we still ask, who created the show?

A comedy series revolving around a single desirable woman could have turned out to be a polemical series or a comedy of ideas/issues which would have turned characters into cartoons or stereotypes. But Brooks and Burns created a family of beautiful characters who in their interaction gave rise to laughter and mirth which ennobled the viewers. Mary Richards made Americans feel good about themselves because she did not raise difficult questions stridently. The comic heroines of Ibsen and Shaw had established a tradition which Mary did not follow, and yet she occasioned the surfacing of issues like divorce and women's rights in a gentle, subdued manner. In one of the episodes[16] Rhoda persuaded Mary to join a divorced persons club called "Better Luck Next Time," and as luck would have it, Mary was elected vice president. Not able to tolerate the burden of untruth, she rose to the podium and declared, "I lied to you. I am not divorced. I never married." That provoked a spate of confessions from the whole gathering except three genuinely divorced people.

There are single women who withhold everything and turn themselves into mean spinsters. Mary had an indescribable self-restraint which she instinctively turned into comic hesitancy. It seemed she had some coiled spring inside her which would let her open up in an uncertain, diffident manner with great comic possibilities. A day after she settled in her Minneapolis quarters, Mary confronted WJM-TV's grizzly bear with a golden heart, Lou Grant, for a job. And when Lou superciliously asked about her age and religion, the coiled spring within her snapped: "Mr. Grant, I don't know how to say this; you're not allowed to ask that when someone's applying for a job. It's against the law." Mary's engaging and affectionate personality and her hesitant reactions to other people's behavior created genuine amusement. As time passed Mary's relations with Lou Grant, Murray, and Ted, constituting the WJM-TV team, began to assume the paradigmatic depth and richness of a family. Lou Grant was married, divorced, and had seen his son-in-law fool around with another woman; but he always came to Mary to cry on her shoulder. Murray pretended to protect Mary and sought protection from her. Ted Baxter, the anchorman who received piles of fan mail, was the butt of the family's jokes. He found it difficult to pronounce Phnom Penh and wished the war were in London because he would have found it easier to pronounce the name. Albany might be in Europe, but Ted was sure that Albania was next door--in fact, the capital of New York. Surrounded by such vulnerable men in the office, Mary had no choice except to mother them into a family. Any attempt to have an affair would have been a disaster.

The other half of Mary's single life was crowded by a single girl, Rhoda, half man-crazy, half food-crazy; and Phyllis, the pretentious, vainglorious mother of a girl. Rhoda and Phyllis never got along with each other, but they both centered upon Mary's after-office life. And their relations were a comic disaster. Once Rhoda persuaded Mary to host an evening get-together. Mary invited her old flame, and Rhoda invited as her date a stranger who brought his wife to the party. The guests thought they would have dinner, although the only edible thing left in Mary's refrigerator was a piece of carrot. They looked for popcorn, which Rhoda, who was always on a diet ("I have to lose ten pounds before my date arrives at 8:30 pm!"), had already finished.

The humor in "The Mary Tyler Moore Show" rose sometimes from the situation, as in a true sitcom (recall the divorce club), and sometimes from the characters themselves, as in the case of Ted ("I have got a good job, good health, a good wife, a fantastic barber"). The judicious blend of character and situation with superb acting of some of the most seasoned professionals from theater and television lifted this sitcom to an art form. If Brooks and Burns had a message, it never clawed at the audience. The function of comedy is to make people laugh. Though no laughter is without a message, the laughter evoked by "The Mary Tyler Moore Show" was full of the milk of human kindness, love, and forgiveness, reminding us of some of the best comedies of Shakespeare. "Thank you for being my family," said Mary when the final curtain fell--in an era when families are breaking apart and humans hide in their foxholes out of fear of their fellow beings.

Sitcom

"All in the Family"

So long as the Archie Bunkers of the world remain a minority, life is a real comedy, but once they begin to gather force you have the makings of the Inquisition, the Star Chamber, the Salem witch trials, McCarthyism, and the Final Solution. When America of the seventies laughed at Archie, there was supreme self-confidence the nation could solve all its problems through liberal democracy. The country had ended its war in Vietnam, and the Nixons were being destabilized in the White House. Everyone was sanguinely awaiting the return to decency once the Bunkers and the Nixons were out of sight. Laughter of the seventies was a kind of comic hallelujah, welcoming the return to sanity through tolerance of plurality. "All in the Family" was like a surgical operation on the nation, and the tumor was found to be benign. It was the patient laughing at his good luck, but the laughter was painful because of lingering doubts.

Were Archie Bunker an abstraction personified and dramatized, probably he would have quickly exhausted his comic energy, but, like Shylock, he refused to be a baited wolf and tore out of the television screen to hurl defiance, slurs, and malapropisms all around. As in the absurd comedies of Eugene Ionesco, the conversations in "All in the Family" began innocently but soon zoomed to dizzy heights of racial slurs, cursing, name calling, or jeering. Of course, the occasion for such provocation was the perpetual presence of Archie's upstart Polish-American son-in-law Mike, who sounded like Meathead to Archie. A personal observation would lead to below-the-belt hits against a whole race:

> Archie: You are the laziest white boy I ever met.
> Mike: You wanna call me lazy, okay. But you don't have to put down a whole race just to do it!
> Archie: I wasn't putting down a whole race.
> Mike: Yes you were. You said I was the laziest white boy you ever met.
> Archie: That's right. YOU!
> Mike: Meaning that the blacks are even lazier.
> Archie: Wait a second, wise guy. I didn't say that. You are the one who said that. I never said your blacks were lazy. I never said that at all. Of course, their systems is geared a little slower than ours, that's all.[17]

Liberal audiences laughed because their suppressed views were comically expressed by someone whom they had rejected as a spokesperson. Episode after episode the clash between Archie and his son-in-law, Archie and his wife, Archie and his daughter, Archie and the rest of America, assumed comic proportion because through him the audiences were whipping themselves for their guilt. Did the liberals understand better and become more forgiving when Edith said to Mike: "Do you wanna know why Archie yells at you? Archie yells at you because Archie is jealous of you. You are going to college. Archie had to quit school to support his family. He ain't never going to be any more than he is right now. Now you think that over."? The audience gave her a standing ovation and applauded thunderously, knowing at the same time that the Archie Bunkers of the world are imperishable and could bounce back. The greater the fear, the louder was the laughter. It was that lingering doubt among liberal viewers (conservatives approved of him) that Archie might have been right which provoked laughter. Consider what Archie had to say in defense of Nixon: "Well, I will tell you one thing about President Nixon. He keeps Pat at home. Which was where Roosevelt should have kept Eleanor. Instead, he let her run around loose until one day she discovered the colored. We never knew they were here. She told them they were getting the short end of the stick and we been having trouble ever since." This subconscious belief on the part of the audiences that they might be racist made them laugh at Archie.

But the sitcom was more than the comic racial bigotry of Archie Bunker. It drew into its comic ambit not only burning topics of the day like Watergate, but also individual problems like Edith's menopause; Mike's vasectomy and impotency; Gloria's miscarriage, hobnobbing with a transvestite, giving up of formal religion, and nude posing; Archie's gambling; a cousin's lesbianism; Gloria's and Mike's marital problems--issues audiences saw as their own regardless of their political ideology. These problems of the Bunker family brought audiences into a communion, a unified consciousness. Recall the scene when Edith faced a rapist who pulled at her zipper:

> Edith: Wouldn't you like some coffee?
> Rapist: I don't drink coffee.
> Edith: I've got Sanka.

> Rapist: I want you.
> Edith: But couldn't we do this without kissing?[18]

Art transmutes ugliness into beauty. This terrifyingly ugly scene of American daily life was transformed into a moment of beauty and pathos. If "All in the Family" tore away the mask of civility by flushing a toilet, it also offered some of the most touching scenes in television drama. Critics have paid much attention to the division of its audiences into liberals and conservatives,[19] but more often this sitcom as a family saga in a comic milieu created a feeling of togetherness and painful awareness of social problems faced by the family as a unit.

The comic family saga was enriched by superb acting by Carroll O'Connor (Archie), Jean Stapleton (Edith), Sally Struthers (Gloria), and Rob Reiner (Mike). In television, as has been observed by several critics, the close-up turns the human face into a universe of feelings, thoughts, and emotions. The face registers the subtlest nuances. It is difficult to fake before the television camera. Most expressive of all was the broad, oval face of Carroll O'Connor. Each muscle in his face had the capacity to twist and twitch with cynicism, jeering, leering, contempt, and deep hatred and disgust. There seemed to be a destiny in the fall of his lower lip, the twinkle in his eye, the raising of his hand in curse, or the pointing of his finger of accusation. Pitted opposite him was his wife Edith, full of quiet and gentle strength, with the self-confidence that common sense would prevail and all would be well with her family. Archie's son-in-law Mike, representative of the rest of the mankind consisting of Hebes, Japs, fags, coons, Polacks, Chinks, Micks, Spicks, etc., knew that his sojourn at the Bunkers' was a temporary affair. He would have his college degree and go away to teach in some university, leaving Archie stewing in his own malapropisms and invective.

Though Norman Lear originally borrowed the concept of this explosive comic saga from a British television comedy, "Till Death Do Us Part," "All in the Family" changed as it ploughed through American consciousness. Sitcoms are locked in formulas, and the humor becomes accepted and anticipated. "All in the Family" kept those gains but occasionally raised the sitcom to the level of serious drama. Its pendulum movement between the sublime and the ridiculous made the sitcom a unique artistic experience.

FOURTH PHASE: SITCOMS WHICH DELIGHT AND INSTRUCT

Bill Cosby: The Comic Godfather of America

In 1925 American radio audiences began to enjoy the hilarious black sitcom "Amos 'n' Andy," which was played by two white actors imitating black voices. The creators Gosden and Correll transplanted it on television in 1953 with real black faces and black voices. Audiences, after they had made the transition from radio to TV version, settled down to enjoy the sitcom till the rise of black consciousness in the sixties provoked a violent reaction against it. The sitcom was taken off the air and out of syndication not only in America but also in Africa and Europe. Its malapropisms and humor anticipated Archie Bunker: "I quote ver-bacon," "A Fisherman's Parasite," "The State to Unlax in," "These kids is smarter than they were in my degeneration," etc. The racist humor of "Amos 'n' Andy" was no different from that of "Sanford and Son," "The Jeffersons," and "All in the Family" except that it was innocent. Blacks felt offended because the civil rights movement of the sixties brought about a shift in their mode of consciousness, and their newly sensitized thinking would not let them laugh at their own kind.

But three years after CBS withdrew the sitcom from syndication, another black man, Bill Cosby, appeared on the comic horizon. Along with him was Lillian Randolph, who had acted Madam Queen on "Amos 'n' Andy." "The Bill Cosby Show" (1969) ran for only three years, but Cosby made his debut as a comic philosopher-teacher, a role which he was to perfect in the eighties as the comic Godfather of America. In the seventies black sitcoms seemed to be splitting off in two directions: one as spinoff or mirror image of "All in the Family," as in "Sanford and Son" and "The Jeffersons"; all these sitcoms have kinship with "Amos 'n' Andy." The other direction is taken by "The Cosby Show" of the 1984-85 season, which hit the ceiling in Nielsen's demographics, dislodging that erstwhile favorite of the audiences, Tom Selleck of "Magnum, P.I.," shown at the same time slot. This success came at a time when many critics had signed warrants for the death of the sitcom in America.

In many ways "The Cosby Show" is more significant than "All in the Family," though it may not generate as much critical literature as did Archie's bigotry. "All in the Family" was a deeply divided, ugly America at its comic best. It was the lot of a white man to show the festering wounds in American society from a comic stance, and the audiences were delighted as much as earlier they had been amused to see black America in "Amos 'n' Andy." "The Cosby Show" rises above the social and ethnic concerns of its predecessors and shows America in the process of healing and integrating.

It is a kind of self-realization that America's salvation lies in rebuilding the family. The way to build the family is through love, care, and hope, with a generous sprinkling of humor born of generosity and compassion. In a way "The Cosby Show" portrays a family in evolution from the Puritan family of early colonial Massachusetts to the present day; today the Puritan God has been replaced by love and laughter.

The Huxtables are a prosperous, upper-middle-class family. The wife is a lawyer, the husband is an obstetrician. One daughter is at Princeton, the second is passing through adolescent loneliness; two younger girls are still at the age of innocence. The Huxtables have a remarkable son, who in one of the episodes responds to a public tribute in honor of his father when Dr. Huxtable cannot attend the function. The Huxtables represent an ideal where both whites and blacks in America aspire to converge, and hence the show's widespread attraction. Brad Darrach calls it a healthy swallow of the milk of human kindness:

> Cosby's success may have changed the game as well as the scores. Before his show hit the air, many viewers rejected primetime television as an electronic guignol of crime, slime, glitz, and glands. "Dynasty" and "Dallas" exalted power over principle and lust instead of love. Blacks complained that they were too often portrayed as whores, pimps, pushers, muggers or noisy dolts like "The Jeffersons." The mortality rate among comedy shows, white or black, was high, and most of those that survived were either smart assed or numbskulled.

> What Cosby offered instead was a gentle, whimsical, warm-hearted sitcom about family life that found humor in the little things that happen in every home and everlasting value in the love and trust that can exist between parents and children. Yes, the family is black, but that fact is totally ignored. No racial jokes are made, no problems of prejudice discussed.... Nobody actually says this family represents the whole family, but the delicious ordinariness of its pleasures and tribulations has given millions a fresh, laughter-splashed perspective on their own domestic lives.[20]

Bill Cosby's comic vision is a re-enactment of the beliefs of the founding fathers that all men are created equal and that the family of man can live on love and understanding-- probably that is the only way. His sitcom is devoid of racist slur, ethnic jokes, or any kind of derogatory insinuation against any community or group. Yet his style, his gestures, his bodily movements, his utterances, are reminiscent of earlier black comedians, and his full-throated belly laugh comes from a man who has not only forgotten his origins but has transcended them without any lingering malice. This comic vision pervades the sitcom and gives it a delightful form. Maybe through "The Cosby Show" audiences are looking for solutions to their problems; though that is not the function of sitcom, it does bring this sitcom closer to daytime soap opera, not in form and substance but certainly in function. Its healing and integrating vision makes "The Cosby Show" superior to "All in the Family," though it must be admitted the latter, because of perpetual antagonism, was the dramatically more interesting of the two.

The networks offered audiences in the fall of 1985 twenty-one new dramatic programs, of which six are situation comedies. Of these, "The Golden Girls" features four older women whose giggles and laughs shame their old age. Nothing is worth crying about, not even when Blanche's catch Harry turns out to be a con man. One-lines and gags range in subject from bladder control and loose dentures to catching a man who "doesn't make noises when he chews." What "The Cosby Show" is to middle-American professional couples raising children, "The Golden Girls" is to aging Americans trying to forget hastening decreptitude and an increasing threat to Social Security. It may be another feather in NBC's cap.

George Burns at ninety is senior America paying its tribute to longevity through laughter. His half-hour anthology series that presents a different story and cast each week is a different kind of sitcom. In fact, we have to redefine sitcom as a genre not necessarily based upon the same set of actions and characters. Television never stops redefining the codes, the modes, and the forms of reality and fiction. Maybe CBS's "George Burns Comedy Week" is an indication of new comic forms to come through cloning, recombination, or spinoffs. Maybe anthologies will return.

Bill Cosby and George Burns have heralded another Golden Age of Comedy different from an era symbolized by "The Mary Tyler Moore Show," "All in the Family," and "M*A*S*H," when America appeared to be doing serious introspection, a kind of collective meditation. In the eighties America is slowly regaining its self-confidence and serenity, and audiences respond to sitcoms which delight and instruct, particularly when the teenagers are round. James E. Gardner,[21] a clinical psychologist and author of The Turbulent Teens, believes that sitcoms like "Facts of Life," "Charles in Charge," and "The Cosby Show" provoke positive discussions between parents and children. Few indeed look at sitcoms from an instructional point of view; but the mode of consciousness is changing and America, from economics to education, is in a mood of self-correction. Comedy prospers at such time.

NOTES

1. Robert C. Toll, The Entertainment Machine (New York: Oxford University Press, 1982), p. 4.
2. Arthur Hough, "Trials and Tribulations--Thirty Years of Sitcom," in Understanding Television, Richard P. Adler, ed. (New York: Praeger Publishers, 1981), pp. 201-233.
3. Horace Newcomb, TV: The Most Popular Art (Garden City, NY: Anchor Press, 1974), p. 41.
4. Ibid., p. 59.
5. Oxford Companion to Theatre, 3rd ed., Phyllis Hartnoll, ed. (London: Oxford University Press, 1977), p. 194.
6. Rick Mitz, The Great TV Sitcom Book (New York: Richard Marek Publishers, 1980), pp. 6-7.
7. John G. Cawelti, Adventure, Mystery, Romance (Chicago:

        The University of Chicago Press, 1976), p. 8; pp. 35-36.
8. Arthur Frank Wertheim, Radio Comedy (New York: Oxford University Press, 1979), p. 380.
9. Gilbert Seldes, "Notes and Queries," Esquire, 25 (March 1946), p. 78, quoted by A.F. Wertheim, p. 381.
10. Robert C. Allen, Speaking of Soap Operas (Chapel Hill: The University of North Carolina Press, 1985), p. 104.
11. Mitz, p. 430.
12. David Marc, Demographic Vistas (Philadelphia: University of Pennsylvania Press, 1984), pp. 112-116; Mitz, pp. 119-124, 297-305.
13. David S. Reiss, M*A*S*H (Indianapolis: The Bobbs-Merrill Company, 1980), pp. 16-29.
14. Ibid., pp. 46-52.
15. Ibid., pp. 96-104.
16. Joel Eisner and David Krinsky, Television Comedy Series (Jefferson, NC: McFarland and Company, 1984), pp. 510-518.
17. Richard P. Adler, ed. All in the Family (New York: Praeger Publishers, 1979), p. 18.
18. Mitz, 258.
19. Adler, All in the Family, pp. 123-139; 139-145.
20. Brad Darrach, Life (June 1985), p. 37.
21. James E. Gardner "Does Your Teenager Need a $95 Shirt or Just Want One?" TV Guide (May 4, 1985), p. 35.

Chapter Seven

THE COLLECTIVE AS CREATOR

* Negotiated Creativity

* The Role of the Producer

* Grant Tinker's MTM

* Norman Lear and the Dramatization of Resentment

NEGOTIATED CREATIVITY

Television creativity is a force emerging from a system of coordination rather than an act of individual creation. This force amounts to rejection of the traditional view of creativity as an activity of a single mind paralleling the concept of the creation of the universe by a single creator. Most of us are trained to believe that the creative imagination leaps and laps over the incongruities of life and imposes order; that creativity and originality make concrete a new order, new relationships, new associations, conceived by a single contemplative mind. Act-actor, creation-creator, deed-doer, medium-producer, cinema-director, novel-writer--these are the familiar designations, and surprisingly they are nothing but derivatives from the notion of immaculate conception. Television technology is challenging the tenet that control and creativity go together. Television reveals that creativity can be an evolutionary process incorporating survival of the fittest and natural selection. The evolution of dramatic genres and dramatic programming since television became a dominant force in American society displays repetitiveness, cloning, spin-offs, recombinants, or originality as functions of survival, much as in biological evolutionism--a reality which denies a single creator-controller. Robert C. Allen's account, "The First Soap Opera: Painted Dreams," illustrates this point more fully. As he says:

> Because the historical import of a first is a retrodictive judgement of historians, contemporaneous accounts are frequently fragmentary--leaving plenty of room for historians to quibble years later over who really was the first to do something and what the person's motives really were. Phillips's "creation" of "Painted Dreams" is detailed in more than fifty-nine hundred pages of first-hand testimony, not because anyone was historically prescient but thanks to a copyright dispute between Phillips and WGN, initiated in 1932 and eventually adjudicated in 1941. The documentary evidence in the case demonstrates <u>the convergence of generative mechanism</u> (emphasis added) discussed above in the genesis of the soap opera form and, for that reason, the futility of trying to assign the creation of the soap opera to the genius of a single individual.... Interestingly, the basis of the suit reveals that even in this embryonic stage of the development of the soap opera form, it was viewed as a set of structural principles that motor narrative and character development.[1]

What Allen says of the first soap opera is equally true of every television dramatic program; and if the collaborators of Aaron Spelling, Garry Marshall, Norman Lear, et al. were to decide the issue of creativity in the courts, probably the conclusion that television creativity is "the convergence of generative mechanism" would be replicated.

The production of television dramatic programming like series, serials, movies, etc., consists of a fiercely contested bargaining process. The parties contesting for dominance are audiences through their surrogates: Nielsen ratings and the FCC; networks and their clients, including advertisers and pressure groups; production companies, which include producers, writers, directors, editors; and many other workers who have dependency relations with the production companies.

The three constituencies of interest create a negotiated public text which has both purposive and symbolic functions in the total context of a society wedded to values derived from free speech and the marketplace. This view of television programming denies any single constituency of interest an exclusive claim to control of the medium; therefore, instead of calling television the producer's medium,[2] which elevates the role of one constituency to hegemony over the whole, it is more appropriate to call television a people's medium--a neutral expression which encourages us to explore creativity in television. This argument also questions the view that "American commercial television programming is basically determined by the three networks,"[3] a statement which denies the role played by the other constituents in shaping the form and content of the public text. Television dramatic programming consists of the following steps:

- Selection of stories, content, form, and format
- Casting
- Directing
- Supervision of cutting, editing, dubbing, etc.

The three constituencies of interest contest and compromise at every step to produce a collective text which entertains and persuades and also initiates "a symbolic process whereby reality is produced, maintained, repaired and transformed."[4] Muriel Cantor has suggested that "the central task of a mass communication organization is to formulate content, which is submitted to an audience."[5] The phrase "submitted to an audience" is well chosen because it establishes a constituency of interest which the expression "the producer's medium" does not include. The formulation of content in dramatic programming begins with the selection and development of a story. At best, the production of dramatic programming from theme to final editing would be under the creative control of an ideal producer, as described by Muriel Cantor:

> The ideal producer would have control of story selection, both theme and content, would be in charge of all other aspects of production, including casting and cutting, and would perform these duties without constraint from the networks and the production company who hires him.[6]

But this ideal producer is not a practical possibility, because in the conglomeration of competing interests that constitutes television as the people's medium, creative control, or decision making, is a kind of floating center in a three-dimensional space positioned by the networks, production companies, and Nielsen ratings (audiences). Any attempt to simplify the issue and attribute creativity and development to one constituency will distort the picture.

James S. Ettema, in an illuminating essay,[7] has utilized Graham Allison's model of negotiation within organization to study creativity in public television. The model beautifully explains the process of negotiated creativity in television as a floating center in a system of coordinate constituencies. The Allison model consists of the following four structures:

1. Constituencies of Interest. In the case of television, they are Nielsen ratings (audiences), networks, and production companies. The three constituencies competing to produce the public text are so structured as to reflect the symbolic and historical (actual) core of American society--i.e., the free marketplace of goods and ideas. For instance, Nielsen ratings are based upon head counts, but not upon the quality of viewers or programs, because in the marketplace what counts is the aggregate, not the Who's Who, of American society. Similarly, networks, like other businesses, are organized around profits, expansionism, and mergers. Individuals in production companies who carry the legends of creators, writers, directors, etc., are as much constrained as is the artist who takes his canvas to the marketplace: the greater the necessity of appealing to the masses, the more the compromise.

2. Differential Orientation of the Constituencies of Interest. The networks, the producers, and the audiences have different orientations which create a clash of interests and the necessity for compromise. Audiences, as markets of taste with a continuous though slow change in their networks of assumptions or modes of consciousness, approach television primarily with the intention of being entertained and informed. Networks, aiming at

profits and prestige, would seek an everlasting formula to entertain the audiences and deliver them to the marketplace. Producers, with artistic aspirations and a desire to deliver a social message mixed with the desire for huge salaries, would not hesitate to introduce themes and contents which would shock public tastes or pander to baser instincts which organized society enjoins them to control.

3. <u>Power</u>. Each constituency's realm has power partly derived from its own base and partly from its positioning vis-à-vis the others. None of the three constituencies could monopolize the power and drive out the others or make them captives because the existence of one without the others is meaningless in a system of co-existence. The struggle for power aims at controlling the floating creative center, which in one dramatic program may be with the producer but might shift to the network in the next program or may be controlled by audiences through ratings, research, and the FCC.

4. <u>Negotiated Creativity</u>. Horace Newcomb and Robert Alley in <u>The Producer's Medium</u> have taken a traditional view of attributing the floating creative center to individuals and have recognized these few individuals in a spirit of praise. Muriel Cantor in <u>The Hollywood TV Producer</u> perceived a continuous struggle between producers and networks. Absent from her work is the third constituency of interest, the audience, which like Banquo's ghost is always present at the negotiating table. While the power of the producers and the networks is known, one does not know what Banquo's ghost wants. The audiences' power comes from their anonymity, their inscrutability, their partial silence, or their misleading feedback via Nielsen ratings. Two parties, the networks and the producers, negotiate the television text for the third party, which, like an absentee landlord, is never present but is always there. Much of the struggle between the three networks and their producers would become unnecessary if somehow there were a method of empirically observing

audiences' changing networks of assumptions or modes of consciousness. In the absence of a reliable methodology, program developers at the production companies and the networks resort to imaginative leaps, trained hunches, or some other arcane method of understanding the audiences. Ratings gauge ongoing tastes and preferences, but they do not explain, for instance, when a program will cease to interest audiences and why or what conservative or liberal social forces might begin to castigate a program's content.

THE ROLE OF THE PRODUCER

The struggle over the form and substance of television dramatic programming among the three competing constituencies focuses on the following television genres:

1. <u>Series</u>: A segmental or episodic narrative in which each episode tells a story complete in itself; the main characters continue from episode to episode. Types of characters and situations largely determine the content of the story. (It is at this crucial stage of decision making that networks and producers mull over and maul each other.) Each episode lasts for a half hour to one hour. Series may be shown daily, weekly, or biweekly. Series could be subdivided into the following categories:

    a. Situation Comedy: "The Cosby Show," "Three's Company," "Golden Girls," etc.

    b. Detective Story: "Crazy Like a Fox," etc.

    c. Police or Adventure Story: "Miami Vice," etc.

2. <u>Serials</u>: Dramatic serials have continuous narrative with opened-end structure. Daytime soap operas like "The Guiding Light" and "General Hospital" exemplify this genre. Daytime serials are aimed at female audiences. Some of them, for instance, "Young and the Restless," are created particularly for young girls. They are slow-paced, problem-oriented stories dealing with drugs, pregnancies, romantic love, power, money, inheritance,

matrimonial infidelities. Prime-time soap operas are glamorous and comparatively fast-paced. The struggle for power and money they depict is often brutal and inhuman because the stakes are high, involving the future of families, nations, and even international personages. "Falcon Crest," "Dallas," and "Dynasty" exemplify this genre.

3. <u>Series-Serials</u>: In 1980 a new kind of dramatic show, "Hill Street Blues," was introduced by NBC. This show has borrowed features from both series and serials. Like the series, each episode is complete; but like a serial, some of the narrative threads continue. It is a unique example of a cumulative narrative trying to reach a resolution. It is also a police story with an attendant sense of humor. It defies categorization and definition.

4. <u>Anthologies</u>. An anthology is held together by a theme but not necessarily by a set of characters. In the fifties and sixties dramatic anthologies were popular. In the eighties a reincarnation of dramatic anthology has appeared on the screen. One example of this is "George Burns' Comedy Week." Shows like "Love Boat" and "Hotel" are essentially dramatic anthologies which have continuity of theme and partial continuity of characters.

5. <u>Variety-Vaudeville</u>. Television versions of this genre, derived from radio and stage, are "People are Funny," "TV Bloopers," etc.

6. <u>Mini-Series and Made-for-TV Movies</u>. While made-for-TV movies are a transplant from cinema, the mini-series is a television created genre. They may be called novel-for-television, or televising the novel. Examples are "Shogun," "The Jewel in the Crown," etc. They are a form of television's epic theater discussed elsewhere in this study.

7. <u>Docudrama</u>. This hybrid genre is a product of cross-fertilization between documentary and drama whose origin can be traced to historical novels and plays, cinema, and radio. There is, however, a

marked difference between docudrama and its ancestors. The television docudrama is of the present and invariably has a rhetorical purpose, a persuasive goal which controls its form and structure. "Fear on Trial" (CBS) and "Return to Earth" (NBC) are examples of this genre.

Of these several television dramatic genres, only miniseries and docudramas are not likely to be based upon formulas; and they demand artistic creativity and freedom. The docudrama, because its rhetorical vision controls its artistic purpose, is bound to invite interference from the networks, and also occasionally to arouse the suspicions of the third constituency (audience), as happened in the case of a docudrama about the Atlanta child murder mystery.

The status of a producer (meaning the nature and extent of his or her creative control) would depend upon which genre is being produced. The creators and producers of "All in the Family" and "Hill Street Blues" could demand and exercise creative control to some extent because the shows were of a different kind, unconventional and innovative. But once the basic format and the nature of the content of a program like "Hill Street Blues" become acceptable to audiences, it does not matter whether the original creators (Kozoll and Bochco) continue with the show because audiences, unlike the readers of a book, are not attracted by the auteurs, producers, creators, or writers.

What is the role of a producer in a medium in which originality and creativity are not of great essence, and imitation, cloning, recombinant strategies, formulaic repetitions are the staple fare? Some statements of producers, though rather dated, are revealing:

> "I both develop and create ideas for production.... The Network created and I developed."
>
> "After the stories I personally see the production to the finish."
>
> "So far as producer's function on this show, it is primarily the supervising of the story materials."
>
> "Every phase of the operation has to be controlled by the producer."

The Collective as Creator

> "Developing the script is one of the most important functions of the producer."
>
> "The story is ground out like sausage, and we ground out the film."
>
> "On paper it was my obligation to develop the stories, but what they let you do are different things."[9]

These responses by producers, reported by Muriel Cantor, to a great extent were re-echoed in another set of interviews by Newcomb and Alley. Producers' claims varied from doing hack work for the networks to near control of the medium, which illustrates the thesis that in television creative control and decision making constitute a floating center.

Control of the floating center of creativity and decision making in TV would depend upon:

1. The dramatic genre. For instance, if <u>War and Peace</u> has to be developed into a mini-series, creative control and decision making would be in the hands of the producer, whose only constraint would be the allotted budget and time. If, however, a new sitcom has to be developed, there is no reason to give creative freedom to a producer because the formula for sausage is known. Grinding of sausage requires no freedom. It requires only quality control.

2. The other factor influencing control of the creative center is the degree of innovation, unconventionality, and freshness required in a dramatic program to hold the audiences. If a formula is successful, the network would not let the producer disturb the status quo. Only in case of uncertainties, when innovations become important to get ratings for the survival of a program or of the individuals in the network, would producers be likely to enjoy more creative freedom. In this regard, Joseph Turow's investigation is very illuminating. Since innovation and unconventionality are aspects of creativity and demand decision making, Turow draws the conclusion that "... unconventional program innovations are most likely to be generated and accepted by

organizations experiencing unusual changes or competitive pressure."[10] He argues that NBC accepted "United States" because the network lagged in ratings, and CBS accepted "All in the Family" because the top management (Robert Wood) thought of boosting the network's ratings. Norman Lear, the producer of "All in the Family," and Larry Gelbart of "United States" got away with creative freedom and control because of their "awareness of having a power base outside the television industry which allowed them attractive work if a network did not accept their proposals."[11] This assertion further illustrates the thesis that creativity in television is negotiated by several parties and depends upon many factors. Even when the producers have creative control in exceptional circumstances, the scheduling of a program could turn that freedom into a meaningless exercise. As Joseph Turow comments, keeping in mind the airing of "All in the Family," "United States," etc.: "The programs were clearly unorthodox, and while key executives had taken the risk of buying them, those same executives and their program committees were hesitant about risking attractive--and valuable--time slots when airing them."

Freedom to create a program does not entail freedom to schedule the program, and it is scheduling which brings the third party to the negotiating table to create the public text.

GRANT TINKER'S MTM

Through his company MTM, Grant Tinker attracted some highly interesting and creative persons like Jay Tarses, Tom Patchett, Michael Zinberg, James L. Brooks, Allan Burns, Steven Bochco, and Michael Kozoll. They gave his company publicly acclaimed and critically valued shows like "The Mary Tyler Moore Show" and its equally illustrious spin-offs "Rhoda" and "Lou Grant," and the unique police drama "Hill Street Blues." The lure for writers and producers to work under the MTM banner was the creative freedom and autonomy which Grant Tinker assured his people under the guise of democratic management. He did not supervise day-to-day development of the story or content and did not confuse his role with that of his writers and producers; probably this management style is what created the illusion of freedom and autonomy enjoyed by his creative workers. But in practice Tinker controlled the broad contours of production by suggesting issues-oriented series and witty and literate comedies for which MTM is known. He exercised subtle creative control over what took shape at MTM, and his low-profile approach and generous habit of passing on credit to his writers and producers was a source of strength for his company. But Tinker knew that creativity in television is a complex evolutionary activity and that few should arrogate to themselves the title of producer, auteur, or creator. As he said:

> MTM was founded on writers, Burns and Brooks being the first two, and then others joined us later and those people became writer-producers. It's particularly important in three-camera comedy, which is evolutionary from the Monday script read around the table till the Friday night we shoot it, that the people who are involved should be all writers. That's what they are doing all week, rewriting the show as things don't work or they see they can improve.[12]

In his own way Grant Tinker tried to describe the nature of the television medium more as a system of coordinate constituencies demanding the merger of creative efforts and individual egos than as a producer's medium.

Grant Tinker began his broadcasting career in 1949 with NBC Radio Network as a trainee in the programming department and continued working there as an operation manager till 1954. After a brief sojourn at Radio Free Europe, he worked for two advertising agencies, McCann-Erickson and Benton and Bowles, where he was engaged in television programming. In the fall of 1961 he returned to NBC, but six years of administrative work at the network persuaded him that he preferred the production of programs rather than the routine administrative work he did at New York headquarters. Though he quit NBC in 1967, it was not till 1970 that Tinker established his own company, named after his wife Mary Tyler Moore, MTM Enterprises, Inc.

Grant Tinker's creative vision centered on exploiting the talented acting of his wife Mary as a comedienne, and he hired the Brooks and Burns team to translate and execute his vision. He passed on his dream to others and watched it take shape as if imagination and fantasy, having split, were nonetheless acting as a creative team. As Brooks told an interviewer, "Grant gave us blanket approval of anything we wanted to do, not just autonomy, but support.... He is a pragmatist with a passion for quality."[13] Within the overall vision of a series developing around the character of an independent-minded career woman, Mary Richards, and her colleagues at a television station, Brooks and Burns exercised their creative freedom under the guidance of Grant Tinker and with the approval of the network-- evidence that creativity in television is a series of compromises. The decision to end "The Mary Tyler Moore Show" (1971-1977) was also Tinker's, not that of writer-producers Brooks and Burns. Tinker had grasped the changing mode of consciousness of the audiences and also the growing maturity of the medium, and he thought it would put tremendous strain on creativity to continue the show in these changed circumstances.

However, "The Mary Tyler Moore Show" birthed a spinoff, "Lou Grant," which, after much struggle against network (CBS) objections and Nielsen's low ratings, went ahead to earn critical acclaim and several awards. "Lou Grant" was about a tough editor of a Los Angeles newspaper who raised controversial issues. Most of the issues raised in the show were topics of the day, and dramatizing them and raising them to the level of public debate made the show very fascinating. In the long run the topicality of the show, the controversial issues it raised, and most of all Ed Asner's personal involvement in the hotly debated issues of the day, as Todd Gitlin[14] has suggested, proved the show's death knell.

Rhoda, a fat, chubby, single, Jewish girl, was a hilarious character on "The Mary Tyler Moore Show." But when Rhoda moved from Minneapolis to New York and started being her own person in another spin-off, "Rhoda," her comic energy got drained on the way. In New York she was slimmer than in Minneapolis, managed to find a husband, and turned her marriage into a celebrated event--no less comic because in her lily-white wedding gown ("Some New Yorker tried to write graffiti on me!") she took a subway to her mother's apartment in the Bronx. After marriage her life returned to normality--boredom, separation, divorce, dating, job-hunting, and more boredom--and left the air. MTM did not know what to do with Rhoda once she left Minneapolis.

"The Bob Newhart Show" was another great achievement of MTM. Its urban wit and charm delighted millions. It had a touch of class. The essence of the show was the comic hostility between Bob, psychotherapist, and Emily, his wife, a schoolteacher. They lived in a Chicago skyscraper and saw humans twisting and turning crazily. Almost everyone needed Bob's therapy session and Emily's mothering. And they themselves needed no less. Their jibes and jabs were delightful:

> Emily: On our wedding night you were stalling.
> Bob: I wasn't stalling ... I just did not want to come on like an animal.

Bob Newhart's pauses reminded one of Harold Pinter's pauses, except that they were funny. In fact he shared his comic uncertainty with Mary's comic hesitancy on "The Mary Tyler Moore Show," which preceded the Newhart show and gave it a kind of continuity. The audiences smoothly glided from Mary Richards' comic fumbling to Bob Hartly's comic stumbling. Mary was not sure how to be assertive in a male-dominated society, and her reactive attempts to walk with pride and dignity sounded funny. Bob's comic pauses were not a mere mannerism but were uncertain reactions to humans who might be tipped over to the other side of normality. His attitude, the way he listened to patients and nonpatients (and occasionally he found little difference), and his well-timed hesitations were the sources of comedy. Bob Newhart's inimitable style was supported by the other well-developed characters who added credibility to a humane comedy full of charming wit. It would be unfair to say that Bob Hartly was a male clone of Mary Richards, but they were certainly born of the same parent, MTM.

Grant Tinker's desire to steer clear of what he called "sizzle shows" and "witless" comedy and to give audiences something substantial which made them think has not been always successful. Comedies like "We Got Each Other," the "Betty White Show," and "The White Shadow" did not catch the audiences' fancy; "WKRP in Cincinnati" was moderately successful. "Mary" and the revival of the older show entitled "Mary Tyler Moore Hour" were hardly received with enthusiasm. The mode of consciousness of late-seventies audiences had changed, and MTM was not listening till it stumbled upon "Hill Street Blues."

While the trendsetter of the seventies, "All in the Family" became easily identified with Norman Lear, it is hard to identify "Hill Street Blues" with any particular individual, either producer or a hyphenate. "Hill Street Blues" is an example of the theory of television creativity as an emergent force in a system of coordinate constituencies. As Michael Pollan wrote in Channels, Fred Silverman, the president of NBC, persuaded Steven Bochco and Michael Kozoll "to produce a new kind of show that he dreamed up."[15] Fred Silverman's dream was articulated and shaped by the Bochco-Kozoll team, cocooned in a production company headed by Grant Tinker, who later occupied Fred Silverman's chair. So who is the creator of "Hill Street Blues"?

The view of television creativity as residing in and emerging from a system of coordinate constituencies in tune with the prevalent mode of consciousness has far-reaching consequences. First of all, it brings television creativity and production closer to events like the Manhattan Project or NASA's program to land a man on the moon. Was Robert Oppenheimer the creator of the first atomic bomb? Was John F. Kennedy, who "dreamed up" the vision of man on the moon, the creator-controller or producer of the first mission? Television programs--informational, journalistic, or dramatic-fictional--are in the nature of the NASA and Manhattan projects. The proper question about such a project is whether it is in tune with the current mode of consciousness. That television programming, as an outgrowth of one mode of consciousness, is the art form of a collective creator does not make individual creativity obsolete; some great works of art and literature will always come from individual creative minds. But television has opened up an alternative mode of creativity as energy developing from a collective wherein each element is conditioned to form a resulting totality.

NORMAN LEAR AND THE DRAMATIZATION OF RESENTMENT

At the peak of his career in the mid-seventies, when six of his comedies were capturing top ratings in Nielsen's demographics, Norman Lear said, "I want to entertain, but I gravitate to subjects that matter and people worth caring about."[16] It was the fine blend of problems and people in a comic theatrical frame which made his television programs significant for 120 million[17] viewers a week. It was a historical event of deep import that one individual intuitively grasped the emerging mode of consciousness of a vast and disparate nation, and could communicate with its millions on issues and topics in a language the genteel and civilized thought beyond the pale of mass entertainment. Yet there was nothing original about Norman Lear. His fame rests on only six comedies: "All in the Family," "Maude," "Good Times," "The Jeffersons," "Sanford and Son," "Hot L Baltimore," and "One Day at a Time"--all of which depict a microcosm of unresolved social conflicts made tolerable only through humor and compassion.

Lear's origins in Russian Jewry may explain his obsession with topicality and his concern to make America more livable through acceptance of plurality. Plurality is the enemy of bigotry. Norman Lear was born on July 27, 1922, in New Haven, Connecticut, of a second-generation Russian-Jewish immigrant family. Instead of turning inward and exploring the ethnic and cultural roots of his people, as members of some immigrant minorities have done, Lear turned to the bewildering variety of his countrymen and confronted them with their problems without condemnation or castigation. He visualized a part of his father's personality in Archie Bunker.

Lear's early life was very undistinguished. Before he could complete his studies at Emerson College, he joined the U.S. Air Force in 1942 as a radio man. After the war he worked in a publicity firm, produced novelty items, worked as a door-to-door salesman, and was a sidewalk photographer. His luck took a turn for the better when, along with his friend Ed Simmons, he wrote a successful skit for a night club entertainer. Soon he was writing for "The Ford Star Review"; "Colgate Comedy Hour," which starred Dean Martin and Jerry Lewis; and many other shows which earned him minor prosperity. But his association with Bud Yorkin, the Colgate show director, turned out to be of great significance to his career; both Lear and Yorkin, through their production company Tandem, spawned many critically acclaimed or denounced films like "Come Blow Your Horn" (1963), "Never Too Late" (1965), "Divorce, American Style" (1967), "The Night They Raided Minsky's" (1968), and "Cold Turkey" (1971). Reviewers called these films tiring; garish; shallow; full of questionable jokes, mockery, and melancholy.

But the sixties, which one might call Lear's film decade, established him as a mass entertainer who would not hesitate in trying "to harness a sweeping satire of American society to his small vehicle," as Paul D. Zimmerman of Newsweek said about him.[18] In this decade he wrote only one script, "Divorce, American Style," which could be called original; all the rest he borrowed and adapted from other sources--a habit of mind he continued in his television decade of the seventies. Apart from his proclivity to adapt materials and storylines, this decade also showed his habit of merging serious themes with laughter--what Michael Arlen of New Yorker called Lear's "jokey topicality."[19] Comic topicality and unfettered and unabashed adaptation, distinguishing characteristics of all mass media entertainment, stood Lear and his collaborator Bud Yorkin in good stead when they hit the idea of Americanizing the British television series "Till Death Do Us Part" as "All in the Family."

Success, however, did not breed originality but only more imitation and adaptation. "Steptoe and Son" became "Sanford and Son," with the Cockney junkmen transplanted to the American screen as black junkmen who used their junkyard as a comic fraud for perpetrating their one-liners and vaudeville jokes that provide comic relief for their black brethren who suffered social neglect for such a long time. (Fred Sanford: "Four men ... four white men. With stockings over their heads. I know they weren't black--you can't get a stocking over one of them naturals.") Through the talented acting of Redd Foxx injustices done against blacks were humorously portrayed. Most of the time it seemed the jokes were contrived and out of place, but they did bring out laughter with a sting. It was not only Fred Sanford's ailing heart and his habit of removing everything from a hotel he visited, but also the way he countenanced whites,

The Collective as Creator 139

which amused his viewers. When his sister married a white man, Sanford called the new husband "Mr. Intermarry," "Paleface," "Snow Whitey," "Honkey," "Color Blind," and "White Tornado." The difference between "Amos 'n' Andy" and "Sanford and Son" was that the laughter in the former was innocent; in the latter it was self-conscious, as if someone were using it as social therapy.

"Maude" was a spin-off from "All in the Family," and the character of Maude was in opposite polarity to that of Archie Bunker. Maude was as bigoted a liberal as Archie was a conservative. Like the other Lear production, "Maude" too dealt with topics like birth control, abortion, menopause, etc., but at the same time explored another obsessive concern of women: aging. Like Archie, Maude was larger than life, and as an extremist liberal she committed the same mistakes and sounded as doctrinaire as Archie. But much of the success of the series came from the talented acting of Beatrice Arthur as Maude. It was her superb sense of timing and her collusion with the audience, as it were, which brought dynamism and humor to Lear's comedy. (A two-part episode called "Maude's Dilemma," in which Maude at the age of forty-seven decided to have an abortion, was a subject of controversy and social boycott by some groups.)

"Maude" produced a spin-off with Maude's black maid Florida entitled "Good Times," though the actual series seemed to mock the title because the poor ghetto family had everything but good times. The only good thing about the series was the mutual love and respect among the family members and the father's wild schemes to get his family out of their miserable situation. In spite of its many afflictions, the family remained together and well integrated--for black audiences an important portrayal because more than any other group they suffer from broken, fatherless families.

Just as Maude, Edith Bunker's cousin, left to start her spin-off show and Florida left "Maude" to create "Good Times," so the Bunkers' neighbors, George, Louise, and their son Lionel left the Bunkers to start their chain-store laundry business and become "The Jeffersons." It seemed that George Jefferson, the vulgar nouveau-riche black who wanted to be considered cultured and aspired to be admitted to civilized society, was nothing but another Archie Bunker with black skin. He lacked warmth, was in the habit of badmouthing his wife and son, called whites names, and treated his maid as a doormat (she in turn hit him in the face). But George, as the series progressed, did not turn out to be another Archie Bunker but became instead a manageable comic nuisance. Most of the comedy in "The Jeffersons" was based upon how the egoistic George got deflated, sometimes by his neighbors Helen and Tom, at other times by his own maid Florence. His wife would join anyone who could bring George to his senses. Yet every episode ended in the celebration of domestic happiness--George in the arms of Louise. And Lear let us see how a rich black family lived as happily as any of us and made us a trifle more tolerant of their aspirations.

By the time Lear was ready to give us Ms. Ann Romano of "One Day at a Time," his audiences had become used to controversial topics like abortion, menopause, sodomy, manic depression, and mental retardation and all kinds of ethnic jokes from both blacks and whites. What he did in "One Day at a Time" was to portray an independent woman who pursued her career seriously as she followed the development of her two growing daughters, while taking her own love life seriously. As a divorced mother she struggled with dignity and developed a quiet strength of character to become her own person. As she told her married lover, "There is something that matters more than you do: my self respect." For Ann divorced life was a course of self-discovery, but only one day at a time.

Norman Lear's success with television audiences of the seventies was due to his intuitive exploitation of the resentment various groups, classes, and social strata had accumulated against each other over a period of decades. He used old-fashioned gags, one-line jokes, vaudeville, and other familiar comic gimmicks to mine the seams of resentment which contending groups in a heterogeneous society naturally build against each other. Television brought all the disparate ethnic, racial, and economic groups to the same screen, where they could see their hateful enemies trounced and deflated. Lear used whites to denounce blacks, blacks to denounce whites, conservatives to condemn liberals, and liberals to condemn conservatives as enemies of the people. But he packed this resentment in humor and compassion, which made his disagreeable characters tolerable if not lovable. In an extremely well-organized society such as America, where social protests are rare and revolution is nearly impossible, one of the ways to release the resentments of those who feel deprived, suppressed, and repressed is through situation comedies which, like boxing and football, are deliberately built and designed to take off the social lid.

There is another reason for the success of Lear's comedies: his superb casting sense and sensibility. A comedy without proper casting can be a great disaster. Excellent casting rescued Lear's humor, which was mostly average and frequently seemed to be tottering. In fact, most of his jokes and themes began to be repeated ad nauseam. His half dozen comedies resembled a palace of distorting mirrors wherein audiences saw their own contorted images and laughed, believing that though there were ghosts and monsters, they themselves were safe. It was a remarkable achievement for a man who invented little and borrowed almost every plot and technique, but had the heart and mind to comprehend in totality the embedded layers of resentment of American society and their dramatic potential.

NOTES

1. Robert C. Allen, Speaking of Soap Operas (Chapel Hill: University of North Carolina Press, 1985), pp. 110-112.
2. Horace Newcomb and Robert S. Alley, The Producer's Medium (New York: Oxford University Press, 1983), pp. 3-45.
3. Muriel G. Cantor, The Hollywood TV Producer (New York: Books, Inc., 1971), p. 207.
4. James Carey, "A Cultural Approach to Communication," Communication, 1975, vol. II, p. 6.
5. Muriel G. Cantor, p. 208.
6. Ibid., p. 14.
7. James S. Ettema, "The Organizational Context of Creativity," in James S. Ettema and D. Charles Whitney, eds., Individuals in Mass Media Organization: Creativity and Constraint (Beverly Hills: Sage Publications, 1982), pp. 91-104.
8. G.T. Allison, Essence of Decision (Boston: Little, Brown, 1971), p. 173.
9. Muriel G. Cantor, pp. 9-14. Also see Muriel Cantor, "The Politics of Popular Drama," Communication Research, 6:4 (October 1979), pp. 387-406.

10. Joseph Turow, "Unconventional Programs on Commercial Television: An Organizational Perspective," in James S. Ettema and P. Charles Whitney, eds., <u>Individuals in Mass Media Organization: Creativity and Constraint</u> (Beverly Hills: Sage Publications, 1982), pp. 107-129.
11. Ibid., p. 125.
12. Newcomb and Alley, p. 226.
13. <u>Current Biography</u> (New York: H.W. Wilson Co., 1982), p. 414.
14. Todd Gitlin, <u>Inside Prime Time</u> (New York: Pantheon Books, 1983), pp. 3-11.
15. Michael Pollan, "Can 'Hill Street Blues' Rescue NBC," <u>Channel of Communication</u> (April/May 1983), pp. 30-34.
16. <u>Current Biography</u> (New York: H.W. Wilson Co., 1974), p. 229.
17. Michael Arlen, "The Media Dramas of Norman Lear," Richard Adler, ed., <u>All in the Family</u> (New York: Praeger Publishers, 1979), p. 117.
18. <u>Current Biography</u> (New York: H.W. Wilson Co., 1974), p. 230.
19. Michael Arlen, p. 117.

Chapter Eight

NEWS AND NEWSCASTERS

* Structure of the Newscast

* TV News as Business, as Show Business

* Can Television Be Fair?

Reliable sources have told us that television images inescapably embody a viewpoint and that traditional ideas about objectivity are false and misleading--we agree.

* * *

What is this thing called news?
Believe it or not, there are no rules.
  --From "Race Against Prime Time"[1]

* * *

Audience: How are these stories chosen and upon what criteria are they chosen? ... In what order? ... Is there an order?

Tom Brokaw: There is no hard and fast mathematical formula that you apply to any given day. Sometimes it's whether or not you have access. Can you get there in time? Can you get a picture out of there? How much does it mean to the entire audience out there? Is it fresh? Is it new? Is it different from yesterday? That's one of the criteria we use in the course of the day. Sometimes, does it move you? Is it so emotional that people are going to be able to get something out of that they can learn about themselves?[2]

The production of television news has something to do with the collective consensus about the normal in a society. The socio-political structures are erected to sustain the normal. News, in a simplistic way, is a celebration of the ideal of the normal or a lamentation for deviation from the normal. The ideal and the deviant create the news in television and other mass media. This simplistic view of the news gathering and selection process does not answer the question about how news items are selected from the myriad of images competing to be picked up by reporters. Is news gathering just like casting a fishing net--catching whatever gets into the net?

The broad consensus in American society is that free enterprise is for the good of all, and that free speech is conducive to the welfare of the individual and the society because it makes possible bringing about social changes through a process of political negotiation and periodic change. This broad consensus has channeled the energies of the ambitious toward unparalleled entrepreneurial achievements; and it has created decentralized freedoms leading to checks and balances, as observed in Congress and other political institutions. This view is further reinforced because American society is a conglomeration of constituencies of interests competing to maximize the limited resources available. The television journalist, therefore, not only reports the ideal of and the deviation from the normal, but also acts as a mediator and an interpreter for various constituencies. As Stuart Hall observed:

> The role of the new journalist is to mediate--or act as the "gatekeeper"--between different publics, between the institutions and the individual, between the sphere of the public and the private, between the new and the old. News production is often a self-fulfilling activity. Categories of news, consistently produced over time, create public spaces in the media which have to be filled. The presence of the media at the birth of new events can affect their course and outcome. The news is not only a cultural product: it is the product of a set of institutional definitions and meanings, which, in the

professional shorthand, is commonly called news-value.[3]

The newsvalues of television journalists support the consensus about the normal in a society, and when they act as interpreter-mediators between various strata of interests, consensus about the core values remains unchallenged. But how does a journalist mediate? If there are ten stories competing for one time slot, how does a television newscaster decide which story to choose?

There are at present two competing theories[4] by which television critics try to explain the professional behavior of newscasters. The manipulative theory of the press states that all newsmen are mannequins and puppets for their employers, and all they do is manage news in a way that hides the truth about the vested interests which pay them. In this view a symbiotic relation[5] exists between the television establishment and the business-industrial complex in America, and so the function of television newscasting is to "routinize the unexpected,"[6] patch up the quilt, and control discontent. Echoing the arguments of Stuart Hall, Gaye Tuchman says that news organizations cast their news nets in well-recognized waters which are indirectly controlled by the public relations departments of the "legitimated social institutions." The assigned function of newsmen is not to report reality, but "through the sources identified with facts, newsworkers create and control controversy; they contain dissent."[7] In other words, the news gathering and disseminating process of the television journalist helps to perpetuate the hegemony of the ruling classes. This manipulative-symbiotic theory is a variation on the theme of base-controlling-superstructure theory, which explains a lot but not the most vital thing--that is, social change. If the government and other establishments manipulate the minds of the people through the media, how could one explain the violent schisms between the press and the government over McCarthyism, Vietnam, and Watergate? To change the topic a trifle, why are the values of American women today so different from those of a generation ago? Is it because women are coparticipating in the legitimated institutions of power, or is it because the birth control pill has liberated them? The neo-Marxist manipulative-symbiotic hegemony theory is useful in studying power structure in a society in stasis, but it does not explain the dynamism of a society in which television, along with technology, plays an important role in bringing about changes. The categorization of news into beats and bureaus and public spaces and time slots which create expectations has something to do with how the human mind works. We impose order upon chaotic flux through classification or categorization of information. Sports, art, education, etc., are categories in capitalistic as well as communistic societies. Classification is simply a method of information processing, of separating news from news, and is not evidence of manipulating people's minds.

The free market model theory treats news as a commodity, which prompts the news establishments to package news in the body of pop star Madonna or the chatty fireside conversation of a beauty queen to attract the largest segment of the audience. The problem for the newscasters, according to this model, is to present the truth as a dramatic spectacle so that the audience can be enticed to watch. But within the package, they argue, lies the kernel of truth--about Lebanon, Nicaragua, black poverty in Mississippi, or $7,600 paid to a defense contractor for a coffee brewer. According to this theory, since the various networks compete for the audience by being first to report on an exclusive basis, the facts cannot be hidden. In fact, it is argued, more and more television stations are engaged in producing mini-documentaries and special reports to expose wayward public officials and keep audiences informed. Partly it is a theory of confrontation between the mass media and the establishment for the public good. American television operates on the assumption that the public interest would be better served by the commercialization of the news and competition in the free market, which is essentially a buyers' market. Since the interest of the owners is motivated by profits, they do not interfere in editorial freedom; they only look at the Nielsen ratings. This model seems to suggest that since American audiences-as-markets are different from their European/Asian counterparts, the news-as-commodity is different in America from what it is in European or Asian markets.

Both theories about newscasting suggest that the newscasters are nothing but spokespersons for either the establishment or the consumers and do not play an active role in the selection and dissemination of news. Missing from both theories is consideration of the journalists' idealism, their compassion, their sense of justice and fair play, and their desire to educate the people. Neither the establishment nor the audiences, for instance, asked for "The Day After" or reports on the horrors of daily life in Beirut. This is what Peter Jennings, ABC's anchorman, has to say about reporting:

> One of the things I really had to decide a long time ago, and I remember the night I decided, we had yet another car bomb in West Beirut ... and we saw violence as we had seen it many times before, but there was one picture of a young child being brought out of a building, down a ladder, put on a stretcher, and I sat there and decided that that one picture was going to tell much more about the story than all of the chaos and the violence again, and I ran [it] at length, all the way down the ladder and on to the stretcher. And the hardest decision for me at that point was to say, do I now sanitize the news because some of you may be at dinner?, but much more importantly, do you have children in front of the television set? I have young children in front of the television and sometimes I just throw them out of the room. The answer is, for me at least, I have to leave it up to you who are parents. We cannot sanitize what is happening in our world. It should not be homogeneous. You should, I believe, see it the way it really is....[8]

Jennings' statement illustrates neither the manipulative nor the commodity theory of newscasting. What is happening in the world, out there, is beyond the control of the establishment or the free market. The newscasters and the television cameracrews, because of their idealism, sense of duty, newsvalue, and the idea of a good news story, select and disseminate news in an order which will maximize their audiences without destroying the broad consensus about the normal or the cultural core or the centralizing symbol. This is not to deny the overt and covert manipulative attempts of the establishment to exercise control over the media either by supplying well-packaged public relations stories or by outright attempts to take over the networks. A Jesse Helms might take over CBS to become Dan Rather's boss, but the ultimate test of a network is its credibility as reflected in Nielsen ratings. If a defense contractor, General Electric, swallows another defense contractor, RCA, which owns NBC, and begins to interfere in the newsroom, the question would be not only whether Tom Brokaw would stay on but whether audiences would stay tuned to NBC. Competition for audiences has become fierce not only among the networks but also among the local stations and the cables. While the total network nightly news audience has been declining steadily since the 1980-81 season,[9] local stations have doubled their news programs. Some of them increased their newscast from an hour to two and one half hours. Because of the many video wire services and CNN as a distributor, local stations feel competent to give news as well as any network. In this environment of cutthroat competition for the loyalty of audiences, the credibility of the network is a crucial factor in determining what is news and what is not news in America.

When an observer leaves the ivory tower of the theoretical models and descends into reality, he finds that the holistic approach to news selection and newscasting becomes a very practical tool of analysis. As stated earlier, television, as a part of the totality, conditions other structures and is conditioned by them and exists in a mutually supportive and hostile environment. It is shaped by the establishment which has created it and in turn shapes that establishment by supporting or opposing it. Its stake is in the normal, derived from the free marketplace of goods and ideas. As an autonomous system, its function is to produce not commodities but information and to act as a clearinghouse of common belief.

The interacting variables in the multidimensional space which transforms an event into television news are as follows: the journalist's idea of a good story; his or her idealism and sense of duty; televisual newsvalue; accessibility; deadline pressure; value for the audience and profitability; institutional manipulativeness; degree of deviation from the normal; degree of idealization of the normal; mode of consciousness of the time; and timeliness. The weight of each interacting variable in the multidimensional event-news space depends upon the context. A "60 Minutes" segment on black poverty in Mississippi, for instance, became meaningful when shown in the context of poverty and hunger in Africa. The notation said: "This is not Africa; this is America." What kind of manipulative or market pressure did "60 Minutes" have in creating this news story? Probably idealism and sense of duty weighed more heavily than profitability or

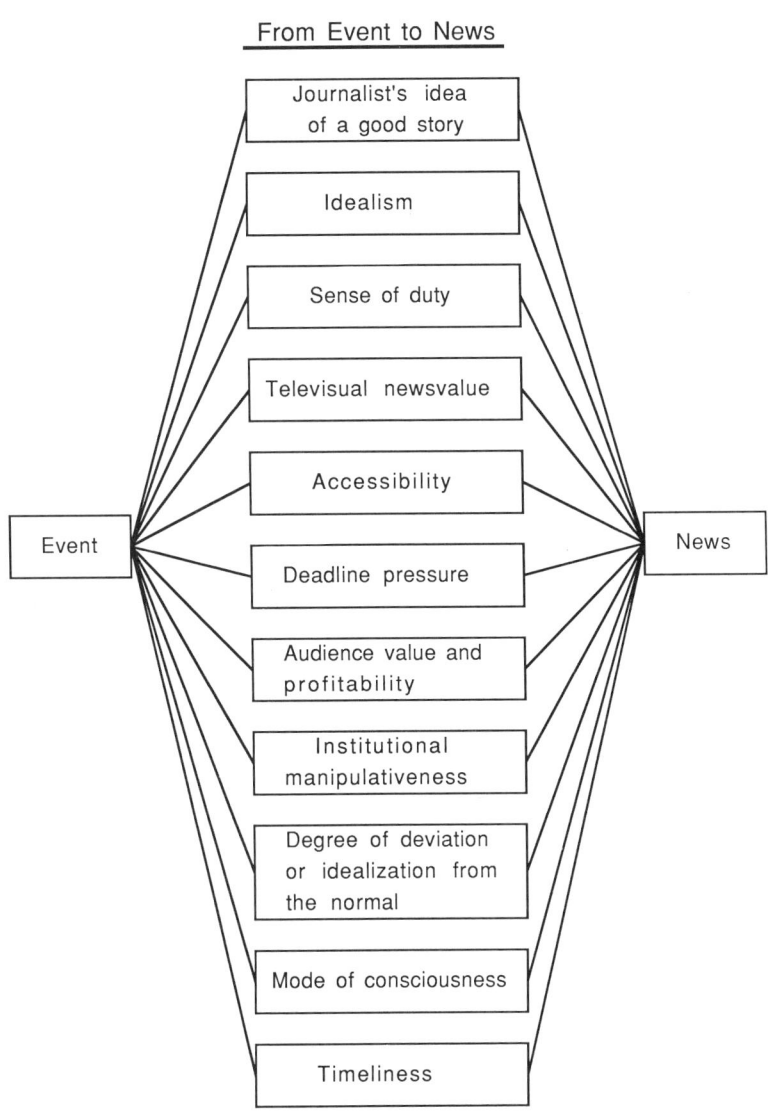

some other variable. In the holistic approach "60 Minutes," by drawing our attention to the degrading poverty in our midst, was creating an awareness so that the normal might be strengthened. It was giving a public voice to people who have fallen short of the American dream.

STRUCTURE OF THE NEWSCAST

In contradistinction to government controlled or owned broadcast systems in other countries, the American broadcast system exists, like any other enterprise, at the mercy of the free market. Its news broadcast structure in the course of the last fifty years has evolved in response to the challenges of the marketplace. To play its specific role as both critic and supporter of the consensus, it functions as informer and entertainer.

Today, in the era of the single anchorman at all three news networks, television newscasting sounds very authoritative, well organized, highly integrated, and credible. Like an English butler who in a dignified mien announces, "Dinner is served," the network anchorman declares in a distinguished, cultivated voice: "Good evening. This is the CBS news with Dan Rather...." During the twenty-two-minute newscast (30 minutes) about fifteen stories, including eight by correspondents, are served to the audience, as it were, course after course. The stories decrease in urgency and end with either a mini-documentary/multipart special report or a human interest story which leaves the anchorman smiling like the Cheshire cat in Alice in Wonderland. "All is under control," he seems to be saying, despite airplane crashes, shootings, etc. In contrast, a newspaper is much less sanguine, more gory and pessimistic.

One reason for this kind of control of the mood in television newscasting is that a single anchorman is in a position to impose a thematic unity on the sequence of the stories constituting a particular day's newscast, and this unity sometimes becomes a reason for the exclusion and inclusion of several items. For instance, Dan Rather, as managing editor of the CBS evening news, has "the final say on what reports are included. He writes or edits all the stories he reads.... During the morning, he takes part in meeting to discuss foreign stories, views three or four in-depth pieces that have been in the works and joins in a conference call with domestic bureaus to discuss story prospects. Typically 36 stories are considered, 16 of them reports from CBS correspondents in the U.S. or around the world.... Stories are told less in terms of officials and more in terms of how people around the U.S. are affected by decisions made in Washington. 'I want the broadcast to have compassion,' says Dan Rather."[10] Peter Jennings and Tom Brokaw also choose stories on the basis of how the stories will affect people's lives, though other factors shown in the model in the previous section are influential. In the long run it is deviation from the normal or idealization of the normal in the society which has a decisive impact on story selection. "News items which infringe social norms, break the pattern of expectations and contrast with our sense of the everyday, or are dramatic, or have 'numerous and intimate contacts with the life of the recipient,' have greater news salience for journalists than others."[11]

Apart from selecting stories as the anchorman perceives their effect upon people, the stories are sequenced in such a terse and dramatic spectacle that an evening newscast seems like the epic theater of Bertolt Brecht--full of music, videographics, on-the-spot live news (sometimes), interrogation of correspondents--all constituting a unified narrative flow. As Paul Weaver stated: "This does not happen by accident; it is intentional on the part of TV newsmen, and the fact that it is intentional is proof that the underlying goal of the television news program is to attain the condition of wholeness, to exhibit theme, structure and unity."[12]

Since the anchorman controls the narrative of the newscast, the viewer, unlike the reader of a newspaper, cannot have a cursory glance over the entire contents to pick and choose items; he or she remains in a state of suspended disbelief, beholden to the tale. The personal authority and voice of the anchorman, his control of the flow of the spectacle in a diegetic-mimetic framework, his implied assurances that the social order is intact, create a sense of security in the audience and confer on the anchorman a tremendous sense of credibility and power. No wonder everyone wants to control Dan Rather, Peter Jennings, and Tom Brokaw--without realizing that the sense of omniscience and omnipotence they exude is due more to the structure of the narrative and the temporal nature of televisual discourse than to their individual genius. If the network evening news were to be extended to one hour and anchored by two or more persons, much of the authority and majesty would vanish. That is the problem with CNN: it is a newscast without authority, though the value of the news as information is the same. If local stations were to change the narrative structure of their evening newscasts, with lone anchormen at the helm, they might pose a serious challenge to the networks, especially now, when cheap television technology and video wire services can provide local stations with live coverage of events anywhere in the world.

TV NEWS AS BUSINESS, AS SHOW BUSINESS

The three network news divisions have discovered that news makes monetary sense. NBC, CBS and ABC news earn about $1 billion in revenues and are big businesses managed by executives who are more interested in making money than in meeting the expectations of the people's right to know. Their emphasis is to treat news as a commodity and to package it in a manner that captures the largest audience rather than to "offer the most comprehensive look at the world around us."[13] Since viewers have shown a great appetite for news and information, networks and local stations have been steadily increasing their time for news coverage in consultation with news consultants who have coined terms like "happy talk" and "cybernetic news." A decade ago, when news consultants were invading local stations with flashy formulas to capture audiences, Walter Cronkite gave a stern warning which today sounds truer than ever:

> Of course ratings are important, and no one--newsman, program manager, salesman or general manager--need hang his head in shame because that is the fact.... But how we get those ratings, what we do to make us competitive, that bothers me, for just as it is no good to put out a superior product if you can't sell it, it is far worse to peddle an inferior product solely through the razzle dazzle of a promotion campaign....
> And aren't we guilty of that when we put the emphasis in our news broadcast on performance and performers, rather than content? Isn't that really

what we are looking for when we examine ourselves to see whether we are indulging in show business rather than journalism?.... It is cosmetics, pretty packaging--no substance ... they've been made suckers for a fad--editing by consultancy.[14]

Walter Cronkite, who affirmed the era of the lone anchorman at CBS and largely shaped broadcast newscasting as it is today, continues to be very critical of deteriorating journalistic standards in television: "Everything is being compressed into tiny tablets.... You take a little pill of news every day--23 minutes--and that's supposed to be enough."[15]

The era of news consultants has dawned even for the networks--they too have started listening to Frank Magid, McHugh & Hoffman, et al. Beautiful people[16] rather than seasoned journalists are being hired by the networks. The networks are being pushed toward total commercialization of the news, slowly losing the public trust. In a July 1985 Gallup Poll, "Confidence in American Institutions," only 29 percent of respondents said that they trusted television news "a great deal" or "quite a lot," as against 35 percent expressing the same opinion about newspapers, even though most people today rely upon television for their news. The more people watch television (an average of seven hours a day) the less they trust the dancing bears. On deeper thought, one might say this distrust is a healthy sign suggesting viewers are not swept off their feet by all the electronic gimmickry, pretty faces, and pretended omniscience of the newscasters. It seems clear that viewers check their information against other sources, particularly the print media, and look for a different version of events. A decade ago viewers would have trusted a television news report more than a newspaper article.[17] Probably, however, it is not quite safe to say that American viewers have become more discriminating and have begun to see how newscasting style dominates substance:

> Thus the style of newscasting may come to dominate the substance of what is communicated. The reality of the news, with its diversity and confusion, is subordinated to the orderliness of the format: 18 bulletins read by the talking head, punctuated by 9 intervals of videotape (selected to provide contrast rather than necessarily to illustrate the latest

or the most important stories, and reflecting camera crew assignments rather than unexpected new developments). The commercials that interrupt this presentation represent the true reality that reminds the viewer that he is still safe in the mainline of U.S. TV prime-time entertainment and not adrift in the turbulent sea of disasters, rivalries, and hassles that constitute the news.[18]

The corrective to this drift toward senseless style would come from the marketplace and other institutional structures with which television has supportive-antagonistic relationships.

Besides loss of confidence in television as an institution, there has been a substantial decline in the total viewership of the evening news from 41.4 percent in 1980-81 to 36.5 percent in 1984-85. This decline is due partly to CNN, the other cables, and local stations' increased newscasting time. But in addition viewers now have greater options and many other things to do with their sets than merely watching the well-packaged news. It is a sign of the times that Ted Koppel's "Nightline" (ABC) was slashed by half: NBC canceled "Overnight" and "First Camera"; and CBS's "American Parade" has not proved much in the ratings. CNN has taken the business of newscasting seriously. Apart from carrying business features, political commentaries, and money matters, it gives two hours of prime-time news from 8:00 to 9:00 p.m. and 10:00 to 11:00 p.m. From 9:00 to 10:00 p.m. occurs "Larry King Alive"--a stimulating interview show. More than anything else, CNN would change the ways of the networks. The dynamic equilibrium of the marketplace is a sink-or-swim situation--there are no state subsidies for survival.

Another disturbing phenomenon in news broadcasting today is the increasing use of video press releases. It is much easier to detect a story based on a press release in a newspaper than in television. The public relations departments of giant corporations are subtly pushing their stories in the local stations and also more subtly in the networks. Because time slots are limited, well-planned and spectacular press releases crowd out genuine news stories that would otherwise find places in a newscast. In 1985, for instance, most local stations and networks aired segments of Disneyland's anniversary celebration, which were based upon press releases. It is very tempting for a station to accept a well made video release rather than to send its own crew to tape the story, particularly when the release seems to be innocent and harmless. But no press release is ever innocent--it always takes the place of a genuine story. A corporation, by spending a few thousand dollars, promotes its product as a news item free of charge, without viewers ever knowing it was not a station-produced story. The trick is to produce a story "that the station can't provide itself, either because it is too expensive, like animation, or it takes special equipment or a considerable amount of time," says George Glazer of Hill & Knowlton.[19] Though newspapers and television stations may not admit it, they do use stories generated by public relations departments, especially when such stories are consonant with the news departments' outlooks. Though every station would like to generate original stories, "economic realities and the sheer impossibility of being everywhere and covering everything may force more and more newscasts to accept free, informative and one would hope, accurate reported items from outside sponsors.... Whether they are being utilized by a small independent station that can't afford another news crew, by a network-owned-and operated outlet on a weekend when news is slow and personnel scarce, or by a cable service as an adjunct to a story, video press releases have insinuated themselves into TV newscasts."[20]

Thus corporate America apparently buys access to the public airwaves not only through advertisements but also through the insidious means of creating institutional news releases to fit the perceived needs of television stations. Between the cosmetic "happy talk" of news consultants and corporate America's attempts at indirect control over news selection, that most pervasive medium television may have ceased to be free, and perhaps audiences are being manipulated. Another important factor in American culture, however, sustains television as a dynamic medium. Though Americans believe that capitalism is a productive system, they have displayed a restrained hostility against big business. The neo-Marxist would interpret this as hostility against a false consensus about the normal in the society. Whatever the interpretation, this hostility gives the networks a motivation and an opportunity to produce in-depth reports not only against big business but also against other establishments--a phenomenon perceived as a liberal bias in television. If one station succumbs to the pressure, others seize the opportunity for an exposé. And since such special reports and mini-documentaries draw audiences, they serve the networks' ratings goals, as shown by two popular and profitable programs, "60 Minutes" and "20/20." In the long run, the ratings and the plurality of channels and programs may be a salvation for audiences caught between various manipulative groups. In order to survive the competition from local stations, CNN, and the video revolution, the networks may shift their priorities and adopt new strategies. "Moving to places: Central America, Africa, Asia--we can follow where the news is and edit stuff on the scene and uplink it,"[21] says a network executive. But since this technology is available to all, it is doubtful if this change alone would be enough.

All three networks are undergoing structural and corporate changes. NBC and ABC have been taken over by General Electric (through RCA) and Capital City Communication respectively, while CBS, though escaping a takeover bid, is undergoing an internal realignment of forces. Burgeoning television and satellite technology will cause further realignments between the networks and their affiliates. No single model is sufficient to describe all the complexities that determine the nature of newscasting.

CAN TELEVISION BE FAIR?

The consensus about the normal is a kind of working alliance which competing groups use to maximize their own resources for survival and dominance. At the heart of every organized structure is power, and power creates patterns of domination and subordination. The very act of organizing creates priorities and hierarchies, inequalities and inequities. Marxists argue that groups or classes are based upon property, and once property is collectivized the classes or groups and the need of organized society itself will disappear --something which has yet to happen in Cuba, China, and Russia. Group interests could be based not only on property but also on color, race, language, religion, ideology, or sex; and this complexity makes a consensus about the normal in a society an inevitable necessity, a question of survival of the whole. Since television is a ubiquitous medium perceived to have a dominant influence on the economic, political, social, and educational aspects of the society, access to it and its control become very important to every group. At any time when television turns its attention upon any group, others are excluded and bias is perceived to have occurred. Bias varies from total exclusion to total condemnation. While criticism of a group is news and evokes a response or countercriticism which also is likely to occupy a time slot, it is the exclusion of certain groups which breeds neglect and callousness. So "no news" in television about a group is not necessarily for the good of that group and may constitute bias.

Bias occurs partly because of the nature of the television medium, which is temporal rather than spatial. In the newspaper stories are sectionalized, paginated, and indexed; and because of the availability of space, a very large number of stories representing diverse opinions and interests can be accommodated. A reader has very great personal freedom in dealing with the plethora of news, features, and columns. According to a recent survey, this plethora is distributed among fourteen sections in American newspapers: Sports, Main Events, Entertainment, Food, Lifestyle/Women, TV/Radio, Second News, Business/Finance, Fashion, Home, Food/Home, Farm, Travel, and Science.[22] "Newspapers," according to Leo Bogart, "representing substantial chunks of the total circulation continue to provide, week in and week out, columns and features <u>that speak to an enormous assortment of segmented concerns on a scale beyond the capacity of other mass media</u>"[23] (emphasis added).

The network news, because of the half-hour limit, the temporality of its narrative, the necessity for spectacle and dramatics (so the temporal spell is not broken during the commercials), imposes thematic unity on the newscast--partly through exclusion of certain (disconsonant) stories and partly through the personal charisma of the anchorman. So the exclusion of stories, source of bias in the network news, is to some extent a function of the newscast's structure which, because of its compactness, drama, and spectacle, creates massive audiences and profits. To democratize the newscast and reduce bias (by exclusion) is the way of CNN, which during two hours of prime-time news covers a large area of "newsworthy" events. But the cost of covering the "newsworthy" events is so large it is impossible for a station not to depend upon gratuitous sources--governments, corporations, well-organized and well-financed pressure groups--

which can tailormake news stories for a station. In place of bias the audience may get product, policy, or institutional propaganda.

All the networks are under pressure to cut their news costs,[24] which would further create exclusion of stories and bias. Other pressures for the exclusion of news stories derive from the networks' close relations with their affiliates, advertisers, and the government, who exercise powerful influences upon them. Regionalization and localization of the news, if that is the trend, might create more bias through exclusion of weaker and underprivileged groups because the local stations are less answerable to public scrutiny than the networks are. Also it is much easier for governments and corporate advertisers to pressure local stations.

One response to this challenge from cable broadcasters and local stations might be for networks to look holistically at the entire week, correlating the evening news with morning news, late night news, weekend features, and interview programs. For instance, the CBS Evening News, the CBS Morning News, and the CBS Sunday News could be integrated with "60 Minutes"--like one whole newspaper, with the evening news as the front page, and Dan Rather instigating and provoking viewers through cross-references to the network's other news and features programs. In addition, redesigning the news format in the context of the whole week and addressing different segments of the community would give a network greater opportunity for indepth reports and mini-documentaries to cover broad areas of newsworthy events. Bias by exclusion would be reduced.

Probing and investigative reporting (the polar opposite of exclusion) is the major cause of accusations of bias against television--it is also the greatest glory of American television. The tactics under attack are the ambush interview (in which the microphone is suddenly thrust into the person's face), hidden cameras and microphones, the reverse shot (in which the question is repeated to record a different response), the staging of an event for camera, the editing of a taped interview to combine several answers in response to one question, the taping of a telephone interview without consent, the use of stock footage for a different interview, etc.[25] But more than the tactics, complaints about one-sidedness and insufficient time and access under the Fairness Doctrine have prompted libel suits against the television networks. Courts have probed the networks about their news-gathering methods and have laid bare their ethical standards.

What does a person do when the television camera shuts him out into oblivion? What does he do when the heat of the camera is on him without his consent? In the former situation, a person might resort to violence, as Cecil Andrews did on March 4, 1983, when he called WHMA-TV in Anniston, Alabama, and said, "If you want to see somebody set himself on fire, be at the square in Jackson in ten minutes...." The camera recorded the unemployed youth's attempt at self-immolation. The mass media, however, discussed the behavior and ethics of the television news staff at WHMA-TV rather than the issue of unemployment in America--a deviation from the normal. Similarly, a midwestern farmer in December 1985 could not accept the foreclosure on his farm; as one man's impotent protest, he gunned down his banker and himself. He too failed to put his problem on the nation's agenda. Deviant behavior becomes newsworthy only when the deviation from the normal becomes a collective defiance with an agenda to change the decision, the controls, or the consensus about the normal in the society. The terrorists in the Middle East and northern Ireland have their agendas, so that their violence is "news" and receives mass media attention.

On the other hand, when privileged groups and individuals in the society step out of normally accepted behavior and cause violence to the consensus--an insurance fraud by a doctor, a general's misleading information about a war, a charge of environmental pollution against a chemical corporation--their behavior becomes newsworthy, and they seek remedy in the courts. The haves fight with money, the have-nots fight with defiance, and both turn themselves into news.

Can television be fair? Television news is perceived to be fair when it reports what it is told to report; but when it assumes an adversarial role and probes beneath the polished surface, it is seen as unfair by the subject of the probe. The pressure of government, big corporations, and advertisers on television newscasters is to reiterate but not to reinterpret what they are given as packaged news. Against this tendency of the establishment to manage news and to control dissent and criticism, there lurks in the heart of every journalist a professional urge to uncover corruption in high places, to discover a Watergate, a My Lai, a sex scandal, and other harvests or legacies of shame. What ultimately comes out of the television networks and the local stations is a product of several kinds of pressures, which makes critics feel that, though the American press is formally free, it is not as free as it pretends to be. The threat of prolonged litigation and expensive libel suits makes the press timid, conforming, and limited in freedom. An associate editor of The New York Times, Tom Wicker, observed that there is a "league of gentlemen" in the country which believes that the government can do no wrong, and that press owners are a part of it:

> The people who run the press--particularly the metropolitan, largely capitalized institutions of the press--are part of it, along with the people who run the government and the major business and the big foundations. This league isn't like a group of industry price fixers who get together every so often and decide on their line. But the members of the league do share a sense of community, a broad common perception of the general interest.... I think the best you can hope for such a press is that on occasion it will see its duties and obligations as a free press clearly enough. The Times's Pentagon Papers coverage was one such occasion. But if you look at the American press as it really is, you will see it's idle to suppose that such a press will be constantly straying off the reservation of the establishment.[26]

From Ed Murrow to the Vietnam War and Watergate to "60 Minutes" and "20/20," television journalism has actually strayed from the reservation of the establishment quite frequently. Whenever this bold act of freedom occurs, however, television is accused of bias. It is followed by a cacophony of criticism and threats of law suits; and then a chill falls on television, and it turns into an entertainment medium. This is its state today. After some time, when the effects of General Westmoreland's case wear off, it will experience a reawakening of investigative reporting, probing documentaries, and hard-hitting features. But the country today is not in a mood of self-criticism. Besides, a social system's tolerance for disturbance is limited. If every year there were a discovery like Watergate, American society would collapse from internal heat.

The very confusion about what is news and what is not news, whether objectivity is possible, whether journalists report facts or give opinions as facts, whether journalists owe their duty to the public or to their employers, whether television is free or indirectly controlled by vested interests, and myriads of other questions about the profession and its practices, make television news not a paradigmatic field where strict policing and gatekeeping are possible. In spite of the seeming routinizing of news into bureaus and beats, in spite of the "league of gentlemen," in spite of the pressure of deadlines which often make critical questioning impossible, there is enough of an ad hoc capability to allow enterprising and critical journalists to go beneath the surface and discover truth. Moreover, journalists, as trained in the United States, believe that the people who exercise power might be corrupt, that big business might be cheating an unwary public, that in an open society the ambitious and scheming may steal and rob, and that they--the journalists--have no choice except to act as surrogates for the public. It is the journalists' uncertainty about goals and objectives, this seeming confusion about their loyalty, which makes conformity and uniformity--in other words, the falsification of reality--almost impossible. From Ed Murrow to Mike Wallace, one sees the periodic withdrawal of TV journalists into silence, but at critical moments in history they have made a significant difference. And in spite of their showmanship, flashy journalism, and theatrics, "60 Minutes" and "20/20" have kept alive the legacy of the early documentary makers. Between them these two programs have covered more than 1,300 stories, presenting exposés about fake pearls, smokeless tobacco, a black engineer falsely accused of robbery, Satanic cults, Scientology, a miracle cancer cure, reporters accepting bribes from industry, Medicaid fraud, the Tonkin Gulf incident, and much more. One might say that they are digging out minor fraud, helping the authorities to police the system and maintain the consensus about the normal in the society. True, television journalists are not revolutionaries who would question the very basis of the society--that function is left to poets and philosophers. But their probes into minor frauds have a mushrooming effect, and they keep alive the legacy of investigative reporting and a critical spirit. Quoting Walt

Whitman, one might say that television journalists remind us that "There is no week nor day nor hour when tyranny may not enter upon this country, if the people lose their supreme confidence in themselves, and lose the roughness and spirit of defiance."27

NOTES

1. John Corry, "TV News: When Expedience Takes Over," The New York Times (December 8, 1985), sec. 2, p. 33.
2. Donahue Transcript #05285, Multimedia Entertainment, Inc., 1984.
3. Stuart Hall, "A World at One with Itself, in The Manufacture of News, Stanley Cohen and Jock Young, eds. (Beverly Hills: Sage Publications, 1973), p. 149.
4. Ibid., pp. 17-32.
5. W. Lance Bennett, Lynne A. Gressett, and William Halton, "Repairing the News: A Case Study of the News Paradigm," Journal of Communication 35 (Spring 1985), pp. 50-68.
6. Gaye Tuchman, Making News: A Study in the Construction of Reality, (New York: Free Press, 1978).
7. Ibid., pp. 210-11.
8. Donahue Transcript #05285, p. 10.
9. "Why TV News Has Been Losing Its Audience," Businessweek (April 16, 1984), pp. 137-141.
10. Alvin P. Sanoff, "How CBS Puts Out Its Evening News," U.S. News and World Report (September 5, 1983), p. 56.
11. Stuart Hall, p. 148.
12. Paul Weaver, "TV News and Newspaper News," in Understanding Television, Richard P. Adler, ed. (New York: Praeger, 1981), p. 282.
13. John Weisman, "Network News Today: Which Counts More--Journalism or Profits?" TV Guide (October 26 and November 2, 1985), pp. 7, 34.
14. Ron Powers, The Newscasters (New York: St. Martin's Press, 1977), pp. 201-202.
15. Newsweek, December 5, 1983, p. 26.
16. For example, former Miss America Phyllis George was hired as co-anchor of CBS Morning News; Kathleen Sullivan was hired by ABC more for her looks than for her journalistic talents; others newscasters have been fired because of their aging looks.

17. "Trends in Public Attitudes Towards Television and Other Mass Media," Roper Organization, Inc., 1959-1980 (New York: Television Information Office, 1981), p. 3.
18. Leo Bogart, "Television News as Entertainment," in The Entertainment Function of Television, Percy H. Tennenbaum, ed. (Hillsdale: Laurence Erlbaum Association, 1980), p. 9.
19. Herman M. Rosenthal, "Beware of News Clips Massaging Your Opinions," TV Guide (April 21, 1984), p. 9.
20. Ibid., p. 46.
21. Weisman, p. 46.
22. Leo Bogart, "How U.S. Newspaper Content Is Changing," Journal of Communication 35 (Spring 1985), p. 86.
23. Ibid., p. 88.
24. Thomas O'Donnel, "Broadcasting," Forbes (January 3, 1983), pp. 216-17.
25. Alvin P. Sanoff, p. 56.
26. "Can the Press Tell Truth?" Harper's, January 1985, pp. 37-51.
27. Ibid., p. 46.

Chapter Nine

TELEVISION DOCUMENTARY IN AMERICAN CULTURE

* Flaherty, Grierson, Vertov
* "March of Time"
* Documentary as Combat-Exposé: "See It Now"
* Documentary as Judgment
* Documentary as an Epic
* Massaging the Message: "The Times of Harvey Milk"
* Minidocumentaries and Counter-documentaries
* The Nation's Conscience Keeper

The American television documentary, in its evolution during the last four decades, has exceeded the functions ascribed to the film documentary by Siegfried Kracauer when he suggested that the purpose of documentary ranged "from detached pictorial reports to glowing social messages."[1] The television documentary has appropriated the role of a crusader, a defender of the innocent, and, sometimes, a people's tribunal and prosecutor. It is exceedingly difficult to define a genre which claims such diverse functions--from redemption of physical reality to salvation here and now. Probably it is easier to appreciate the role of the television documentary in American culture if we assess the contribution made to the genre by pioneers of the documentary movement on both sides of the Atlantic.

FLAHERTY, GRIERSON, VERTOV

Robert Flaherty, the first American documentarist of significance, is remembered for his classic "Nanook of the North," made in 1922 about Eskimo life in northern Canada. In this documentary, by breaking away from the travelogue tradition of film and by filming "an episode from many angles and distances, seen in quick succession,"[2] Flaherty created a possibility of drama in the life of people as they actually lived, not posed for the camera. His purpose was to show the "former majesty and character of these people, while it is still possible--before the white man has destroyed not only their character, but the people as well."[3] Flaherty's style has been called romantic and idyllic, and all his later works like "Moana" (1927), "Man of Aran" (1934), and "Louisiana Story" (1948) show the same desire to celebrate the beauty of primitive and rustic people in their natural habitat. Today Flaherty's documentary tradition is seen in the National Geographic Society's series titled "Explorer" and in CNN's "Portrait of America" series. Even Jacques Cousteau's television series about undersea life is an extension of Flaherty's exploratory idea, enhanced by modern x-ray cinematography and new sophisticated lenses which can reach anywhere and reveal hitherto unexplored realities.

While Robert Flaherty was exploring the lives of primitive people in the frozen north and tropical Samoa, John Grierson was turning documentary into an instrument of British trade and imperialism: "So to the ends of the earth goes the harvest of the sea," read a subtitle in "Drifters," 1929. "Drifters" was as much a tribute to British workers as it was propaganda for its sponsors, the Empire Marketing Boards. Similarly, "Song of Ceylon" (1937), directed by Basil Wright, was a very beautifully executed documentary; of course, behind the facade of Buddha was the tealeaf, whose production and sale were controlled by the British. Another great achievement was "Night Mail" (1936), directed by Harry Watt with a narrative written by poet W.H. Auden. While Robert Flaherty was a poet exploring the beauty of man and his surroundings, John Grierson and his followers, such as Paul Rotha, initiated a school of thought advocating that documentary should be used as a tool for social propaganda. For Flaherty the documentary was a revelation; for Grierson it was a benevolent intervention, always accompanied by the voice of authority. Grierson used the poetic to serve the rhetoric of the ruling class, while for Flaherty poetic truth was itself an end and a means to human compassion.

But the political climate of the age favored use of the documentary as propaganda tool. In Soviet Russia Dziga Vertov made new uses of film footage by turning it into newsreels designed to indoctrinate people in Communist ideology. Paul Rotha described Vertov's documentary method as "a scientific, experimental study of the visible world.... It sorts the pertinent from the irrelevant and places it on the cinema screen."[4] For a Communist idealogue like Vertov, the "pertinent" and the "irrelevant" became keys to the restructuring of social reality through interpretative editing of newsreels, transforming them into a voice of the revolution. Vertov called his manifesto "Kino-Pravada" (film truth) based upon "fragments of actuality." These "fragments of actuality" had to be edited and thematically organized into the whole truth reflecting Soviet reality.[5] One of Vertov's most praised documentaries was "One Sixth of the World" (1926), in which he used subtitles with telling effects. The documentary was an invocation and paean to the various peoples and nationalities of Communist Russia, who number one sixth of the world. Vertov's kaleidoscopic and reportorial documentary style had a great impact on documentary technique. Other film makers and documentarists in Russia, such as Lev Kuleshov, V.I. Pudovkin, and Sergei Eisenstein, also made new uses of images, close-ups and other kinds of shots; by exploiting imagistic similarities and dissimilarities they produced new meanings and emotions. The reconstruction of the historical events of the Russian Revolution became a challenging task for these film makers and documentarists, as we find in <u>Potemkin</u> (1925), <u>Ten Days that Shook the World</u> (1928), and many other films by Sergei Eisenstein. According to Paul Rotha, these documentaries present not only historical actualities of the revolution but also a political point of view obtained by giving the material a dialectical treatment. As he says, "It is creating a form of documentary approach which gives new meanings to familiar things; not representing persons and things as they are, but relating them in such a manner to their surroundings that they temporarily are transformed by the powers of the film into material which can be shaped to take on different significances according to the director's aim."[6] In theater a Communist playwright, Bertolt Brecht, was experimenting with other techniques to create "defamiliarization" to produce what he called an epic realism--which makes people think. Given this legacy, it would not be far-fetched to say that the cinéma-vérité of the 1960s owes much to Vertov.

During World War II, every warring nation turned the documentary into an instrument of propaganda and training, to churn out soldiers and war goods and to maintain public morale. Out of these propaganda efforts emerged new techniques, enriching the documentary repertoire. For example, Leni Riefenstahl's Triumph of the Will (1935) was a partially-staged documentary which created a powerful mystique about Hitler and the Nazi Party. What mattered was not the historical actuality or the creative interpretation of actuality, as Grierson would have it,[7] but the creation of a mystique to communicate a new collective identity to the German people. A similar attempt to create a mystique was seen in a recent documentary, "The Times of Harvey Milk" (PBS, 1985), about a self-confessed homosexual public official of San Francisco, though it must be said that the documentary was not based upon staging so much as upon manipulation of the stock footage and creative use of the camera. A similar effort to create a halo and mystique is seen in docudramas, especially those about members of the Kennedy clan.

In Britain, which has a proud tradition of documentary making, Paul Rotha and others attained new possibilities in documentary technique by introducing the voices of common people interrupting the narrator and thus heightening his final authority, as we find in "World of Plenty" (1943). Intercutting the voice of the common man with that of the narrator is today used not only in documentaries but also in news magazines like "60 Minutes" and "20/20."

In the United States during World War II documentarists like Frank Capra, John Ford, John Huston, et al., made many innovative uses of visual, sound, and editing techniques in manipulating war footage to compile documentaries; they also used the semi-dramatization techniques of "March of Time" to achieve their directorial purposes. American documentarists did what their counterparts in Germany and Russia were doing--that is, in the words of Time publisher Henry Luce, "fakery in allegiance to the truth."[8] Documentaries beginning with Vertov's "Anniversary of the Revolution" (1919) and continuing through Frank Capra's "Why We Fight" (1944) were compilation documentaries based upon archival research, editing techniques, and other special effects.

"MARCH OF TIME"

Along with the heritage of Grierson, Flaherty, and Vertov, the television documentary had another fecund source of creative ideas, "March of Time," which enlightened and stimulated American audiences from 1935 through 1951. The producer of this documentary, Louis de Rochemont, wanted to reconstruct the context and the essential framework of a newsworthy event and also to reveal the event's larger significance. Paul Rotha described de Rochemont's method as applying "partly the same naturally shot material which is the stuff of the newsreel, and partly staged scenes with both real people and actors ... to present an event in relation to its background--an approach that calls for a considered restatement of fact."[9]

In the mixing of news actuality and staged reality, "March of Time," in both its radio and film versions, made its great contribution by arousing the audience's awareness and heightening their consciousness about the issues facing them. Its greatest impact was felt, however, when it shed its multi-story news magazine format and adopted a single storyline (1938), which is the essence of the documentary. Its first documentary, "Inside Nazi Germany" (1938), used the dramatic technique of staging to bring out the inherent drama of the rise of Hitler in Germany and of his followers in the United States. While Vertov, Eisenstein, et al., rearranged and reassembled fragments of actuality to create new truth, de Rochemont re-enacted and re-created reality through impersonation and staging. He moved the documentary from the photographic naturalism of Emile Zola to the dramatic realism of Henrik Ibsen. Both naturalism and realism searched for truth, and de Rochemont combined both to deepen the audience's perception of the problem; in the process he raised many controversies and also the spectre of censorship. This line of development in the American documentary, which uses staging, re-enactment, and dramatic reconstruction, has evolved now into a widely accepted though controversial, television genre, the docudrama.

Cinéma-Vérité and Direct Cinema

As distinct from the compilation method of creating, interpreting, and manipulating reality for different social and political purposes, and the impersonation and staging techniques of "March of Time," there arose two different styles of documentary called direct cinema and cinéma-vérité. These two styles became possible partly through availability of the modern technologies of the lightweight hand-held camera, synchronous sound, and the zoom lens, which, according to Stromgren and Norden, help the documentarist to "capture unplanned, uncontrolled, ongoing events with maximum flexibility":

> Because of the lack of preplanning and the difficulty in anticipating the complexion and direction of events, the films resulting from these two approaches are often marked by shaky camera work and ineptly composed, out of focus, poorly-lit shots. Sound is often characterized by occasionally inaudible dialogue, distracting noises, and long periods of silence. But such "raw" characteristics, considered flaws in other forms of film making, have come to be heralded as the proofs of authenticity and spontaneity. They help preserve not only the details of actuality, but also its unforeseen ambiguities, hazards, and contradictions.[10]

The technique of direct cinema and cinéma-vérité can be seen in the prime-time police drama, "Hill Street Blues." The direct cinema approach, wedded to high-tech photography, produced a remarkable documentary titled "The Silent Scream," which seemed to tilt the argument in favor of the anti-abortion movement in America. A compilation documentary would have sounded propagandistic; but "The Silent Scream," based upon a direct cinema approach of recording unvarnished reality with nonauthoritarian narration by an expert surgeon, Dr. Bernard Nathanson, has given a proof of new truth. Pro-abortionists have not come up with a counter documentary proving there is no life in the womb.

Direct cinema is a comparatively nonobtrusive, observational approach which waits for drama to happen rather than provoking it as cinéma-vérité does through interviews and confrontation. Direct cinema is grounded in the belief that an observer changes reality by his intervention and therefore must remain detached and distant. Cinéma-vérité is closer to the participant-observer approach that the only way to know truth is to get involved. Cinéma-vérité necessitates interviews, which lead to viewer empathy and involvement in social change--thus bringing cinéma-vérité closer to the goals, though not the techniques, of Vertov, Eisenstein, and Grierson. Thus the two documentary approaches which evolved as antitheses to the compilation approach have enriched the documentary heritage of American television. However, the distinction between the two approaches, according to television historian Erik Barnouw, is critical:

> The direct cinema documentarist took his camera to a situation and waited hopefully for a crisis; the Rouch version of cinéma vérité tried to precipitate one. The direct cinema artist aspired to invisibility; the Rouch cinéma vérité artist was often an avowed participant. The direct cinema artist played the role of uninvolved bystander; the cinéma vérité artist espoused that of provocateur.[11]

Some of the well-known practitioners of direct cinema are Richard Leacock, Maysles brothers (Hillary Harris, Albert and David), Don Pennebaker, Robert Drew ("Primary," 1960), and Frederick Wiseman ("High School," 1968). Cinéma-vérité's prophet was Jean Rouch, a Frenchman known for "Chronicle of a Summer" (1961); and in America Peter Davis's "Hearts and Minds" (1974), a documentary about the Vietnam War, is well known.

DOCUMENTARY AS A COMBAT-EXPOSE: "SEE IT NOW"

"See It Now," the Ed Murrow-Fred Friendly documentary series during the fifties, had a seminal influence on television documentary form and structure--apart from confronting the controversial issues of the decade and the menace of the time, McCarthyism. The documentary series, by plunging into the age's heart of panic and fear, emerged as a contributory factor in making television a dominant force in the shaping of American political life and culture. Just as in the sixties and seventies it charted the course of the Vietnam War and influenced its outcome, in the fifties TV helped McCarthyism bury itself in its own excesses. "See It Now" as a documentary series achieved its goal by intensifying actuality to the brink of drama, involving people and turning their consciences into decisive battlegrounds.

"See It Now" (CBS), introduced by Murrow and Friendly in 1951, took its own time to grow out of the heritage of "March of Time" and the newsreel into in-depth probing of something beyond the immediate and newsworthy. By the time it developed a single story format (1953), it was ready to confront its viewers with the issues of civil liberties and McCarthyism. Its first meaningful moment occurred in the case of Lieutenant Milo Radulovich, accused by the Air Force of hobnobbing with his own parents who were suspected of radical leanings. As Erik Barnouw says, "All were aware that Murrow was not merely probing the judicial processes of the Air Force and Pentagon--a quixotic venture few broadcasters would have undertaken at this time--but was examining the whole syndrome of McCarthyism with its secret denunciation and guilt by association."[12] The cancer was spreading in every organized branch of public and private life, and the time had come to stop its menacing growth. By their intentions and deeds, Murrow and Friendly turned their documentary into a crusade against the injustices of the high and mighty. The Air Force, consequently, declared Lieutenant Radulovich as no security risk.

Their success against the Air Force led Murrow and Friendly to explore civil liberties issues at Indianapolis and segregation at Clinton, Tennessee, and finally to confront the victorious advance of McCarthyism. The documentarists allowed different interviewees to speak their minds and offered their own editorial comments. They developed the technique of the cross-cut interview which, as A. William Bluem explains, "involved the procedure of recording many interviews at greater length to be shot-gunned throughout a program."[13] The technique is now commonly used by news magazines like "60 Minutes" and "20/20" and by many other in-depth television reports. To achieve their editorial goals, particularly in the case of McCarthyism, they used juxtaposition of film clips to heighten dramatic effect by contrast and reinforcement. "See It Now" rose to be a crusader, standing in defense of Dr. Robert Oppenheimer and other innocents in America. Its greatest contribution, however, was that "by virtue of its recognition of television's intrinsic characteristics of intimacy and immediacy in presentation, it did what no printed or verbal form of communication could do [as] well--involve people in events at maximum level of identification."[14] Murrow and Friendly made television profound.

DOCUMENTARY AS A JUDGMENT:
"THE UNCOUNTED ENEMY: A VIETNAM DECEPTION"

This 1982 CBS documentary would be valued in television culture more for its contribution to opening up the debate about such time-honored standards for libel as "actual malice" and "reckless disregard for truth"--which the Supreme Court's 1964 New York Times v. Sullivan verdict created to protect the press--than for its historical revelation about America's most traumatic war. The ninety-minute documentary was an accusation against one man, General William C. Westmoreland, commander of the U.S. forces in Vietnam from 1964 through 1968, that prior to the 1968 Tet offensive he lied to his countrymen about actual enemy strength. The CBS documentary's sharply worded, accusatory thesis was that the general had participated in "a conspiracy at the highest levels of American military intelligence,"[15] to suppress facts about the enemy and to create false hopes that America was winning the war. If the documentary had merely revealed statistical discrepancies, the seventy-year-old general would not have stirred from his silent retreat, and the mass media would not have been divided over the issue of war once again. What aroused the nation about the general's $120 million libel suit was the stated conclusion that there was "conspiracy." The report, based upon interviews with more than eighty people, tried to establish that there were a half million Viet Cong troops engaged in war at the time of the Tet offensive; and that the general, in order to please President Johnson and his own supervisors in the Pentagon, had concocted a lower figure of about 300,000. He also disregarded the guerillas and irregulars, who constituted a great source of strength for the Viet Cong and whose defeat in the Tet offensive did not bring about the end of the war.

The documentary, broadcast in January 1982, did not convince mass media critics. The first shot was fired by TV Guide's article entitled "Anatomy of a Smear," which prompted an internal investigation by CBS; its sober determination was that use of the word "conspiracy" was not justified. The author of the TV Guide article, Don Kowet, subsequently wrote a book, A Matter of Honor, in which he maintained his charge that the CBS documentary violated the tenets of fairness in investigative reporting and that the documentary was wrong. His own book, however, contained many deficiencies. Though the subsequent libel suit brought by Westmoreland against CBS was withdrawn because it would have been impossible for the general to prove "actual malice" and "reckless disregard for the truth," the documentary had an unintended effect: it provoked the public to question the credentials of the media and their pretension to fairness. If the general could lie, so could the mass media. The three-year debate concluded: watch the watchdogs, who are big business now.

DOCUMENTARY AS AN EPIC: "VIETNAM: A TELEVISION HISTORY"

This thirteen-part documentary about the Vietnam War was an epic of sorrow and compassion. Unlike Peter Davis's "Hearts and Minds" or Emile de Antonio's "In the Year of the Pig," it did not point an accusing finger at or level blame against anyone. On the contrary, the total impression viewers got from the monumental documentary was that of a battleship which rushed to rescue a small boat caught in a destructive hurricane and in the attempt was nearly destroyed in that terrible storm. As in a classical Greek tragedy, events were not of the protagonists' making, yet were inevitable--the Americans were irrevocably sucked in. Today the United States, like some mythological god, sits on a stone on the shores of the Pacific brooding over what might have been. The documentary did create that state of collective catharsis which ennobles tragedy, and to that extent it was a great success. If, however, it was meant to stand in historical judgment, apportioning blame and unearthing the villains, the documentary was a terrible failure. We must look to "The Uncounted Enemy" or earlier judgmental documentaries like "Hearts and Minds," to identify the causes and villains of the war, which cost America 58,000 lives and terrible shame and humiliation.

"Vietnam: A Television History" was produced by PBS-affiliate WGBH in Boston in association with Britain's Central Independent Television and France's Antenne 2. Produced at a cost of $4.6 million, it took executive producer Richard Ellison six years to complete. It achieved its nonjudgmental and nonaccusatory purpose by structuring a balance of contending goals: the viewpoints of both Vietnamese and American policy makers; Vietnamese soldiers and American G.I.s; Vietnamese villagers and Americans who watched the war in their own living rooms. In an accusatory or ambush type of documentary the rhetoric is sharply cut with the reality, but in "Vietnam: A Television History" the rhetoric supported the view that everyone had been caught in a destructive hurricane; viewers were left to assess the damage caused by blind forces, a state of affairs which precluded their making judgments or indulging in self-castigation or self-pity.

Like a true history, the documentary did chronicle the events of the war. The opening episode recounted the century-long brutalities of French colonial rule in Vietnam; death due to starvation of two million Vietnamese during and after World War II; and Ho Chi Minh's alliance with Russia and China. The second episode, centering on the battle of Dien Bien Phu (1954), showed the flight of the French from Indochina. The third program showed the spectacularly horrifying scene of a Buddhist monk immolating himself as a protest against Ngo Dinh Diem's government, and Diem's loss of credibility in the United States. That was the year when John F. Kennedy was exhorting Americans, "Ask not what your country can do for you ..." and Martin Luther King, Jr. was sharing his dream. It was idealism at home and butchery abroad. The death of these dreams led to the Great Society of Lyndon Johnson, a president who emerged in the fifth episode as less of a hawk than as a confused man caught in a maelstrom. Subsequent programs showed the Vietnamese point of view; the spillover of the war into Laos and Cambodia; the Tet offensive; prolonged peace negotiations; and the ultimate American withdrawal. All thirteen episodes were replete with heart-wrenching scenes of both Vietnamese and Americans suffering the agony of war.

Chronicling the events of the war (based upon 200,000 feet of film footage procured from eleven countries and 5,000 pages of transcripts of interviews)[16] did serve a historical

TV Documentary in American Culture   175

function. History has three purposes, in order of importance: (a) to chronicle, (b) to explain, and (c) to predict and warn. It was in its functions of explaining and predicting that "Vietnam: A Television History" failed. Absent from the documentary was a proper context indicating America's larger aim to checkmate Chinese expansionism from the Himalayas to Korea and how the Americans succeeded in that larger goal. America lost Vietnam but gained China--that is the untold saga. Post-Vietnam China is confused ideologically, is on the capitalist path, and is pleading for American technology and markets.

Although by its judicious balancing, varied perspectives, and multipolarity the documentary succeeded in leading the viewer to understand and not to judge harshly, it nevertheless failed to fix responsibility and warn about the future. And as a documentary it failed to initiate a debate in the light of America's temptation in Latin America. "Vietnam: A Television History," as a television epic created in the spirit of what Milton called "calm of mind and all passion spent," was a great success, but it was not a history.

MASSAGING THE MESSAGE: "THE TIMES OF HARVEY MILK"

Harvey Milk's colleague and assassin Dan White committed suicide on October 21, 1985; three weeks after his death PBS showed a 1984 Oscar-winning documentary on the life and death of the gay saint of San Francisco. The artistic beauty of the documentary, with the slow, sad, and moving voice of narrator Harvey Fierstein, touched the viewer's heart and imagination. Had this documentary been shown before the panic of AIDS had overtaken America, the documentary would have communicated its message of tolerance for homosexuals and recognition of their contributions to the society. But when the politicians are (at least privately) saying, "Shoot them," and even parents refuse to accept sons suffering from AIDS (as a 1985 television movie <u>An Early Frost</u> brought home to us), the emotions created by the documentary become ambiguous and uncertain. The documentary re-created the life of San Francisco in 1978 by the use of still photographs, archive footage, interviews, the tape-recorded will of Harvey Milk, and the statement of Dan White. The slow-motion cinematography showing Harvey

Milk making prophetic gestures was lyrical in effect; the
candlelight procession and the mob violence which set police
cars ablaze were spectacular. Interviews with Harvey Milk's
colleagues and friends and President Carter's statement asking voters to turn down Proposition 6 (which would have
denied gays their rights) added depth to the documentary.
Had this been the age of art for art's sake, an Oscar Wilde
would have hailed the documentary as a great achievement.
But the public's mode of consciousness had changed since
1980, when AIDS appeared on the scene, and gays became
suspect. Today San Francisco is not the Mecca of liberal-
ism, but a suspected cesspool of a fast-spreading fatal
disease. The message of the documentary was lost because
the deviants of the society seemed to threaten the accepted
normal way of life. Maybe in another age the message could
be resurrected and the documentary could plead its case.

MINIDOCUMENTARIES AND COUNTER-DOCUMENTARIES

A minidocumentary is a series of investigative reports
focused on a single theme and presented as a part of the
daily newscast, in segments of three to five minutes, over
two or more successive days. A minidocumentary might be
presented by a local station or by a network. Its avowed
purpose is to examine a weakness of the community in order
to attain its amelioration. Since the minidocumentary is part
of a daily newscast, it bypasses the sponsor and the advertiser; according to the rules of the game, they are not supposed to interfere in newscasting. This form of documentary,
disguised as serialization of news or special reports, belongs
to the tradition of news documentary and investigative reporting of Frederick Wisemen ("High School," "Law and Order,"
"Hospital"), David Wolper ("Biography"), and others. In its
impact, however, it differs from a full-length documentary
since it deals with a limited problem requiring immediate attention and redress. It adds prestige to the local station
and draws a larger audience; and through the snare of
serialization it retains the audience's loyalty. Since the
reach of a newscast is much greater than that of a full-
length documentary, the episodic documentary, piggy-backed
on the newscast, is viewed by a large and disparate audience at the news hour. Among topics that minidocumentaries
have investigated, according to Stanley Field, are housing,
welfare, emergency ambulance service, the energy crisis,

mercy killing, illegal aliens, rape, alcoholism, child abuse, and fraudulent promoters.[17] Since these are recurring problems, the task of the minidocumentary is never done; and the stations, lured by newer audiences and high ratings, will always be tempted to produce a minidocumentary.

A reporter working on a minidocumentary normally uses the cinéma-vérité approach, which, as discussed earlier, consists of pursuing a crisis until all its dimensions are revealed fully. Investigation is based mostly upon interviews with victims, sufferers, and perpetrators. Since time for each segment is limited, there is little chance of visual pyrotechnics, and the documentarist goes straight to the heart of the matter. Because of their serial nature and the paucity of artistic quality, minidocumentaries never reach the status and historical importance of full-length documentaries like Ed Murrow's "Harvest of Shame" (CBS, 1960), Jay McMullen's "Biography of a Bookie Joint" (CBS, 1960), or Peter Davis' "The Selling of the Pentagon" (CBS, 1971). Minidocumentaries act only as modest exposés which obligate local communities to solve the problems. If a local problem has national significance, a network may offer a full-length documentary to allow the problem to enter national consciousness. Many minidocumentaries have led to definitive actions.[18]

A minidocumentary, because of its structure, meets its obligation under the Fairness Doctrine by inviting proponents of opposing viewpoints to respond. Most often such responses are incorporated structurally into the minidocumentary. Theoretically, a full-length documentary should also create conditions for the right to reply; but in practice this has been difficult, though Murrow and Friendly and many others did give opportunities to the opposing sides to state their cases. Documentaries have been mostly one-sided affairs, thus unintentionally violating the spirit of the Fairness Doctrine. But lately, as James Traub reported,[19] the offended parties have been taking advantage of the right to reply in the form of "counter-documentaries." It was an unprecedented gesture of self-confidence and fairness, opines Traub, that NBC and PBS invited two right-wing groups, the National Conservative Political Action Committee (NCPAC) and Accuracy in Media (AIM), to air their views. NCPAC responded on March 20, 1985, that because of Mikhail Gorbachev's close association with the brutal Soviet dictator Yuri Andropov, the new Russian ruler must have similar traits: like master, like protégé. NBC's special reporter John Cochram in Moscow based his assessment of the Soviet leader on casual conversations and observations indicating that Gorbachev's wife loves literature and music and is very personable; Gorbachev was viewed as utterly polite and looking like an Anglo-American. He and his wife were compared with the Kennedys. JFK was gracious and tough; he was also brutal and unscrupulous, as the Bay of Pigs incident showed. Therefore, if Gorbachev is like JFK, the United States should be very careful; and NCPAC, even though one may not like the association, had a point, a warning: a ruler of one-sixth of the earth cannot be soft.

AIM's counter-documentary "Television's Vietnam: The Real Story," which was presented on June 26, 1985, by PBS as part of a larger program, "Vietnam OP/ED--An Inside Story," was polemical and accusatory, as expected. While the thirteen-part series "Vietnam: A Television History" offered a case history of a tragedy for which no one was to blame, AIM's counter-documentary was an anti-Communist statement. Both NBC and PBS served the people well by inviting the conservatives to express their points of view. The debate, as they say in the British Parliament, shall continue.

DOCUMENTARY AS THE NATION'S CONSCIENCE KEEPER

Television documentary as it developed in America during the last four decades has become a powerful means of influencing public policy and effecting change in the people's perceptions and consciousness. It is also a comprehensive instructional tool which quickens the learning process. This universal range of functions--from description to normativeness, commentary to castigation, actuality to dramatization --has not made it easy for scholars to define the boundaries of this unique television genre. Every crisis in American culture since World War II has called forth documentaries which have not only recorded the deeds and misdeeds of this great civilization, but have also transformed the past into the perpetual present: today's documentaries become stock footage for tomorrow's documentaries. The viewer, while watching a documentary, is alternately detached and involved--responses which drama or film or a conventional newscast cannot elicit well--because past and present in a documentary exist on the same plane of the viewer's consciousness. Normally, history is regarded as the past, something which existed and has become only a reference point in the vastness of time past; but documentary, itself a form of history, arrests the dramatic in the historic and transforms it into the present. Examples of this phenomenon include Claude Lansman's profoundly sorrowful Holocaust memoir, "Shoah," which was built on the voices of the past living in the present; Ken Burns' biographical documentary, "Huey Long," about the Louisiana politician (1883-1935) who emerged somewhat as an American version of a fascist; Cheryl McCall's "Streetwise," which by using cinéma vérité technique brought out the lives of the homeless in Seattle; CBS's "Dinosaur!" (1985), a reconstructed, dramatized, fictionalized account of the existence of primordial creatures that became extinct because of "nuclear winter," a well-chosen contemporary phrase with an apocalyptic ring that makes dinosaurs our close cousins. Since television is a medium for cinema documentaries also, the distinction between the two media is only academic because what begins with the purpose of selective viewing eventually ends up as public communication.

In functions ranging from John Grierson's "the creative treatment of actuality" and Paul Rotha's "the use of film medium to interpret creatively and in social terms the life of people as it exists in reality" to apocalyptical warnings in seemingly instructional documentaries like "Dinosaur!" and many National Geographic "Explorer" series, the documentary has used a rich repertoire of techniques: capturing the dramatic in the mundane; creating new reality by reassembling the "fragments of actuality"; hieroglyphic-like montages; shotgun interviews; creative editing; yoking the poetic to reinforce the rhetorical; a direct cinema approach of unobtrusive recording of unfolding events; the cinéma vérité method of provoking crisis to unearth reality; and varied roles for the narrator, from authority to raconteur, from instructor to prophet. This variety has enabled documentaries to be profound without being obscure, to describe the indescribable, and to give expression to the inexpressible. Television documentaries, because they are predicated upon public communication and public truth, turn private sufferings into universal experience for the masses, without, however, reducing the complexities of the experience. Thus it becomes rather difficult to appreciate the deprecatory voice of a great scholar like Wayne C. Booth when he observes:

> The screen thus re-inforces a general trend in <u>all</u> media toward simplification and polarization of the unlimited complexities of our lives. As citizen of the country presented to me by TV, whether that documentary is literally [about] the United States of some imagined world, I learn quickly that all problems could be solved simply, if only other people would think about them the way I am being taught to do <u>now</u>. It is no news to say that anybody who reads a book--any book, even the most distorted on any subject will be appalled by the simplification of that subject in any movie or TV program. There are simply no movies or TV programs, regardless of the depth of chosen subject, that make intellectual demands of the kind expected of even the most watered down philosophical or scholarly text, or of the printed fiction that critics take seriously.... But all evidence so far suggests that the medium of TV itself for some reason <u>builds in</u> a contempt for us and our life. When anything we care for passes through its hands, what comes out is a single statement: None of this matters very much.... Video culture is, by contrast, a culture of the superficially informed, the hasty, the indifferent.[20]

Booth associates obscurity with profundity, which he seems to say can be attained through the written word only. True, television abhors obscurity; and as a medium it attains profundity through simplicity, juxtaposition, contrarieties, dramatics, a Gestalt of the spoken and the visual--and by hurtling viewers through multiple perspectives, as some of the best documentaries covering topics from McCarthyism to the Vietnam War have done. Booth is concerned about the thirty-second commercial, but he refuses to look at the Holocaust or the creation of the universe in his living room.

In the documentary form television achieves its profoundest expression, which urges humans to social action and change and to contemplate truth as John Keats contemplated the Grecian urn. The poet in Robert Flaherty seized a moment and turned it into an eternity. The rhetorician in

TV Documentary in American Culture 181

John Grierson perceived reality as change and progress. The range of thought and emotion expressed in TV documentary has been varied and profound. Since its beginning the documentary has been engaged in a search for the lasting and the progressive. It has kept the debate alive and the status quo in a state of disturbance.

Much of the future of this flexible form will depend upon technological developments in computer and video. Documentary developed when early photo-essay journalism was wedded to time and motion, to sound, and to the point of view of a narrator. Today high-tech video and computer simulations and graphics are helping documentarists to reconstruct events as they might have been. For instance, in "Creation of the Universe" (PBS, 1985) author-narrator Timothy Ferris attempted to explain the modern scientist's quest for a unified theory of the universe. He explained through computer simulation and videographics the four fundamental forces--gravity, electromagnetic force, weak force, and strong force, the latter two within the atom and the former two in the universe--and how scientists are trying to find a single equation, a single force, the scientific equivalent of the Judeo-Christian God. The documentary would not have been possible without the latest technology, which was used not to reconstruct or dramatize the past but to regress into a time when space, time, and matter were in their infancy.

From "Nanook of the North" to "Creation of the Universe" is one documentary strand which has been woven into the public consciousness. The other strand, which began somewhere with "March of Time" and has continuously probed and questioned societal values from "Harvest of Shame" to "Legacy of Shame" (CBS), has kept American society in a state of ferment--which is the secret of its vitality. From explorer to guerrilla,[21] the American documentarist has played the role of a benevolent vigilante and has helped keep this complex society sane. One wonders what the course of German history would have been if Leni Riefenstahl, instead of creating the Hitler mystique, had spoken like Mike Wallace or Roger Mudd:

> Defending the country not just with arms but also with ideology, Pentagon propaganda insists on America's role as the cop on every beat in the

world. Not only the public but the press as well has been beguiled, including at times, ourselves at CBS News. This propaganda barrage is the creation of a runaway bureaucracy that frustrates attempts to control it.22

The American television documentarist today is the chorus and the conscience keeper of American society.

NOTES

1. Siegfried Kracauer, Theory of Film: The Redemption Physical Reality (New York: Oxford University Press, 1960), p. 194.
2. Erik Barnouw, Documentary (New York: Oxford University Press, 1974), p. 39.
3. Ibid., p. 45.
4. Paul Rotha, Documentary Film, 3rd ed. (New York: Hastings House Publishers, 1952), p. 244.
5. Adams Sitney, ed., Film Culture Reader (New York: Praeger, 1970), p. 362.
6. Paul Rotha, p. 94.
7. John Grierson "The Story of Documentary Film," The Fortnightly Review, 1931, p. 121, quoted in A.W. Bluem, Documentary in American Television, p. 207.
8. Barnouw, Documentary, p. 121.
9. Paul Rotha, p. 117.
10. Richard L. Stromgren and Martin F. Norden, Movies: A Language of Light (Englewood Cliffs, NJ: Prentice-Hall, 1984), p. 224.
11. Barnouw, Documentary, pp. 245-255.
12. Erik Barnouw, Tube of Plenty (New York: Oxford University Press, 1975), p. 175.
13. A. William Bluem, Documentary in American Television (New York: Hastings House Publishers, 1965), p. 99.
14. Ibid.
15. "A TV Monument to the 'TV War,'" Time (October 3, 1983), pp. 76-77.
16. "Battle Lines Are Drawn," Time (October 14, 1984), p. 79.
17. Stanley Field, The Mini-Documentary (Blue Ridge Summit, PA: Tab Books, 1975), pp. 237-238.
18. Ibid.
19. James Traub, "Counterfeit Documentaries," Channels of Communication (May-June 1985), pp. 58-60.

20. Wayne C. Booth, "The Company We Keep: Self-Making in Imaginative Art, Old and New," Daedalus (Fall 1982), pp. 44-47.
21. Barnouw, Documentary, pp. 262-286.
22. Marvin Barrett, ed., Survey of Broadcast Journalism, 1970-1971 (New York: Grosset and Dunlap, 1971), pp. 151-171; quoted in Barnouw, Documentary, p. 282.

Chapter Ten

THE POETICS AND THE RHETORIC
OF DOCUDRAMA

* The Roots of Docudrama

* The Fear of the Genre

At the heart of a television documentary is a pressing social problem which cries for solution, and the documentarist, through creative interpretation of the fragments of actuality, aims to change public priorities. By contrast, a docudrama, which rearranges actuality into a dramatic structure--rising action, crisis, and resolution--purports to theatricalize the individual's will to action and the attendant consequences. In a documentary the viewer is given an outside point of view, and through the seeming objectivity his consciousness is awakened and he is prepared for action. In docudrama the viewer, through his faculty of empathy and identification, is at the center of the dramatic action, feels the full emotional impact of the human will to action, and vicariously shares the consequences. In historical and chronicle plays of the Renaissance the protagonists seemed distanced because of the passage of the centuries. Though the chronicle plays turned the historical past into the present, they always evidenced the burden of history. Shakespeare's _Henry IV_ and _Richard III_, Marlowe's _Edward II_, and other historical plays created by the University Wits of the Elizabethan era had a sense of distance built into them because of the remoteness of the past. But today's television docudrama deals with the topics of the day, or of the very recent past, to which we have been witnesses.

Because a docudrama is produced after the events have been recorded, discussed, and evaluated--and as they

are in the process of being archived--it seems to challenge
the truth and disturb such guardians of truth as journalists,
critics, police, and politicians. A docudrama demands reas-
sessment, re-evaluation, and retrial in the theater of public
consciousness; because of the nature of viewer empathy and
identification, the genre is more involving and persuasive
than a documentary or a newscast. One docudrama is more
powerful in its social impact than a thousand nights of Dan
Rather or Mike Wallace broadcasts. An arrogant and self-
righteous newscaster might say that the camera never blinks
and, therfore, the newscast is the truth and the only truth.
A docudrama seems to say "probably this is how it happened,"
and it enhances and reinforces the plurality of thought; in
the hands of responsible producers it could be a great instrument of social justice. It must be remembered that the
aims of a docudrama are not artistic but rhetorical. Poetics
and dramatic structure are used to create a new rhetorical
vision, to purify the image of a protagonist, or to rechronicle
events in order to rebuild and refurbish the public image of
a significant individual or group. The rituals of drama are
used to question the status quo, to bring about a change, or
to establish and maintain power. These purposes are accomplished by offering alternative interpretations and newer
possibilities. Since docudrama serves free speech, and by
drawing a large number of viewers also serves the marketplace, its place in American culture is assured. The
networks, because of the lure of ratings, will be commis-
sioning more and more docudramas and will thereby indirectly
enhance free debate and free speech.

THE ROOTS OF DOCUDRAMA

The chronicle and historical plays of the sixteenth
century dramatized historical material and drew heavily on
the histories of Raphael Holinshed and Edward Hall. As the
form developed it gained in dramatic unity in the works of
Christopher Marlowe and William Shakespeare. Dramatic emphasis shifted from the actualities of historical accounts to
the study of human character, its strengths and weaknesses.
Allardyce Nicoll says in British Drama that history or chronicle plays were popular because the form "allowed of bustle
and action, partly because it could mingle together thoughts
serious and merry, tragic and comic, and partly because
there had come over England in those years a wave of patriotic

sentiment."[1] Apparently, the chronicle or history plays took much liberty with historical material because their chief aim was an in-depth probing of human character--not coopting the functions of history. Their legacy passed on to the historical romances and novels of William Thackeray and Sir Walter Scott; and the emphasis on either adventure or the study of character also continued. But readers never mistook the historical plays or historical novels as histories. The tradition of history plays encouraged the development of the idea of dramatized actualities, and docudrama.

In American culture "March of Time," "The Living Newspaper," and Armstrong Circle Theatre have played a great part in the growth of the television docudrama. The radio version of "March of Time" in the Depression era used actors to give listeners a dramatic presentation of the news. One reason for using actors instead of the actual persons was the lack of mobile and easy-to-handle equipment. Another reason was that documentary as a pure genre, free from the encumbrances of drama, had not emerged as yet. When "March of Time" was transferred to the cinema screen its popularity soared, and millions of people watched the reenacted and dramatized versions of actual events. Producer Louis de Rochemont thirsted to get behind the news to capture real events by the reconstruction, re-enactment, and staging of reality. Even today the audience's appetite is increasing for news, and for fiction that heightens the reality behind the news, according to a noted historian:

> Today the television audience has an insatiable appetite for news, hence a natural receptivity to complex and controversial issues--even when they appear in the guise of primetime entertainment. Viewers want to be informed no less than readers. True, you may say, but how can a drama-- specially a TV docudrama, with its composite characters, rearranged events and commercial interruptions--possibly convey the nightmarish reality of the Holocaust? To that, I can respond that fiction has long been a worthy partner of history in the search for verity. What factual account of Napoleon's invasion of Russia can equal "War and Peace"? So it is with the literature of the Holocaust; and so, too, I've discovered, can television treat the subject in fiction as powerfully as it does in fact.[2]

The Poetics and Rhetoric of Docudrama

Though "March of Time" used actors and reconstructed and staged events, it did not adopt a true dramatic structure, at the heart of which is a crisis demanding a resolution. One might argue that drama can exist without resolution, that a television soap opera is not predicated upon closure, but even the soap opera does promise a resolution which is, however, eternally postponed. "March of Time" was not dominated by a single dramatic crisis with inevitable consequences. It was both an impure form of documentary and an undeveloped docudrama.

Just as in "March of Time" dramatic elements and techniques were used to reconstruct and reinterpret reality, so in the theater some producers used documents and other naturalistic techniques to offer a point of view or to promulgate certain social and political ideas. In Russia during the 1930s the workers' theater was of this kind, as were many theater productions--like "Triple-A Plowed Under," which explained problems arising out of the Agricultural Adjustment Act of 1933--in the United States in those days. But the emergence in 1935 of "The Living Newspaper," which was funded by the federal government to support unemployed theater workers and artists, was an important development in the growth of reality drama. "The Living Newspaper" was sponsored by the Newspaper Guild. It was designed by playwright Elmer Rice, and like a newspaper, it had a full editorial staff. The newspaper consisted of a series of scenes developed around an important news item and accompanied by projected pictures and narration, an episodic style which on its surface reminded viewers of Bertolt Brecht's experiment in epic realism. But the way news stories as scenes were strung together implied a thematic treatment and a point of view which made "The Living Newspaper" a theater documentary rather than a docudrama. Scenes were enacted not by the actors but by "impersonators." In docudrama we have actors who carry out the will of the characters and face the consequences.

Bertolt Brecht's "documentary theatre" was a reaction against the grotesque emphasis on the emotional practiced by traditional Aristotelian theater. This tradition he called "culinary theatre"; in its place he wanted to establish a dialectical theater for the rational man who could confront social problems with detachment. Since traditional drama made a "massive assault on emotions" and created a "kind

of hypnotic trance in the audience,"[3] Brecht introduced
documentary elements into his plays to create "verfremdungeffekt" (distancing or alienation) in the audience.
But unfortunately, instead of reducing the emotional impact
of his plays, the documentary devices added to it--something
which explains the force of docudrama. Brecht later modified
his views and acknowledged the place of empathy in drama,
but only "a legitimate kind of empathy," a natural unity of
thought and feeling which impels us to the utmost exertions
of reason--a reason which purges us of our feelings. Though
Brecht's "cool" theater was a failure, he left a rich legacy
which the docudrama has yet to exploit fully.

What the television docudrama does is to infuse the life
of drama into journalistic facts, so that audiences see events
and their human agents afresh. Docudrama transfers the
center of gravity of an historic event from the critics to the
audiences. The dialectical interplay between mimesis and
diegesis which is the essence of docudrama gives television
audiences a different image of reality and invites them to
participate in its unfolding processes.

Another important source which contributed to the development of docudrama was Armstrong Circle Theatre; it
made its network debut in 1955 and continued until 1963.
By rearranging and reordering indisputable facts it sought
to establish dramatic plots in the form of crisis-resolution.
The aim of the producers, David Susskind and Robert
Costello, was to find a plot in the documented facts which
resembled the theme of a typical American success story:
obstacles overcome, hope fulfilled, courage, honesty, and
love rewarded. A. William Bluem says that in order to ful-
fill their aim of combining "fact and drama--to arouse interest, even controversy, on important and topical subjects,"
the writers were "sometimes pushed to create real or composite
characters which were founded upon accurate factual observation, and yet also had range and depth as characters in
their own right."[4] Of course, the passage of time has dis-
proved Bluem's prescriptive statement that documentary and
fiction drama should not be mixed but should exist separately.
Television does not recognize anyone as its prophet and continues creating new genres from the old.

Other influences enhanced the acceptance of docudrama
as a television genre. In the 1960s docudrama developed

strongly in West Germany, and playwrights used recent historical events to fix responsibility for Nazi atrocities on the perpetrators of the crimes. Of these docudramas, Peter Weiss's "Marat/Sade" (1964) and "The Investigation" attained international renown and respectability. Heinar Kipphardt's "The Case of J. Robert Oppenheimer" (1964) was later developed into a mini-series docudrama "Oppenheimer" (1982).[5] Some early Hollywood films of a biographical nature, like "The Story of Louis Pasteur" (1936), "The Life of Emile Zola" (1937), and "Young Mr. Lincoln" (1939), set the scene for reconstructed and enacted historical realities and made them acceptable to American audiences.

Thus by the mid-1960s television docudrama, which received its sustenance from theater, radio, motion pictures, and Americans' natural hunger for the historical (as evidenced by the attendance at museums and the popularity of historical fiction), was ready to enter the public consciousness as a source of entertainment and information. During the next decade (1966-67 through 1977-78), according to Thomas W. Hoffer and Richard Alan Nelson,[6] the public and commercial networks increased their docudrama quarter hours from 119 to 2,227. Public interest is still unabated. Some docudramas like "Adam" (1983) were among the top ten shows of their seasons.

THE FEAR OF THE GENRE

One reason for the genre's tremendous popularity is that viewers are given to see a dialectical interplay between mimesis and observation. Mimesis is the basis of all imaginative arts, but mimesis alone does not create art. It is the imaginative and playful imitation of reality guided by an artistic vision and a moral force which brings forth great art. From Homer and Shakespeare to the creators of the soap operas, we see how imitation of reality is given imaginative wings to give us intimations of something beyond reality. It is worthwhile quoting Polish director Jerzy Grotowski:

> Every performance built on a contemporary theme is an encounter between the superficial traits of the present day and its deep roots and hidden motives. The performance is national because it is a sincere and absolute search into our historical ego; it is

realistic because it is an excess of truth; it is social because it is challenge to the social being, the spectator.[7]

Television docudrama, based upon empirical observation of actual historic events, confronts audiences with the deeper truth of hidden motives and allows them the pleasures of a detective in the process of discovery and of a spectator (who knows the conclusion) enjoying the performance. No other television art form provides viewers with this complex aesthetic pleasure of simultaneously questioning the hidden springs of their society and enjoying the rituals of performance. This combat between liturgy and topicality is a constant source of enjoyment for the viewers of docudrama.

Probably another reason for the genre's popular acceptance is that events which constitute the basis of docudrama occur over a period of time and build into a chronological sequence or spatial jumble in the minds of viewers. The viewer's consciousness is normally fed bit by bit (or is it byte by byte?) by mass media and interpersonal communications. But docudrama challenges this sequential build-up and provides an alternative view of topical reality by presenting a simultaneity of sensory impressions constituting a unified consciousness. The reality of the docudrama challenges the reality of the rational man--the journalist and the critic especially--and explains why most people steeped in print culture feel so disturbed by this hybrid genre which presents topical reality as a revelation, an all-embracing Gestalt. Critics have objected to docudrama as being neither fish nor fowl. As A. William Bluem opined: "On the one hand, its commitment to the faithful duplication of events and people limited its freedom as drama; on the other, the use of actors and theatrical conventions deprived it of any validity as documentary ... that documentary and fictional drama not only cannot exist side by side in television, but can better strengthen and inform each other only when they do exist independently."[8] For the faithful depiction of events we should go to the historian. If we go to the documentarist, it is for a fresh insight into events because, by rearranging events and reassembling fragments of actuality following his own design, he gives us a new, creative interpretation of reality. A docudramatist, similarly, rearranges events in such a manner as to perceive a crisis and a will to action through the eyes of a protagonist and gives us a glimpse of reality from another angle. The question is, whose truth should be accepted: that of the historian, the journalist, the documentarist, or the docudramatist? Perhaps one dubious consolation of living in a closed society is that there are no such contending truths--it is the party's truth or the theologian's truth, whatever the case. An open, pluralistic society should create conditions for multiple perspectives.

Of course, from "Collision Course" (ABC) to "Sadat" (Columbia Pictures), the docudrama has raised many controversies, but most of them have been about details omitted, condensed, or exaggerated. General MacArthur and President Truman both left their memoirs, and each account differs from the other. Writer Ernest Kinoy gave his own account of the collision between these two powerful historical personalities, and, even though he might have invented some scenes, he brought forth the conflict in dramatic terms. Because of the demands of the documented facts, the mimesis cannot deviate much except to dramatize a significant fact. Astronaut Edwin Aldrin, whose book was turned into a docudrama titled "Return to Earth," had only a minor complaint about it: "On the whole, I'm satisfied with the picture, but condensation alters the truth. For example, you are left at the end thinking I'm still a mixed-up guy emotionally, when by now I'm actually recovered and coping quite well. Also, there is a romantic scene at the end in which I am walking down a beach, hand in hand with my ex-wife. It never happened that way. I had already told her I wanted a divorce and was going to marry someone else."[9] "Return to Earth" dramatized Aldrin's will to succeed as a man in space, though fringe details could have been managed differently. What mattered to viewers was one astronaut's modern version of heroism.

Sometimes a docudrama purifies the image of a protagonist in order to dramatize the most significant truth. For instance, the 1970 docudrama "Kent State" portrayed the turmoil on American college campuses, of which Kent State was an example. In order to achieve this larger aim, the producers altered and purified the image of the four boys killed by National Guardsmen. The docudrama, for instance, portrayed Bill Shroeder as an all-American boy, responsible, mature, apolitical, vulnerable, and unsure about his membership in ROTC;[10] but those who lived and worked with him drew a different portrait of him. But the purpose of the docudrama was not to purify the individuals but to portray the state of university campuses during the Vietnam War era. A docudrama creates problems for those who, having witnessed certain details of the events, swear by the truth, forgetting the docudrama's larger design and purpose. Objections were raised against the docudrama "Sadat." Those who knew Egyptian presidents Nasser and Sadat were less than pleased by their portrayals. In life Nasser was a towering figure with a pan-Arabic vision; the docudrama made him look ridiculous. There were other disconcerting inaccuracies, like Sadat kissing his wife in public, something which Moslems are forbidden to do. Of course, Sadat made peace with Israel with the support of the people of Egypt, but human motives are always intermixed. Sadat was not far above the temptation of glory; he did emerge as a giant on the Nile. In any case, this was an American cultural product and not an instrument of foreign relations or a propaganda film.

Some critics have questioned the desirability of showing a docudrama like "The Atlanta Child Murders." Between 1979 and 1981 several black children disappeared and were found murdered in Atlanta. There seemed to be a regular pattern to such killings, suggesting the handiwork of the same killer. When in 1981 police apprehended Wayne Williams on a bridge over the Chattahoochee River, the police, the politicians, and the media sighed with relief that an explosive racial problem had been solved. Surprisingly, the murders and the disappearance of children stopped after the arrest of Wayne Williams. Fiber evidence conclusively linked the culprit with the crime, and Wayne Williams was convicted speedily. The docudrama of writer-producer Abby Mann ("Judgment at Nuremberg") questioned whether law enforcement personnel had asked all the valid questions about the nature of the evidence involved; or was Williams' conviction a hasty political solution to an unsolved criminal problem? After all, in the Lindbergh child murder case, too, everyone seemed to be sure that the culprit was apprehended and punished; but doubts began to resurface that an innocent person might have been punished. What Abby Mann accomplished through his well-researched docudrama (based on 600 interviews and three years of research) was to create a doubt--not to give Wayne Williams the benefit of the doubt. Critics feared that viewers would get the impression that Williams was innocent. The

The Poetics and Rhetoric of Docudrama

docudrama, however, gave viewers a chance to look at the motives of the prosecutors; and also gave them a critical consciousness about the judicial process. The docudrama transferred the judgment to the viewers. It became another piece of evidence.

Whether docudrama should be produced about people on trial is a matter of station policy and free speech, but the genre surely keeps debate alive. At best we can criticize a docudrama on the basis of factual inaccuracies and omissions, which every form of artistic composition (particularly one which combines rhetoric with poetics) necessitates. Anyone who is familiar with the sources of a particular docudrama can find error, and that's what the best critics have done so far. Take the case of TV Guide critic David Shaw's commentary that "Robert Kennedy and His Times" omitted the invasion of Cuba in 1961 (the Bay of Pigs) and the United States role in the 1963 assassination of President Ngo Dinh Diem of South Vietnam. He called the docudrama sanitization of U.S. foreign policy and rhetorical purification of Robert Kennedy's image.[11] A similar commemorative effort was seen in NBC's 1983 three-part docudrama "Kennedy," which succeeded in creating the Kennedy mystique without, however, glossing over the dark spots of JFK's career. The docudrama was written by British novelist Reg Gadney and directed by Jim Goddard. In the background of the Kennedy drama was the sinister shadow of FBI Director J. Edgar Hoover, who kept dossiers on everyone whom he wanted to control. And then there was the First Lady, Jackie Kennedy, whose fine excess charmed people the world over. One wondered how the writer obtained those intimate conversations unless as a dramatist he used the dramatic license of mixing historical facts with fiction. From the Inauguration through the Bay of Pigs and the Cuban missile crisis to the assassination, the docudrama created the majestic awe of a royal president whom American refused to forget. If the purpose of the producers was to give viewers a historical analysis of the thirty-fifth presidency, probably a documentary approach would have brought about better results. "Kennedy" as a docudrama was commemorative and ritualistic in spirit. Even the dark spots which the British writer and the director would not hide added to the legend of JFK.

In the case of NBC's "John and Yoko: A Love Story" (1985), what mattered to viewers and John Lennon's devotees

was not the biographical details but the mystique which the
celebrated musician and his avant-garde Japanese artist
wife created through their art and political activities. The
docudrama covered a period of fourteen years, beginning
with the Beatles' 1966 triumphant tour of the United States,
John's encounter with Yoko in a London art gallery, their
fiery affairs, Yoko's divorce and custody battle, their marriage, a drug bust, Yoko's two miscarriages, immigration to
the United States, surveillance and threats of deportation,
1973-1975 separation, reunion, and John's assassination.
These were the documented facts which, through the music
of the Beatles and John Lennon and Yoko Ono, as well as
the romantic dialogues, were given dramatic structure and
form. Viewer interest focused not on how true were the
facts, but on how intense were John's and Yoko's lives, how
their love and music created a unified consciousness in a
generation on both sides of the Atlantic. The viewers' desire was to share the mystique or relive an era. And the
ritualistic communion was established. If there was any
serious flaw in the docudrama, it was John Lennon's summary death, which was a great dramatic opportunity un-
realized.

The issue, therefore, is not of "fake realism" or the
commercial exploitation of viewers,[12] but of the larger truth
and total impression which a docudrama creates. Though
"Shogun" and "Roots" are not docudramas according to our
definition of the genre, the inaccuracies found by many
scholars and critics[13] did not hinder the emergence of historical truth about seventeenth-century Japan or colonial
America, respectively. The fear that docudrama, by communicating fictional occurrences and bias as facts, might
mislead audiences is overly solicitous and misplaced. Docudramas do not serve as "surrogate reality,"[14] but they do
heighten certain aspects of reality, as does any other form
of public discourse. For instance, even if the British writer
were totally and factually true to American history in "Kennedy," he could not have been accurate enough because the
syncopation of time, condensation and selection of material,
and imposition of a crisis-resolution structure and a form-in-
suspense would have created an historical unreality. When
we experience reality, time is of the essence; drama is nothing but the reshaping of historical time in a form that allows
the dramatic experience to be felt as a totality, a simultaneity, a unified consciousness, a destiny. In docudrama, the

The Poetics and Rhetoric of Docudrama 195

two planes of reality, the topical and the dramatic, create a kind of complex seeing, or alternative perceptions. The historic Robert Kennedy, who played a significant role in the Bay of Pigs, and the ritualistically purified Robert Kennedy of the docudrama exist together in the viewers' consciousness, illuminating each other--what was and what might have been.

What about young viewers whose first intimation about the Kennedy clan is only through the docudramas? Might not they form a wrong impression of the historical events? To say so is to beg a question because the function of docudrama is not to assert historical truth, but to show viewers a realm of probability which is neither exclusive nor exhaustive and to leave room for further interpretations. That is why "The Atlanta Child Murders" was culturally so important: because it left an unresolved question about the infallibility of the courts. If it muddied the case for the prosecution, let the prosecutors present foolproof evidence. Speedy justice, kangaroo courts, racist juries, etc., do constitute a deep inheritance in American culture, and hence the importance of retaining doubt. The documented events of contemporary history become a kind of paradigmatic structure against which the docudrama is played, and the viewers' response is deepened. "John and Yoko" depicted the Immigration and Naturalization Service threatening to deport the musicians unless they gave up their anti-war, anti-Nixon political activities. A few weeks before this docudrama was aired, viewers had seen how another nonconformist immigrant religious leader in Oregon was obligated to leave the country. When audiences saw John Lennon under surveillance, fretting and fuming that his telephone was bugged, their response to this paradigmatic structure was deepened. Audience involvement means that television docudrama deserves much greater attention than the perfunctory, supercilious notice some critics have given it by calling it another commercial gimmick of the networks to seduce viewers eighteen to forty-nine years old.

Briefly, the view that docudrama restructures contemporary events of public significance into crisis-resolution dramatics, centering on the individual's will to action, has some consequences for students of television culture. First of all, it excludes mini-series like "Roots" and "Shogun" as docudramas because they, like Arthur Miller's "Crucible," are not based on contemporary events. They do not evoke contemporary memories; they belong to a genre called the historical fiction mini-series. This definition also excludes dramatic monologue based upon some factual events--a monologue is not drama. Also, those programs which have verifiable historical facts but only imaginary characters are to be excluded from this category because docudrama is essentially concerned with the lives of people who actually lived and asserted their will to action and with the attendant consequences. This definition, however, puts us in a quandary about a mini-series like "Mussolini: The Untold Story" (NBC, 1985) or a movie like <u>Gandhi</u> (1982). "Mussolini" was a docudrama mini-series for the Italians who were his contemporaries and experienced the historical events; <u>Gandhi</u> was a docudrama biography for the people of India, which explains why so many Indians protested that the movie/docudrama was inaccurate. For Americans who were not participants in those events, "Mussolini" was just a mini-series, and <u>Gandhi</u> was a straightforward movie. Television is no respecter of definitions and continues to mix genres and create new types, leaving us with only a working definition of docudrama. If after a century, for instance, another version of "Robert Kennedy" were shown, it would be a historical mini-series or a movie rather than a docudrama because the condition of contemporaneity of events would not be met.

A docudrama is culturally significant because by reshaping real lives and topical events in a crisis-resolution structure it gives us another intepretation of and commentary upon the lives and times of those individuals--and of our own. The ultimate test of docudrama is whether it sends viewers back to study history and historians to reopen the dialogue in a society wedded to the ideology of the free marketplace of ideas.

NOTES

1. Allardyce Nicoll, <u>British Drama</u>, 5th ed., (New York: Barnes and Noble, 1963), p. 84.
2. John Toland, "A Noted Historian Judges TV's Holocaust Film," <u>TV Guide</u> (February 13, 1982), pp. 6-8.
3. Keith Dickson, <u>Towards Utopia</u> (Oxford: Oxford University Press, 1978), p. 163.
4. A. William Bluem, <u>Documentary in American Television</u> (New York: Hastings House Publishers, 1965), p. 193.

5. Robert B. Musburger, "Setting the Stage for the Television Docudrama," Journal of Popular Film and Television, 13 (Summer 1985), p. 93.
6. Thomas W. Hoffer and Richard Alan Nelson, "Evolution of Docudrama on American Television Networks: A Content Analysis, 1966-1978," The Southern Speech Communication Journal, XLV:2 (Winter 1980), pp. 149-163.
7. Jerzy Grotowski, "Towards a Poor Theatre," in Bernard F. Dukore, ed., Dramatic Theory and Criticism: Greeks to Grotowski (New York: Holt, Rinehart and Winston, 1974), pp. 985-995.
8. A. William Bluem, p. 193.
9. Bill Davidson, "Fact or Fiction--Television Docudrama," in Richard P. Adler, ed., Understanding Television (New York: Praeger, 1981), p. 251.
10. Louis P. Cussella, "Real-Fiction Versus Historical Reality: Rhetorical Purification in 'Kent State--The Docudrama,'" Communication Quarterly, 30:3 (Summer 1982), pp. 159-164.
11. David Shaw, "Danger! Please Don't Mix Facts with Fiction," TV Guide (April 20, 1985), pp. 5-7.
12. Paul Klein, "Programming," in Steve Morgenstein, ed., Inside TV Business (New York: Sterling Publishing Company, 1979), pp. 21-22.
13. Dan Slater, "Historians Assess 'Shogun,'" Journalism Quarterly 59, pp. 648-651.
14. Lance Morrow, "The History Devouring Device: Television and the Docudrama," Media and Methods 15 (October 1978), pp. 18-20.
15. Paul Klein, "Programming," pp. 21-22.

Chapter Eleven

THE MINI-SERIES: EPIC IN THE AGE OF TELEVISION

* The Problem of Adaptation

* The Narrative Structure of the Mini-Series

* "The Jewel in the Crown" and the American Audience

* The Narrator as an Intruder, as a Noise

* "The Thorn Birds": An Epic of Sin and Suffering in the Vatican Backyard

The mini-series is a television created genre; it never existed before 1970. It is a lengthy, complex, dramatic narrative predicated upon a closure. The viewing time may extend from five hours to eighteen hours, from two nights to several nights, depending upon whether the mini-series is aired on a commercial network or on PBS. "The Jewel in the Crown" lasted for fourteen hours, spread over as many weekly episodes. "The Winds of War" (ABC, 1983), an adaptation of Herman Wouk's 1971 novel, extended to eighteen hours. The sleazy "Lace" (ABC, 1984), however, was limited to only five hours but hit a mega-audience. The mini-series' complexity depends upon its length, which does not, however, promise profundity.

Like the soap opera, the mini-series has enough leisure and opportunity to develop the characters, the situation, the total ecology and milieu--the paradigmatic structure of the story. Since, unlike the soap, it is not an open-ended structure, it is comparatively fast-paced and races to a closure, thus giving viewers the pleasure of completing a form. A made-for-television movie or a conventional film negotiates many compromises with character and story development in order to make sense of the visual narrative. But a mini-series has the potential of being as profound as an epic or a great novel--as audiences discovered in "Roots" and "The Jewel in the Crown."

One might hypothesize that a television genre will survive in America if it is both culturally and commercially significant. Culturally, the mini-series as a genre is very important because its multipart form makes possible in-depth treatment of any historical and social theme. During the last decade, apart from the path-breaking "Roots" and "Shogun," one has to think of "Masada," "Jesus of Nazareth," "Nicholas Nickleby," "Brideshead Revisited," "The Thorn Birds," "The Jewel in the Crown," "Holocaust," "George Washington," "Fatal Vision," and many others--some of them British imports. Of course every culture has its biological orifices from which come sleaze like "Lace," "Mistral's Daughter," etc., but these are part of the cultural continuum.

The age of the mini-series began, not with "Roots" in 1977, but a year earlier with the twelve-hour adaptation of Irwin Shaw's "Rich Man, Poor Man." Its commercial success led to its cloning as "Rich Man, Poor Man--Book II," "Beggarman, Thief," and so on. In 1985 the pattern was repeated in "Hollywood Wives," "Hollywood Wives II," and "Hollywood Wives III." The commercial networks look for a recipe to repeat till audiences get tired of the concoctions. But a recipe is not a genre, which may be defined as a set of creative possibilities from which various recipes and formulas can be drawn for specific needs. The networks might exhaust a few recipes, but the larger possibilities of the genre are potentially very rich, as audiences discovered in "Roots," in which they saw not only a family saga but a permanent structure being established in their culture. It is unpardonable to talk in the same breath about the historic "Roots" and the tawdry "Lace"; but, surprisingly, their narratives were motivated by similar questions. "Roots" asked, "How did Kunta Kinte come to America, if not as an immigrant?" "Lace" (Lili) asked, "Which one of you bitches is my mother?" In a perennially intermixing culture, where open marriages and promiscuity are not frowned upon, where men walk out on their women, where single parenthood is a viable phenomenon, the question of legitimacy, the search for one's mother or father, has become an obsessive concern, a surface structure. "Lace" was a mock epic wherein the theme of roots and legitimacy received semi-pornographic treatment. In "Roots" the possibilities of the mini-series genre were used to enact an historical epoch as a mass ritual; in "Lace" the possibilities were used to satisfy a collective voyeuristic urge. Both of these mini-series drew enormous audiences, and one can understand the networks' search for the mega-audience through a "Lace"-"Roots" combination and permutation of theme and treatment.

The networks look for a vast canvas peopled by characters whose activities cause tremors not only in audiences but also in Nielsen ratings. PBS has near-captive audiences who have become culturally conditioned to accept every British import as superior; the commercial networks have to earn their audiences. CBS broadcast "Kane and Abel," based on British author Jeffrey Archer's best-selling novel. The mini-series celebrated Americana in epic and melodramatic proportions. It spanned six decades and showed the lives of two persons born on different continents but destined to meet in a headlong clash within the framework of America's open society and capitalism. This mini-series, with superficial biblical references, was a piece of American history unfolding against the background of atrocities committed on the European continent. "Kane and Abel" exemplified a melodrama cast in a mini-series structure. "Fatal Vision" (1984) was a docudrama in a mini-series form. Television has a strange appetite for mixed genres; it does not respect purity of form. As stated earlier, the mini-series is only a set of (in)exhaustible creative possibilities. The complication of the yarn, the vastness of the canvas, and the need for a large audience make the form inevitable.

Another spectacular series of epic scope was CBS's "Space" (1985), based upon James Michener's novel: the telecast spanned five nights and thirteen hours and was a feast of science, adventure, and history. The epic drama began when an American engineer went to Germany after World War II to persuade German rocket experts to come to the United States to help build its space program. The tale followed many subplots, trials, and tribulations and culminated in America's victory and "a giant step for mankind." A made-for-TV movie would have chopped off most of the book's yarn; but the mini-series, without causing boredom, added to the rich visual texture and depth of human relationships.

If an epic is defined as a long narrative poem in elevated style that recounts the deeds of a legendary or historical hero, or as a novel or drama that suggests grandeur in the scale, scope, and profound human importance of the subject,[1] then ABC's eighteen-hour adaptation in 1983 of Herman Wouk's 1971 novel The Winds of War was a true television epic. The network chose this subject of worldwide scope in order to earn a substantial rating to justify an expenditure of $40 million, but their commercial purpose served the cultural purpose of bringing a well-known book to the audience. The month of February is a "sweep" month, when the ratings of local stations are measured and their advertising rates are decided. In order to capture top ratings in the "sweep" month, the network started a publicity blitz, educating people about the times and the leaders of World War II. They also made a short documentary about the war in an attempt to raise viewers' awareness about Wouk's historical epic of love, war, and adventure. The story was told from the point of view of a U.S. Navy captain, Victor Henry, a participant-observer-narrator who was an attaché in Berlin. As viewers learned, the Soviet-German Non-Aggression Pact freed Hitler to launch the war and was followed by the invasion of Poland, the fall of France, the Battle of Britain, the German invasion of the U.S.S.R., Pearl Harbor, and the U.S. entry into World War II. But interweaving these historical events were many subplots which gave the epic its human side and depicted the profound tragedies suffered by the characters as individuals rather than as faceless masses. One of the subplots revolved around Victor Henry's son Byron, who loved a Jewish girl, Natalie, the niece-secretary of a historian living in Europe. During the German blitzkrieg the lovers consummated their marriage. Though the Jewish theme was persistent, it did not dominate the mini-series. The making of the mini-series was a gigantic task requiring two years. Herman Wouk himself wrote the script and, along with the producer-director Dan Curtis, created an absorbing visual narrative of epic proportion.

The important point is that the commercial greed and the ratings war of the networks are turning them to subjects of great cultural and historical significance. The auctioneer and the artist both can find a bargain in the mini-series.

THE PROBLEM OF ADAPTATION

While commercial networks adapt only best-selling novels for mini-series, PBS producers adapt only those books that have been read and critically acclaimed by the literary establishment on both sides of the Atlantic. The purpose of the television adaptation of a serious novel as a mini-series is to draw into the orbit those readers who have heard about the book, read the reviews, but never had the time and courage to actually read the book. According to James Traub, a well-received PBS mini-series, "especially on 'Masterpiece Theatre,' can lift a classic book from plodding respectability to minor cult status."[2] Evelyn Waugh's Brideshead Revisited has been selling very well since it was adapted for the mini-series. Because The Citadel was produced as a mini-series (1983) the publisher, Little, Brown and Co., issued many other titles of A.J. Cronin. Robert Grave's I, Claudius and Paul Scott's The Jewel in the Crown, too, showed remarkable surges in print sales after each mini-series was aired.[3] According to Karen Johnson of Boston station WGBH, books "extend the life of a transitory television event and they supplement the content of the show and they help promote the show."[4] This is a very superficial explanation of why audiences turn into readers. Probably the truer explanation is that the novel and the mini-series present two perspectives on reality, and moving from one perspective to another deepens critical understanding. Intuitively, a reader-viewer realizes that exclusive dependence on a particular medium gives a partial view of reality, and hence he moves from one medium to another. Just as highbrow intellectuals and serious readers move from a novel to the mini-series or vice versa, the common reader of the best-sellers, for the same reason, moves to and from between the written and the televisual. If a PBS mini-series boosts the sale of a forgotten classic into the hundreds of thousands, the commercial network adaptation of a popular work sends the sales figures sky high. Might one say that the mini-series are turning Americans into readers--of pulp novels today, and maybe of T.S. Eliot tomorrow? But that's only a point of view: that the greed of the commercial networks is driving people to reading just as the greed of American capitalists is creating jobs and plenty of material goods.

Bob Sumner reported in the Publishers Weekly that television became a central factor in some of the books published in the South.[5] He mentioned that after the docudrama "The Atlanta Child Murders" was aired in April 1984, Chet Dettlinger's book The List, which had been ignored by reviewers, picked up a hefty sales volume, even though Abby Mann's docudrama was not based upon Dettlinger's book. The case of "Andy Griffith Show" is stranger than fiction. The top-rated show of the sixties was turned into a book by Richard Kelly titled The Andy Griffith Show, which received wide critical acclaim and brought audiences back to the reruns of the old show--making it a kind of cult. This is a new cultural phenomenon: that television adaptation, instead of turning the viewers into a nation of "videots," is changing them into readers. Even if Wayne C. Booth is correct in his view that television trivializes everything,[6] he cannot regret that more people read books today than ever before. We can teach people how to read, but we cannot legislate what they should or should not read.

How serious is the problem of adaptation? Does it trivialize the original version? It is worthwhile quoting the novelist A.H. Hotchner, who adapted several works of Ernest Hemingway:

> There is probably no form of writing more perilous by nature than adaptation: if the dramatic version succeeds, the author of the original novel or short story is hailed for indestructible genius; if it fails, the writer who adapted it is blasted for defaming the master. The adapter lives under the gun.[7]

Hotchner's concern is with the original writer and the adapter's loyalty to the writer's vision. But for an adapter who works for a commercial network the major problem is how to win the viewer's loyalty, or when to provide an enticement in the story, so that the mini-series does not lose the audience. Since an adapter works for a network or a production company, he or she would follow the pressure of the demographics as interpreted by the programmers rather than the author. A PBS adapter, not being accountable to the marketplace, has a freer hand--which explains why the narrative structure of the PBS mini-series is so different from that of the commercial networks.

A.H. Hotchner has simplified adaptation into five types:[8] the scissor adaptation, which requires simple excising of surplus time and pasting together what's left; the distilled adaptation, which demands reworking for the length of time required (this method worked for Hotchner when he adapted Hemingway's For Whom the Bell Tolls); the expanded adaptation, which is the reverse of the distilled adaptation (this method is used for adaptation of a short story into a movie); the straight conversion, when the original material is perfectly suited to television drama. But few past writers wrote novels with television in mind. Some of today's popular novelists write as if they were doing so for straight adaptation. Sidney Sheldon's novel fit into the five-hour (A Rage of Angels) or the nine-hour (Master of the Game) mini-series. A reader can visualize his novels in twelve-minute segments spread through three nights. There is another kind of adaptation Hotchner calls wild adaptation, entailing the conversion of the original work into a musical (Lewis Carroll's Alice in Wonderland into a musical by Irwin Allen) or a ballet (Shakespeare's Romeo and Juliet into a ballet by Tchaikovsky and Prokofiev).

An adaptation can hardly be satisfactory to the writer unless the writer himself becomes the adapter. Hotchner quotes the wrath of Hemingway: "You write a book that you like pretty good over years and then you go and see them do that to it, it's like spitting in your father's beer."[9] (Maybe Hemingway used another word instead of "spitting.") Some other serious readers believe that there should be no violation of the original text, which would make television adaptation almost impossible and may amount to cultural regression because the readership of a telecast book, as evidenced by library loans or bookstore sales, increases substantially after the program has been aired. Apart from the wrath of the purists against adaptation, an adapter faces some practical problems when converting material for televisual dramatization. The pleasure of reading a novel lies not only in pursuing the story but also in multiple perspectives, shifting points of view, streams of consciousness, flash forward and backward, and richness of style, which includes the author's play with the language. The television adapter has to invent televisual correlatives for the myriad creative and imaginative devices at the novelist's command. The adapter creates new scenes, deletes some material, adds visual descriptions, and introduces composite characters to straighten the story material, so that the viewer, who unlike the reader can neither go back nor pause, follows the story line easily. This revising was one of the problems with "The Jewel in the Crown" and with adaptations of many other novels like Wouk's The Winds of War--novels not written for the home screen. In the case of The Winds of War, originally British writer Jack Pulman was contracted to write the script of the mini-series, but after his sudden death Herman Wouk himself took over the script. Adaptation of his own work, under the guidance of director-producer Dan Curtis, came as a revelation to the writer. It is instructive and illustrative to quote from an article about Herman Wouk and his struggle with adaptation:

> A key element in the novel was the ironic perspective of the apocryphal German General Von Roon, who narrated the historical passages. Pulman maintained that Von Roon's literary irony could not be preserved and that his insights ought to be dramatized in scenes showing world leaders in action. "It was a hell of a shock to me," says Wouk. But within a day Wouk had concluded that it was "a craftsman-like stroke that cut to the heart of the matter."[10]

Herman Wouk, after the adaptation, became a television proselyte, as his own remarks show:

> Only 15% to 20% of the material in the book is on the screen.... The film medium can say a lot more in a hurry. The attack on the refugees fleeing from Cracow to Warsaw was built sentence by sentence in the book in order to engage the reader's imagination. In a few seconds on the screen, however, you have flames, zooming planes, horses rearing, people falling.... I was in virgin territory and tried to end each episode with a cliffhanger.... Curtis showed me that although you might break at a high point, it was really one flow of a

> narrative, just like the novel.... Film almost always simplifies, and this is a simpler version of my story, my people and the history. But within those limits, it is faithful.... A 2-1/2 hour feature film would necessitate a terrible sacrifice of character and depth.... You watch it as you read a novel, in several sittings.... [Television] may be emerging from the nickelodeon era. It is a plastic, versatile medium--far more than the feature film--but is still in its early stages.... It is evident that the medium can do projects of substance. We're trying to take a medium that is so important in people's lives and do something first class that really matters.[11]

These are the beautiful thoughts of a good writer who, having undergone the tortuous creative process of adaptation (which some people call hack work), has come to understand the medium's cultural and historical importance: that a television mini-series based upon an acclaimed work might be a window for viewers to look beyond and a temptation to explore the original. As a limited analogy, compare the mini-series to the reproduction of a painting by a great master which might prompt some viewers to go to the museum to see the original.

THE NARRATIVE STRUCTURE OF THE MINI-SERIES

A narrative consists, first, of a story plotted as a chain of events, actions, or happenings which reveal themselves through the characters and their environment; and, secondly, the shape or form the story assumes--that is, its discourse in a particular medium. When a narrative is adapted from any medium to television, only the story is transferred to the television screen; television creates its own discourse from that story. Within the structure of the original narrative the story elements may be reordered and given a new coherence when adapted for television as a mini-series. Seymour Chatman expresses the relations diagrammatically as shown on page 207.[12] Chatman distinguishes between story and discourse: "The what of narrative I call its 'story'; the way I call its 'discourse.'" The shape of the discourse is what earlier in this book was called "form-in-suspense," that immanent presence, an incompleteness destined to

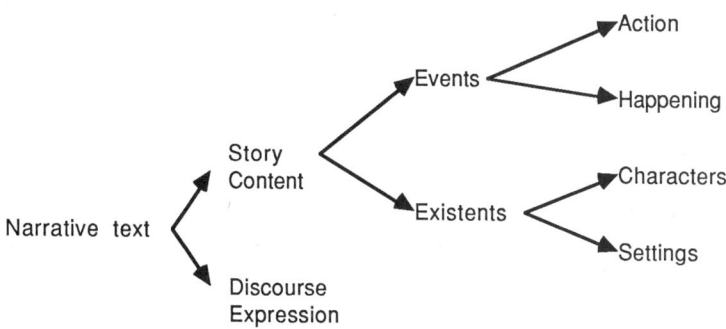

Chatman's relation of story elements
as seen in mini-series

completeness--which is a source of aesthetic pleasure for the audience.

The shape of the discourse is partly medium dependent and partly story dependent; since what is transferred from a novel to the mini-series is only the story, the television medium and the structure of the mini-series ultimately determine the discourse. For instance, though the story of Conran's novel Lace (about three girls who decided to get pregnant, giving Lili her problem as to which of the three was her mother) was the same in the book and the mini-series, the shape of the discourse, which is a source of pleasure, was different in the two media. And that explains why viewers move from televisual discourse to printed discourse--not for the content, but for the form-in-suspense. "Narratives are communications, thus easily envisaged as the movement of arrows from left to right, from author to audience ... what is communicated is story, the formal content element of narrative; and it is communicated by discourse, the formal expression element. The discourse is said to 'state' the story...."[13] Since a narrative is a totality in which each element conditions, and is conditioned by, the others in a dialectical relationship, adaptation from novel to mini-series changes the shape of the discourse and hence the narrative. Adaptation, therefore, is reinterpretation and recreation of a different narrative from the original, though both narratives belong to the same story domain. What is significant to the narrative as televisual discourse is its televisual logic, its thematic unity and credibility. Since a mini-series is a sequence of segmented episodes, punctuated by commercials with their own narrative properties and spread over several nights, the problem of viewers' commitment is of great concern; and this concern finds expression in the mini-series' structure. Mere logical clarity, thematic unity, and credibility may not bring the audience back the next day. Therefore, mini-series in American commercial television are designed as episodic clusters of suspense and surprise. From exposition to involvement to crisis to climax to resolution is quite a challenge even for a two-hour feature film, but for a twelve-hour mini-series spread over six nights exposition to resolution cannot be maintained without thinning out the tension and suspense and losing the audience. Consequently, the traditional diagram of a well-made movie changes in the case of a mini-series:

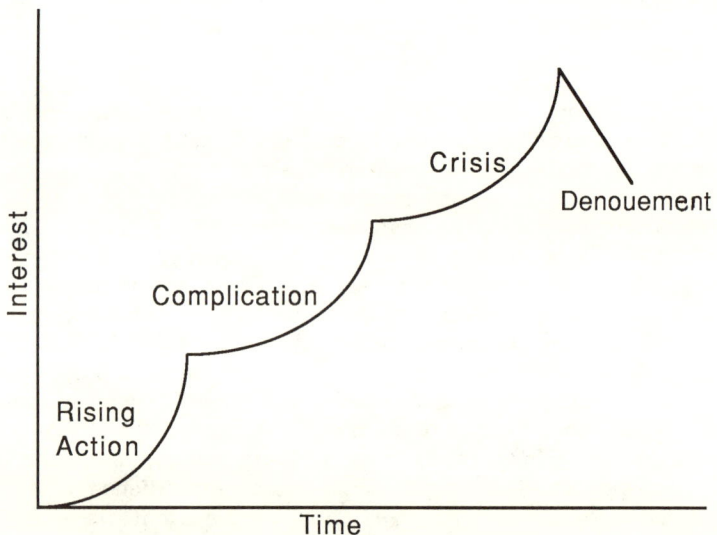

The Tempo of a well made movie.

One might envisage a mini-series as a limited serial consisting of short plays, or playlets, each lasting about twelve minutes with its climax when the commercial break occurs; each twelve-minute segment alternates with a three-minute commercial break. In an episode of three-hours there would thus be nine segments of twelve minutes each--hinging on an intriguing question, a puzzle, a suspenseful moment, an unfulfilled expectation with a promise. In the case of NBC's seven-hour mini-series "Mussolini: The Untold

TEMPO AND STRUCTURE OF A NETWORK TELEVISION MINI-SERIES

"MUSSOLINI: THE UNTOLD STORY"

21 mini-climaxes and 3 cliff-hangers

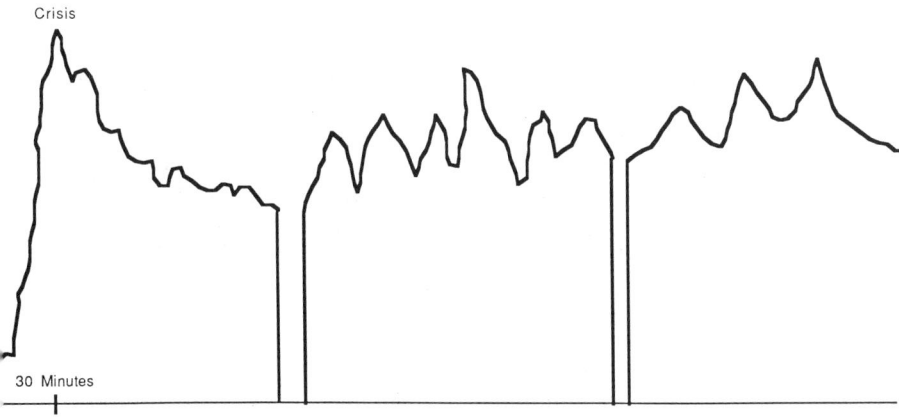

Crisis

30 Minutes

EPISODE ONE

Opens in 1922 as Mussolini, by using the strong-arm tactics of his monstrous black shirt power, establishes dictatorship. "Italy shall have an empire". He sees himself as Caesar and is hailed as Il Duce. The crisis occurs in the first 30 minutes.

EPISODE TWO

He is hailed as peace-maker (Munich, 1938) but is confused by Nazi dictator's cunningness. He is drawn into war and destroys his country.

EPISODE THREE

Torn between his wife and mistress, his son dead, his Fascist regime in ruins, he is reduced to a figurehead ...until his own people hang him and his mistress upside down in a public square.

Story" (November, 1985) there were twenty-one mini-climaxes, and three major cliffhangers coinciding with the end of each episode. As Dan Curtis told Herman Wouk, a break in the narrative flow at any high point creates a desire in the audience to return to the narrative and see it completed. Whether this desire for the fulfillment of a narrative, the completion of an incompleteness, is due to some feeling of guilt or to some hidden spring of aesthetic pleasure is a moot point and beyond the scope of this study.

Most mini-series begin on a Sunday evening, which is considered the family evening in America and has the highest viewing audiences. It is during the first night that the audiences get involved with the characters, get hooked on the narrative, and the hook gets deeper on each subsequent night. Since many viewing options are available to American viewers and remote control makes it easier for the viewer to change the channel, the mini-series must catch its audience in the first thirty minutes--that is, by the third segment of the first episode. The same may not be the case in Britain and other countries where audiences are blessed with fewer channels. When discussing the shape of a narrative discourse, the important question is not only, "What are the structural properties of the mini-series?" but also, "Why is the structure so peculiar to the American mini-series?" The narrative structure of the American commercial mini-series is determined by where the state of technology intersects the controlling center, the free marketplace of goods and ideas. No other television genre so well illustrates the main thesis of this study that all cultural forms in a society are determined by the state of technology and the controlling center; and since technology is only a state of permanent change, the mode of consciousness (episteme) is never static --the narrative structures are never abiding even when they are culture bound. The narrative structures of a nation, whether mimetic or diegetic, fictional or realistic (journalistic, historical, official), are in a state of permanent flux. Narrative structures are the signs of the time; knowledge of them could help us in the historical reconstruction of a society at a particular time. In "Mussolini: The Untold Story," screenwriter Stirling Silliphant, by reconstructing European era as told to him by Mussolini's eldest son Vittorio, not only entertained us, but also through a segmented narrative created forms or surface structures which invite deeper probing into our own society.

The mini-series has not seriously challenged Aristotle's model: an imitation of an action that is one and entire, the parts of it being so connected that if any one of them be either transposed or taken away, the whole will be destroyed or changed. For whatever may be either retained or omitted, without making any sensible difference, is not properly a part.[14] But adaptation does necessitate transposing the parts--truncating them or even inventing new ones, and all this shapes the discourse anew. Sidney Sheldon's novel-based nine-hour mini-series "Master of the Game" was a popular hit in defiance of the Aristotelian model. Part I introduced a wealthy South African family whose fortunes were based upon the diamond trade; part II almost abandoned the storyline of the first part; and part III took a different turn. Yet the three parts worked together because of suspense, surprise, dramatic tension and televisual logic.

The mini-series, though it starts with immediate crisis, has a narrative progression built on a kind of episodic roller coaster: tension and suspense, achieved through intercutting between incidents; crosscutting from detail to detail; composition, montage, editing, and manipulation of the camera. All these substitute for a well-integrated plot. A story is a sequence of events not necessarily related causally; plot requires cause-and-effect relations. One might say, every plot has a story, but every story does not necessarily have a plot. The oft-quoted distinction is, "The King died and then the Queen died" is a story; "The King died, and then the Queen died of grief" is a plot.[15] Television seems to destroy the distinction between story and plot because juxtaposition, simultaneity, montage, and other cinematic devices (constituting televisual logic) suggest causal links between events. In television story is the plot.

"THE JEWEL IN THE CROWN" AND THE AMERICAN AUDIENCE

As a television mini-series "The Jewel in the Crown" (PBS), however well designed,[16] beautifully made, and cinematically epic, was essentially regional and provincial in scope. It lacked universal appeal. It had a great appeal for the British because India will ever remain a structural component in the British historical experience. Unlike the film Gandhi--which despite only three hours of narration (against the mini-series' fourteen hours) successfully embodied a universal experience and had worldwide appeal--"The Jewel in the Crown" had a narrow point of view: the British experience in India at a particular time in history when the British were puzzled about Gandhi as a political phenomenon, the phenomenon which neither Paul Scott's novels nor the mini-series show. The question is, why did the American audience take so much interest in the mini-series when the intelligentsia, even in India, were indifferent to it? Before any attempt is made to answer this question, let's consider the substance of this mini-series.

"The Jewel in the Crown" is not a fictional account of the decline and fall of the British Empire. It is the vision of a writer who, instead of looking at the British Empire from the majestic Himalayan heights, decided to look at the intercultural tapestry formed of lives of ordinary British and Indian people during and after World War II whose petty acts of omission and commission gave rise to extraordinary consequences which the fragile intercultural framework could not contain. The narrative was fueled by the rape of an English woman, Daphne Manners (Susan Wooldridge), who came to experience India sensuously ("I love the smell of India") and fell in love with an attractive native, Hari Kumar, whose education in England had made him a misfit everywhere. A British officer, Ronald Merrick (Tim Piggot-Smith), who was born in a wrong British class and bore a grudge against everyone in England, came to India to protect the empire and the honor of English women. Particularly, he was fond of Daphne, who preferred the contemptible Indian, much to the wrath of Merrick, who was on the lookout for an opportunity to twist his poisonous fangs into Hari Kumar and the rest of his race. When Daphne was gang raped, Merrick seized the opportunity to incarcerate Hari Kumar. The dominant structure in the story is how Merrick brutalized Hari Kumar through physical torture and legal trials; and how at the end he himself was brutally murdered at the hands of a cultist group. But before Merrick met his brutal end, he moved from one posting to another, from police department to the army; his malevolent shadow was felt everywhere. Merrick watched the portents of infatuation between another Englishwoman, Sarah Layton, with another Indian, Ahmed Kassem--and let out a warning. Merrick married Sarah Layton's younger sister, a war widow, who earlier had tried to immolate her own child in some superstitious fire ritual. But fire burned every home and street in India on the eve of independence. Then there was the sweet, pathetic missionary schoolteacher, Barbie (Peggy Ashcroft), who had nowhere to go, neither to England nor India. Erupting from the mini-series were black-and-white newsreels of the empire on victorious march, proud and condescending toward its subjects. And then there were Indians butchering Indians--Moslem against Hindu, class against class. All this gory drama of political hatreds, personal passions, homosexual carnality, and petty domesticity of the English ladies was played in a setting of most beautiful lakes and mountains, drenched in the Indian sun, creating thousands of shadows and myriads of colors. India fascinated and repelled the British, and they did not know how to accept her--that is the theme of the mini-series, which the producers, Christopher Morahan and Jim O'Brian, faithfully expressed.

Paul Scott was an army officer in India for a few years, and The Raj Quartet ("The Jewel in the Crown" takes its name from the first book of the set) is an objective correlative of that experience. The novels portray this experience through a complex structure of flashbacks and flashforwards and multiple perspectives, and the story moves tortuously in a labyrinthine manner. In order to transpose it to a televisual correlative, the producers straightened out the complex temporality of the story and transformed it into straightforward chronological and anecdotal order without sacrificing much of its original beauty. The pleasure one gets from The Jewel in the Crown is different from the kind one gets from the mini-series. At times one had a feeling that the too leisurely pace of the mini-series was proving a drag on the emergent meaning. But Britain's Granada Television has a different value of television time from American network television, where every minute must be counted and paid for. Probably the American network adaptation of Paul Scott's monumental work would have brought about surprisingly different results--maybe better for the American audience because their narrative expectations are different.

THE NARRATOR AS AN INTRUDER

This brings us to the role of the compere, Alistair Cooke, in the "Masterpiece Theatre" series. Every work of fiction on which a mini-series is based has an implicit or explicit narrator. A reader does not need an outside agent to tell him how to read a book. Based upon mutually shared cultural codes and modes of consciousness, the reader and the author enter into a dialogue. When a work of fiction is turned into a television mini-series, the producer assimilates the narrator's voice and guides the viewer through the audio-televisual narrative. The television mini-series has built-in structural devices which lead viewers from one episode to another. Why is it necessary to have Alistair Cooke explain to viewers what to look forward to and how to understand a mini-series? By adding his interpretation and telling us how to see things he imposes his own meaning on the narrative, which diminishes the viewers' pleasure in making sense out of the mini-series. Or, to frame the question differently, why have American viewers accepted the condescending attitude of this no doubt highly sophisticated and ultracivilized Anglo-American gentleman when his interlocutions are absolutely disruptive, if not insulting?

What we call the American experience consists of many structural components, of which Britain is one that easily translates into the American cultural code. Some historical experiences will be forgotten in course of time; for instance, when the Vietnam generation fades away, the experience will become a dim memory. But Britain, like immigration, the family (legitimacy, fatherhood, motherhood), slavery, and Christianity, constitutes a deep structure. When such structures interact with the state of technology, they create the American mode of consciousness (episteme), that way of thinking, feeling, and beholding the world which is peculiarly American--no one else can have it. This heritage explains why Britain evokes such a strong response in the American collective psyche and why cultural communication is so effective. When viewers watched "The Jewel in the Crown," they vicariously shared the British experience in India. A French mini-series about the colonial experience in Algeria, for instance, may not evoke the same response in American viewers because France is outside America, whereas Britain is within America. No wonder Prince Charles and Princess Diana have such a strong emotional pull upon the American people. Watching the "Jewel" might have brought Americans closer to Britain, but India is a faraway country.

Because Britain is a deep structure in American culture,

Alistair Cooke, in spite of the fact that he is more of a communication "noise" and jars the mini-series narrative, has been accepted as a constant presence on "Masterpiece Theatre." We feel the weight and authority of this most cultivated English gentleman in our living rooms, and we are afraid that it might be impolite to ask our guest to leave us alone. After all, Alistair Cooke has been there for a half century interpreting the American experience for the British and the British experience for the Americans--as the Manchester Guardian's correspondent, the host of NBC's "Omnibus" (1952-60), the narrator of the BBC-produced series "America: A Personal History of the United States" (1972-73), and now as the compere of "Masterpiece Theatre." His books have been on the best-seller list, and he has won many Emmy awards and generous praise from all shades of critics. Robert G. Kaiser once observed in the Washington Post that "Alistair Cooke covers a story the way a short dress covers an attractive girl."[17] Should not that effort be left to the viewers?

"THE THORN BIRDS": EPIC OF SIN AND SUFFERING IN THE VATICAN BACKYARD

Go to Sophocles or to Shakespeare to experience tragedy and to feel the inexorability of fate. But in the age of television a viewer may have sufficient excuse to be satisfied with its modern equivalent in the television version of Colleen McCullough's novel The Thorn Birds. The ten-hour family saga (ABC, 1983) was located in an outpost of the Catholic Church, a sheep ranch in Australia. The mini-series was about corrupting wealth, forbidden love, sin, and retribution --themes common to great literature of the past, but treated in the four-night visual epic in the framework of an enveloping bushfire, illicit pregnancies, a bloody encounter in the wilderness, and the drowning of a young priest. Everyone in "The Thorn Birds" seemed to be walking on live embers, trying to quench or escape fire.

The Vatican legate sent his promising, handsome disciple, Father Ralph, to the Cleary's vast sheep empire so that the aging matriarch might be persuaded to leave an inheritance to the church. But the matriarch, instead of dying, began to lust for the priest: "I have always loved you --so much that I could have killed you for not wanting me....

Inside this stupid body I am still young, and I still want you, O God, how much." Father Ralph, however, had developed deep fatherly affection for little Meggie, whom he watched grow from infancy to puberty; in the rose garden, when he explained to her the meaning of womanhood, their innocence changed into a hesitant flame and then to a destructive fire. They sinned passionately and suffered deeply. It was a relentless tragedy, not in the Greek sense, nor in the Shakespearean sense; but it did intimate such tragedy. The epic of human passions and will at cross purposes unfolded amid beautiful vistas of countryside, a sheep shearing contest, and elaborate religious ceremonies. It gave a glimmer of hope that the television genre might be a great way of bringing audiences back to their sets night after night. The executive producers, Stan Margulies and David Wolper ("Roots"), did not employ actors with Australian accents. In fact, the series was filmed in California. That turned out to be a great dramatic opportunity because since the setting did not draw attention to surface signs and symbols, viewers confronted the deep structure of the miniseries--the icy imperial will of the Catholic Church against the human need for love. The mini-series was a metaphor for a recurrent pattern of institutional domination over individuals who have no choice except to submit or to perish.

Because time and audiences are key factors which shape a television mini-series, sometimes commercial television has an advantage over those television productions PBS borrows from British television. There was a sense of urgency in "The Thorn Birds" which viewers missed in "The Jewel in the Crown"; one wonders how David Wolper might have handled Paul Scott's novel to suit the culture of the marketplace.

NOTES

1. M.H. Abrams, A Glossary of Literary Terms, 3rd ed. (New York: Holt, Rinehart and Winston, 1957), pp. 49-50.
2. James Traub, "Intrigues of the Story Trade: How Mega-Books Become Mini-Series," Channels of Communication (March/April, 1985), p. 26.
3. Ibid.
4. Ibid.
5. Bob Sumner, "TV Issues Central in Some Southern

Books," Publishers Weekly (April 17, 1985), p. 94.
6. Wayne C. Booth, "The Company We Keep: Self-Making in Imaginative Art, Old and New," Daedalus (Fall 1982), pp. 44-47.
7. A.H. Hotchner, "One Thing After Another--the Adaptation" in The Eighth Art (New York: Holt, Rinehart and Winston, 1962), p. 71.
8. Ibid., pp. 71-72.
9. Ibid., p. 88.
10. "In Virgin Territory," Time (February 7, 1983), p. 74.
11. Ibid.
12. Seymour Chatman, Story and Discourse (Ithaca: Cornell University Press, 1978), pp. 19, 26.
13. Ibid., p. 31.
14. S.H. Butcher, Aristotle's Theory of Poetry and Fine Arts (London: McMillan, 1923), p. 31.
15. E.M. Forster, Aspects of the Novel, (London: Edward Arnold & Co., 1927), p. 82.
16. Susan Todd, "The Jewel in the Crown: The Raj Quartet Comes to Masterpiece Theatre," Theatre Crafts (January 198?), p. 24.
17. Current Biography Year Book (New York: The H.W. Wilson Company, 1974), pp. 83-88.

Chapter Twelve

THE TELEVISION CRITIC AS A SOCIAL PROPHET

* The Issues

* Standards and Practices of a Good Critic

* Ideology, Idealism, and Ideal Types

THE ISSUES

Though we do not expect the television critic to provide the rich assessments of a literary craftsman, we do hope that he or she will guide us through the maze of television programs wherein Americans spend more than seven hours a day and seem to have no control. Television is not only drama, music, film, and dance, but also a magic casement onto the world of news, rituals, game shows, sports, business, and politics. It has become a chief negotiator and interpreter of reality, as we found in the 1985 Beirut hostage crisis. When a television critic assumes the role of a well-informed connoisseur of popular arts, he or she leaves much unsaid because the beat is so vast that the talents and training needed to do justice to this multidimensional medium are nearly impossible to attain. The path of the critic's consciousness leads not only to the convergence of political, social, and moral values, but also has the possibility and the obligation of social prophecy. Television encompasses so much of social reality that only a critic with a refined sensibility, a sense of history, and a trained intuition can correlate the interplay of variables and constants and foresee events as they cast their shadows before the passage of time. It is in this sense that a television critic is a social prophet without, however, relinquishing the traditional functions of informing, evaluating, documenting, applauding, and reprimanding. Because television criticism is immature at present and audiences are heterogeneous and dispersed, the television critic has not played as serious a role as a traditional critic of the theater whose voice is heard and whose opinion can make or break a play.

There is another reason why the television critic does not have the same status and power as a theater or a literary critic. In a society where the marketplace is the controlling symbol and the ultimate force in determining all human activities, the humanist critic has to yield place to the empirical critic whose methods are derived from quantification of observations and the realm of probability. No wonder A.C. Nielsen's ratings, with an unbiased and scientific facade, have become the chief television arbiter today. At present television critics, who primarily belong to the print establishment, see their role as that of an adversary against the TV establishment as a whole, with the latter seeing this danger and trying to manipulate the critics through public relations gimmicks of gifts and glitter. The audience and the industry both listen to Nielsen ratings; and the humanist critic's voice, backed by neither a credible model of criticism nor any vision or prophecy, is a voice in the wilderness.

The first step in training a television critic in the television establishment should be to distinguish the critic from a reporter, who records and documents events as they develop. A reporter has to keep his sources alive, and if he assumes the role of critic his honesty and forthrightness might threaten to dry up information sources. An industry with billions of dollars at stake cannot suffer a few smart pen-pushers to get away with carping criticism and would certainly unroll a red carpet before anyone masquerading as a critic. Therefore, a critic must be a person of unimpeachable integrity--a quality not related to money because critics are poorly paid, but a product of one's love for the calling.

A television critic's respect for his or her profession will be greater if he or she understands the magnitude of the issues involved. Society faces several major areas of concern because of television's overwhelming presence:

   1. <u>Television's Creativity and Innovation</u>: Every

season hundreds of new television programs are offered to American viewers, including series, serials, made-for-TV movies, regular films, and mini-series. The outpouring is prodigious and mostly disappointing because the television establishments exclusively listen to A.C. Nielsen's ratings. The humanist critic, with a value system not based upon quantification, feels excluded because he cannot instantly demonstrate the depth of viewers' feelings or tastes because his judgement is not the product of audimeter or electronic scanner. If the critics' opinions saved programs like "All in the Family" and "Hill Street Blues," their collective opinion could also help eliminate the general poverty in television programs, provided they have a capacity for vision and prophecy. The networks spend about $150 million[1] a year in developing new programs, and they are more interested in capturing Nielsen's demographics than in listening to the enlightened but ineffectual voices of the critics. The critics fight against the philosophy of the "least objectionable programming." What is good for the normal curve is not necessarily good for the humanist critic, though it need not be always so, as "The Cosby Show" demonstrates. High-quality programs as well as low-quality programs can produce high ratings on Nielsen's scale, which makes ratings not necessarily the only arbiter of public taste. The humanist critic with a vision should be the arbiter.

2. Television News: A critic whose expertise lies in television entertainment may find the broadcast news production system beyond his or her reach, and he or she may wonder about the millions of dollars star newscasters take home. Television news is a serious business whose profitability depends upon ratings, and the competitive pressure turns newscasters into star performers. The area of concern is whether the television news can be news and whether the newscasters can be interpreters of news for the audiences. Apart from the print model of news presentation, what are the other ways of informing audiences about world events? How adequate is the TV method of news presentation? These are some of the questions critics ask.

The field of television newscasting touches sensitive issues like the Fairness Doctrine and the First Amendment. The FCC demands constant attention from the critic because its deliberations affect the future of the nation relating to the foundations of the free marketplace of ideas and the listeners' right to know. The deregulation policy of the Reagan administration needs attention, which fortunately is one aspect of television criticism not touched by Nielsen ratings. No critic of sound mind can practice his or her art without sufficient knowledge of constitutional law arising particularly from the First Amendment. A television critic trained in the entertainment arts may lack the expertise required to discuss policy issues and the problem of television news as news.

3. The Social Impact of Television: A film or theater critic's responsibility ends with aesthetic evaluation of the artistic product, but a television critic cannot escape the social responsibility of assessing the immediate and the long-term effects of programming because television shows are repetitive and ritualistic and millions are exposed to them. The issues involved are violence and its impact upon children, excessive advertising on children's programs, racism, sexism, misrepresentation of minorities and women. A humanist critic cannot afford to express his or her opinion on these issues without arming himself with empirical evidence. Here a humanist critic breaks bread with a social scientist and makes a judicious use of data to support arguments.

4. The Issues Arising from the Emerging Television Technologies: Not only are news and entertainment being transformed by the converging media and the emerging technologies, but also our daily lives are being imperceptibly changed because of the onrush of new technologies: DBS, MDS, videotext, VCRs, videogames, etc. A television set is a receiver as well as a monitor. A television critic cannot rest content unless he or she senses the deeper significance of the new, ever-expanding beat. In this role he or she becomes a futurist, explaining the conflict between technological developments and the broadcasting system based upon the Fairness

Doctrine. In a manner of speaking, traditional criticism is free from the responsibilities of being worldly. Television criticism extends the traditional role of the critic to the social issues which are inevitably discussed in the medium. In order to be effective and powerful, a television critic has to discover a voice of authority through commitment to high standards and sound practices.

STANDARDS AND PRACTICES OF A GOOD CRITIC

Traditionally, criticism of the arts has served a useful function in stimulating a level of learned discourse to maintain cultural standards. It has not been free from the taint of propagating and perpetuating orthodoxy, but bold and courageous critics have recognized creativity and good taste everywhere. However, the audience for the traditional arts was small, homogeneous, and knowledgeable. The critic whose refined sensibilities were attuned to the art as well as to the society became an interpreter of concrete reality, and his or her voice was heard with respect. But neither the critic nor the arts have ever immediately affected society, though their activities may have long-delayed consequences (England, for instance, will be known not only for her empire but also for Shakespeare). As Moses Hadas says in "Climates of Criticism":

> Where a product is exotic or revolutionary and addressed to a limited and homogeneous audience of sophisticates, criticism interposes a useful barrier against these qualities but affects the general level of taste only indirectly. But where the product is of a traditional kind and its audience large and heterogeneous, criticism becomes an essential safeguard.... The larger and more indiscriminate the audience, the greater the need to safeguard and purify standards of quality and taste.[2]

The problem of standards of quality and taste in television criticism is not limited to creativity and entertainment, but, as discussed in the previous section, also extends to newscasting, freedom of speech, regulation and deregulation, the social impact of commercials, and new technologies. The interplay of variables determines television creativity in the long run--and, in consequence, our living room environment. Television, therefore, demands from critics much more than mere maintenance of good taste. Not all critics will have the aptitude and training to master the intricacies of such diverse areas of social concerns, which necessitate specialization and development of expertise.

A good critic should begin with the basic requirements of respecting at least the tremendous potentials of the medium --the music, the profusion of colors, the intimacy of human relationships, the close-up of reality, the monitoring of reality as live action, the splicing and juxtaposition of shots to modify or create new meanings, the metonymic syncopation to condense information, etc. Such superior knowledge about the medium and its unexploited potentials will be a source of strength for the critic in applauding and reprimanding. Along with examining the existing potentialities, the critic should see the impact of the new technologies on the present television culture--in this sense he or she is a seer and a prophet.

A sensitive television critic should master a comparative study of the arts in television and in the traditional medium of theater, and should educate audiences about how television modifies and redefines the received traditions. Watching King Lear on television creates different emotions from watching it on the stage, and the critic should explain the sources of aesthetic pleasure in each version. The question of adaptation from literature to television, theater to television, and film to television is another fascinating facet of criticism. Great epics and mythologies of the world have always been close to the masses; but now television's new genre, the mini-series, has enabled millions of people to enjoy great works. A critic should explain what we miss by not reading, for instance, Anna Karenina, and what we actually gain by watching it on television. He or she should be so deeply immersed in the rich artistic and literary heritage of the human race that the present should be a constant source and temptation of comparison. The critic's every remark should be anchored in the fullness and richness of the past as a living presence, as a totality where time has been annihilated.

A discriminating critic should be a watchdog for historical truth and accuracy, especially in documentaries and docudramas. He or she should question the methods of data collection, the nature of evidence, and the process of reaching conclusions. He or she may compare investigative reporting with similar in-depth reports in newspapers and magazines in order to question the accuracy of the television reports. In this way the critic can check the arrogance of television newscasters, interviewers, and documentarists when they make large claims--the camera never blinks. This role turns the television critic into a researcher trained to examine public records, files, and other documents. Documentaries, when properly structured, have great rhetorical force, and their immediate and delayed impact could be very great; hence the necessity of checking their accuracy.

A critic with a sense of television history would not only compare one season's programming with that of another, but also would point out why certain forms and genres have ceased to be popular. He or she would tell us why Westerns are no longer popular or why "Lou Grant," "The Mary Tyler Moore Show," or "All in the Family" are watched now only as reruns. He or she should examine the changing mode of consciousness, the way people see things, and peoples' collective fantasies or totality of perception, which would explain their urge to see certain genres but not others. In this way the critic can become an interpreter of our time and its zeitgeist, with an authority, in the words of Edward W. Said, "to stand between culture and system ... to stand close to ... a concrete reality about which political, moral, and social judgments have to be made and, if not only made, then exposed and demystified."[3]

A great critic would occasionally become a naïve observer, an outsider or alien, as it were, to view television's reflected social reality from a fresh angle. An act of estrangement, as Bertolt Brecht suggested, from the overwhelming immensity of television would enable the critic to see society's general drift and its periodic and repetitive performance, such as presidential inaugurations, political conventions, pageants, and awards, and to give detached and amused accounts of these rhymes and rhythms which keep the people waiting today for the Super Bowl and tomorrow for Christmas.

Can a television critic be indifferent to the warnings of the social scientists that television has now taken its place with education and parenting in shaping the destinies of our children? Bad television programs may nullify the effect of good parenting and education; for children of troubled families, bad television might even aggravate the problem. No social scientist has ever called the televisual medium neutral; the success of television advertising is the proof. Television criticism cannot remain detached from the increasing protests of parents and teachers and must establish a dialogue with these concerned constituencies so that problems are understood in proper perspective.

IDEOLOGY, IDEALISM, AND IDEAL TYPES

A complete critic fine-tunes his or her sensibilities by immersion in the classics of art, music, and literature, and in the knowledge of historical movements and crucial technological developments. Moreover, he or she learns to interpret the language of social scientists and empiricists, not with the idea of coopting them, but to enrich a humanistic approach. To avoid dogmatism, cynicism, and the sin of glittering generalities, the critic tests conclusions repeatedly, knowing that the certainties of today might become the superstitions of tomorrow. As Littlejohn says:

> The writers I'm referring to are very bright people, aware of and excited by contemporary culture, but in vital contact with past history as well. They can seem almost magically creative and free, and yet they are careful and correct in their use of language that allows them their extraordinary insights into what they discuss.[4]

How does a critic develop "insight"? We call a critic "insightful" when he or she illuminates those aspects of an event which we, due to the lethargy of the senses and excessive familiarity, fail to grasp in deeper significance. But can a perceptive critic be an insightful seer without values which not only illuminate the critical path, but also awaken sympathies and emotions and give the critic a voice of gusto and authority?

A critic's attitude towards television culture predicated upon a personal value system will raise questions about his or her ideological commitments. Can a person of taste and values be free of ideology? Ideology, broadly speaking, is concerned with patterns of dominance and their social, political, and moral consequences in the society. We call a critic liberal or conservative within the framework of the dominant cultural paradigm of the free marketplace of goods and ideas in American society; but a critic could also be classified according to class, sex, or race. Without an ideological commitment, how can a critic look at the annual American ritual of the Miss America Pageant, for instance? Is it a celebration of the budding beauty of feminine America or America's acculturation and conditioning for the <u>Playboy</u> philosophy? How far should a television critic go? Should he or she be limited only to evaluation, reporting, documentation, explication, and illumination?[5] Criticism without commitment is vapid, irresponsible, and immoral.

Acceptance of ideology as a commitment will eventually lead the critic to advocate ideal types of television programs to which he or she will compare the present actualities and point out possibilities missed or not realised. As Michael Harrington writes in <u>The Other America</u>, "My standard of comparison is not how much worse things used to be, it is how much better they could be if only we were stirred."[6] A television critic should be aroused to sublime wrath when he or she finds the chasm between the actual and the possible too wide. A network of television critics "stirred" and aroused may draw the viewers' attention to media degradation, create collective dissatisfaction with present programming, and force a change.

According to one critic, the method of ideal typing[7] which originated with Max Weber is a sophisticated mode of analyzing television programs. For example, when we study Elizabethan drama we understand how Shakespeare and his contemporaries deviated from the ideal type and recreated the tragic mode anew, thus enhancing the possibilities of the tragic form. Similarly, the soap opera as drama should be ideal-typed to extract and abstract a purified and ideal form which all the soap operas converge upon and diverge from. For example, one way of understanding "All in the Family" is to compare it with the historical comic genre; another method is to imaginatively create a comic television genre-- the ideal type--and to compare the sitcoms of today with this ideal type. As Christians and Carey say: "Each richly interpretive type can be deployed as a device for assessing the direction of contemporary history so that in the service of reason and freedom men and women might better grasp the impact values governing their lives."[8]

Thus governed by the ideal of the "service of reason and freedom," the televison critic whose intellectual training encompasses the humanities and the social sciences constantly compares the actuality of television with the ideal possibilities; and in the process applauds the creative, reprimands the makeshift and mechanical, and thus helps viewers to understand the drift of their lives. As an individual of refined sensibilities and broad sympathies, the television critic becomes a social prophet--in the marketplace.

NOTES

1. Reflections on Television (New York: CBS/Broadcast Group, 1984), p. 4.
2. Moses Hadas, "Climates of Criticism," in The Eighth Art (New York: Holt, Rinehart and Winston, 1962), pp. 15-16.
3. Edward Said, The World, the Text, and the Critic, quoted by Caren J. Deming, "On the Becoming of the Television Criticism," Critical Studies in Mass Communication, 2:3 (September 1984), 324.
4. David Littlejohn, "Thoughts on Television Criticism," Understanding Television, Richard Adler, ed. (New York: Praeger, 1981), p. 168.
5. Mary Ann Watson, "Television Criticism in the Popular Press," Critical Studies in Mass Communication, 2:1 (March 1985), p. 66.
6. Michael Harrington, The Other America (Baltimore: Penguin Books, 1963), p. 24.
7. Clifford G. Christians and James W. Carey, "The Logic and Aim of Qualitative Research," in Research Methods in Mass Communication, Guido H. Stemple III and Bruce H. Westly, eds. (Englewood Cliffs, NJ: Prentice-Hall, 1981), p. 356.
8. Ibid.

Chapter Thirteen

THE WAYS OF NIELSEN

* Television Audiences as Markets of Taste

* Ratings

* What Ratings Measure and Measure Not

* Guardians of Public Taste

* Some Facts About Television

TELEVISION AUDIENCE AS MARKETS OF TASTE

Few people ever go to the theater in search of new ideas. An audience in search of theater wants to be amused and thrilled, and its members submerge their separate identities and become simply a crowd, if the theater experience is worthwhile. The same phenomenon occurred in Roman amphitheatres when the cries of innocents were drowned in the din of cheering and hysterical crowds. We see the same at bullfights, rock concerts, and football games today. From the ancient theaters of the Greeks to the modern whirlwind musical tours of Michael Jackson and Boy George, the emergence of crowd personality depends upon two factors. One, the members of an audience must leave their homes to go to a specially constructed place; two, the experience should be so exciting and amusing that audience members lose their powers of independent and rational thinking, becoming impassioned with emotions or helpless with mirth. A supreme example of the emergence of crowd personality is found in

Shakespeare's <u>Julius Caesar</u>, when Mark Antony's words
"Friends, Romans and countrymen" changed the perception
of history. The nonmedia audience was large, ranging from
50,000 in ancient Greek theater to hundreds of thousands in
Oriental theatres. Special settings, time, and space maximized acoustics and reception. Rank and status in seating
arrangements did not always play a role. The occasion was
either uniquely created or occurred cyclically in the form of
religious festivals. Members of the audience gathered to
feel terror, pity, relief; or to laugh, cry, or admire. The
individual self was lost in the larger communal self. The
same phenomenon is observed in today's rock concerts or in
religious revivals. This kind of audience, tied to a locale
and an occasion, which has always existed in different cultures and tends to be a crowd, differs from the television
audience.

Television viewers are not an audience in the same
sense that a Broadway theater audience for <u>Cats</u> is an audience. Yet the television audience becomes a collectivity (in
Stephenson's sense of convergent selectivity:[1] Coke Is It;
The Pepsi Generation), when, for example, the Olympics are
broadcast, because a sense of occasion is created through
publicity. But the experience is not the same as sitting in
the colosseum when Nero, with an imperial gesture, asked a
gladiator to save a victim, followed by an immense sigh of
mass admiration. Watching the Olympics on television, we sit
alone with a can of beer and popcorn, not as members of an
audience of 100 million people. Market researchers like Nielsen tell us the next day that we were part of that vast audience. We never feel the terror, the pity, the thrill, or
the infectious laughter of the crowd. We are alone with our
own little sovereignties--a remote audience condition never
experienced before by any collectivity. It is only by stretch
of imagination and with extreme reservation, and because of
the limits of language, that we call television viewers an audience. This collectivity is formed "either in response to
media content and defined by attention to that content or
one that exists already in social life and is then 'catered
for' by a particular media provision. Not infrequently, it
is inextricably both at the same time."[2]

Denis McQuail's view about the duality of the audience
is a helpful starting point. It suggests the contours, but
not necessarily any inner structure, of that collectivity. The

essential qualities of the television audience are its dispersedness, its amorphousness, its lack of self-awareness, and its own oblivion--characteristics which as an audience or a collectivity it does not share with a movie audience, a concert audience, or a theater audience. A member of a television audience cannot surrender his individuality to the crowd personality because he is not part of the physically localized audience; he is less manipulable because he can ignore the message since he is not under group pressure. It is unimaginable to turn such dispersed entities as television audiences into socially active groups because they lack "a degree of self-consciousness, a common identity, and possibilities for interaction internally and for influencing the communication supply";[3] though at a lot of big crowd events, huge TV screens show the action. This dispersedness produces a sort of hybrid audience.

It is difficult to define the television audience because of the profusion of channels, cables, and media products, as well as the multiple uses of television sets as videocassette recorders, video game players, and computer terminals. But we can conceptualize television audiences as markets of taste.[4]

Taste is preference for material goods and cultural patterns which one cultivates according to one's mode of consciousness and material resources. It may not necessarily have any correlation with one's class or socio-economic status. Taste for country music, for instance, cuts across all classes of demographics, as does taste for horse racing or video games. Tastes as preferences exist, can be cultivated, and also can change. Tastes are not fashions; they are more abiding and are assertions of one's individuality. An affluent society like America encourages and recognizes tastes; recognition leads to empirical observation, quantification, indexing, and lastly to prediction. Prediction serves the free marketplace of goods and ideas.

Tastes are overlapping. One's taste for the Playboy channel may coincide with one's taste for fields and streams. Or, putting it the other way round, a black, a Hispanic, a WASP, and a lesbian may all enjoy Pavarotti. As a society becomes more affluent, it develops pluralistic taste cultures which break down the barriers of ideological and class orthodoxy. Empirically, it is very productive to look at television audiences as markets of multiple tastes, overlapping, crisscrossing, changing, and ever threatening the dynamic equilibrium of the marketplace. From the traditional concept of an audience as localized, centralized, capable of being emotionalized into a fickle-minded crowd or into a social action group, we have conceptualized television audiences as unselfconscious collectivities of tastes--aggregates for Nielsen, but richly spoiled individuals with the power of remote controls, viewing and half-viewing, sovereigns in their own homes expecting their good taste to be served. As Himmelweit and Swift say, "The media form part of the background rather than the foreground of the leisure life and interests of adolescents and young men: they are used far more than they are valued."[5]

In closed societies where taste pluralities are not permitted and in underdeveloped societies where poverty of resources does not encourage taste differentiation it is possible to create mass societies, and to keep them bound to ideology or religious orthodoxy. In other words, taste plurality as an audience concept is a function of the free marketplace of goods and ideas. When the marketplace is not free, tastes shrink into a mass. Again, tastes are linked with a society's mode of consciousness, of which values form a part. The way we beautify our lives, entertain and inform ourselves, depends upon our mode of awareness. As George H. Lewis has put it, "Distinct, recognizable taste cultures form because choices of content from a culture are not random, but patterned."[6] The patterning of taste culture is determined by a society's mode of consciousness, which has a symbiotic relation with its centralizing symbol--in America, the free marketplace of goods and ideas. Thus the television audience as a taste plurality, or market of tastes, is free from the taint of class or ideology, is not ethnocentric, is amenable to Nielsen ratings, and in the long run is predictive of future trends.

Three broad theories have influenced audience research:

1. <u>The functional theory</u>: Television viewers watch programs and are persuaded to the extent programs and messages serve their informative and entertainment needs. William Stephenson's play theory,[7] with its twofold purpose to foster the audience's mutual socialization through convergent selectivity and to exercise social control, falls into the category of functional theory.

2. <u>Dissonance theory</u>: Viewers pay selective attention to messages and select those messages which fit into existing cognitive and emotional patterns. Man is a rationalizing animal.

3. <u>Learning theory</u>: Viewers, in order to make sense of the world, seek information. Man is a rational animal and bases his decisions on information.

Based on these theories, audience research can be summarized as follows:

1. Television viewers are not necessarily obstinate. They will watch and listen to people of different opinions and different tastes. Audiences look for rewards. Cost-benefit analysis is silently operating in viewers' minds. Dissonance will not bother them if it is rewarding. Audiences learn even from contradictions.

2. Perception is functional and subjective. Audiences perceive to satisfy cultural needs and tastes, or to order environmental messages or TV programs in such a way as to fit into their existing patterns and become more supportive and acceptable.

3. Social approval of the televisual communicator by audiences makes programs and messages more acceptable. Viewers not only want to be informed and amused, but also want programs to follow the norms of good taste and morality and perhaps other societal values. In short, audiences do not expect televisual communicators to violate their mode of consciousness.

4. Since television audiences are delocalized, demassed, dispersed, and are not subject to crowd effect, the problem of persuasibility is quite serious. Research suggests that personality traits like intelligence and anxiety have curvilinear (inverted U curve) correlations with persuasibility. The intermediate level of viewers' personality traits are highly correlated with persuasibility.

Considering the abiding nature of tastes, the absence

of crowd effect, the "sovereignty" of the viewers at home, and the casualness with which TV messages and programs are treated, we shall examine the significance of the methods of Nielsen and Arbitron ratings.

RATINGS

Television stations thrive on selling "time" and delivering audiences to advertisers, who, because of their profit motive, keep the economy on a steady keel. This total commercialization of television is not a universal practice; in fact, it is peculiar to America. Since governments do not subsidize television and monopoly is anathema in American culture, stations have no choice except to commercialize time by luring audiences through programming methods. Because of their different demographics, psychographics, and life styles and the competitiveness of stations, audiences are seen as fragmented. The fragmentation is increasing partly because of the wider choices available to American audiences and partly because of newer uses for a television set. To gain a share of the potential audience in such a highly competitive market becomes largely a function of programming. Cost (CPM, cost per thousand of viewers) would eventually depend upon the advertisers' ability to reach the audiences. But the quantitative aspect of an audience is not the only consideration while purchasing television time. The cost also depends upon the buying power of the audience. A million HUTs (households using television) in Los Angeles have more buying power than the same number in West Virginia.

The commercial value of television time is tagged to audience variations at different times of the day, the buying power of the available audience, and the advertiser's market interest area. Program sponsorship, station break spots, and participating announcements are the legitimate ways of inserting messages, though viewers must be aware of underhanded practices like "payola" and "plugola" in which a product is gratuitously mentioned or shown on the television screen.[8]

The advertisers, networks, and program suppliers demand empirical information and evidence as to whether a program actually reaches the targeted audiences and how the audiences respond to messages. Therefore, measurement of estimated audiences, their demographic composition, and their behavioral responses in the forms of recall, purchases, or knowledge levels have increasingly become the concerns of media research companies like A.C. Nielsen and Arbitron which, in the tradition of Ford and General Motors, are national institutions. Eighty companies at present conduct research on various aspects of audience, media, market, and programming relationships. Pretesting of not only commercial but even noncommercial programs has become a necessity because of the massive costs involved and the risk of failure. The success of "Sesame Street," for instance, was due to year-long pretesting and research into all aspects of the program. Quantification of behavior and messages is riddled with difficulties partly because no direct causal links can be established between the two variables and partly because of the problems associated with sampling. In spite of the limitations, measurement of audiences as reflected in ratings is the only dependable--rather, the least objectionable--method of explaining and predicting audience trends.

It is important to understand some of the concepts which constitute the basis of the rating methodology:

Rating: The estimated percentage of viewers or households tuned to a station or a network for five minutes or more during an average quarter hour of the reported time period for the population in question.

Rating is calculated as a station's or network's actual audience divided by the total number of television households.

$$\text{Rating} = \frac{\text{Viewers or Household Viewers}}{\text{Total TV Households}} \times 100$$

From a sample of 1,700 TV households (Nielsen's sample) if 340 households were tuned to ABC, then

$$\text{ABC Rating} = \frac{340}{1,700} \times 100 = 20\%$$

Since the total number of television households in the United States is approximately 85 million and ABC's rating is 20

The Ways of Nielsen

percent, the total number of households tuned to ABC is 17 million.

> Share: The percentage of those television households reached by a station or a network which were actually using television during a particular time period.

Rating is based on total television households, while share is based on households using television (HUT):

$$\text{Share} = \frac{\text{Viewers or Household Viewers}}{\text{Households Using TV (HUT)}} \times 100$$

Suppose out of a sample of 1,700 television households, 900 households used television during a time period (others were not in use). Out of 900 HUT, 340 households viewed ABC.

$$\text{ABC} = \frac{340}{900} \times 100 = 37.8\%$$

While ABC's rating is 20 percent, its share is 37.8 percent. Trade journals report it as 20/37.8.

This estimated rating and this share are subject to standard error caused by the sampling error and other limitations.

> Standard Error: The measurement of the sampling variability because the audience estimate is not based on an actual census of TV households but on a sample of TV households.

$$\text{Standard Error} = \sqrt{\frac{p\,(100-p)}{n}}$$

p = % of viewers
n = sample size

In the case of ABC, standard error (SE) would be calculated as follows:

$$\text{SE} = \sqrt{\frac{20\,(100-20)}{1,700}}$$

$$= \pm\,.97$$

This is the value of one standard error. It means ABC's rating range is 19.03 to 20.97 percent. If we want to reduce this margin of error by half, we have to increase the sample fourfold. There is one more point to be considered. One standard error gives us a 68 percent level of confidence. It means that 68 times in 100 measurements we would capture the "true" percentage in our range. In other words, if we accept an ABC rating of 19.03 to 20.97 percent as true, then we run a risk of 32 percent. In order to reduce this risk to 5 percent, or to have 95 percent level of confidence, we must take into account two standard errors.

$$\text{The value of 2 SEs} = 2 \times .97$$
$$= \pm 1.94$$

So ABC's rating would be 18.06 to 21.94 percent. This would give us a confidence level of 95 percent or a risk of 5 percent if we accept this estimate.

Similarly, in order to have a 99 percent level of confidence, or to take a 1 percent risk, we need to consider 3 SEs. Nielsen ratings have 68 percent level confidence; or, they have 32 percent risk involved.

> Area of Dominant Influence (ADI): A geographical area constituting all those counties in which a commercial station and its satellites garnered a maximum of television viewing hours. Each county in the United States is a part of only one ADI.

Nielsen calls the Area of Dominant Influence a Designated Market Area (DMA) and defines it as "generally a group of counties in which stations located in the Metro Area achieve the largest audience share."[9]

> Metro Area: Consists of the town, county, and other areas in close proximity to the station. Nielsen calls it the central city of the market corresponding to the Standard Metropolitan Statistical Area as described by the U.S. Office of Management and Budget.

> Adjacent ADI: Areas of influence which are adjacent to a station's ADI.

> Total Survey Area (TSA): A geographic area

comprising ADI, Metro Area, and Adjacent ADI in which, according to Arbitron, "Approximately 98 percent of the Net Weekly Circulation of commercial home market stations occurs, exclusive of counties located outside the local market area reached solely by satellite transmission."[10]

Cume: The cumulative unduplicated audience consisting of an estimate of those viewers who watch a program for at least five minutes during a reported daily segment. For example, if seven viewers watch CBS Evening News for five minutes, they will be counted as seven. But if one viewer household tuned to CBS News for five minutes Monday through Sunday, it would be counted only once.

HUT: Households using television is the estimated percentage of television households using at least one set for five minutes during an average quarter hour.

Quarter Hour Audience: The number of unduplicated viewers who watched a station for five minutes within a particular quarter hour. This is the basis of Average Quarter Hour Audience and shows (viewers') loyalty to a station.

Television Household: An estimate of the number of households having one or more TV sets. It is estimated that there are more than 84.9 million TV households in the United States.

Daypart: A part of a television day for which an audience estimate is calculated; for instance, 6:00 p.m. to 8:00 p.m.

Television Data Base

The Bureau of the Census, trade associations, and many private agencies collect data which market researchers use as a base to build upon and to investigate their own problems. This data base gives market researchers a geographical distribution of the population, including such demographics as sex, education, race, age, occupation, and income. Apart from the demographic indicators there are economic indicators like auto registrations, retail sales volume, agro-industrial production, etc. This information base helps advertisers and programmers to construct messages and programs that match the material and cultural needs of the audience.

For television audience research the data base consists of the number of television sets in a well-defined market; the ratio between television households and total households is called penetration or saturation.[11] Sydney W. Head has suggested that the following five questions should be asked when interpreting television ratings:[12]

1. What criterion was used for counting an audience unit in or out of this particular audience?

2. What was counted as an audience--a whole household or an individual--and if an individual, were any age limits imposed?

3. The audience for what broadcasting entity was measured--a station, a network, a group of stations, a program, a group of programs?

4. Were audience members outside of homes counted as well as those in homes?

5. What time base was used--instantaneous, average, or cumulative?

Sampling

Audience ratings research done by A.C. Nielsen, Arbitron, or any other market research firm depends upon sampling. Statistical procedures have become so refined that a sample of 1,700 television households or 3,200 television user diaries could represent a population of 85 million television-using households in America.

This representativeness is achieved by the random sampling method. According to Fred F. Kerlinger, random sampling is "that method of drawing a sample of a population so that each member of the population has an equal chance of being selected."[13] Elaborating further the principle of

The Ways of Nielsen

randomization, he states, "since in random procedures, every member of a population has an equal chance of being selected, members with certain distinguishing characteristics--male or female, high or low intelligence, Republican or Democrat, dogmatic or not dogmatic, and so on and on--will, if selected, probably be counter-balanced in the long run by the selection of other members of the population with the opposite quantity or quality of the characteristics."[14]

Since the selection of sample members depends upon chance and every member of the television households universe has an equal chance of being selected in the sample because of randomization, the mathematical laws of probability become operative. This enables us to generalize from a sample to the whole population. For example, if 20 percent of a sample of 1,700 was watching "Dallas" on one Friday evening, then we can safely estimate the total population watching "Dallas" to be 17 million with ± .97 SE and a confidence level of 68 percent. This confidence level could be increased to 95 percent or 99 percent by counting two or three SEs, respectively.

In actual practice a modified form of random sampling called multi-stage area probability sampling procedure is used. A.C. Nielsen defines area probability as one in "which the sampling frame consists of small areas and each area is selected with a probability equal to the proportion of the total housing units in the area." If New York accounts for 10 percent of total housing units in the United States, then approximately 10 percent of Nielsen's sample will be from the New York area. Multistage sampling consists of four steps:[15]

1. The selection of counties within the country

2. The selection of census block groups within the counties

3. The selection of blocks from the block groups

4. The selection of housing units within each block

The A.C. Nielsen media research group uses two national samples. One is for the National Television Index (NTI), consisting of approximately 1,700 households tuned to network shows, which provides information about the percentage of households tuned to network shows. The other national sample is collected for National Audience Composition (NAC). This sample consists of 3,200. Each member is required to keep a diary. This sample provides information about who is viewing what. The sample design has a provision for systematic replacement of the households over a period of five years for the National Television Index and three years for National Audience Composition. NTI and NAC research results are combined four times a year to compile Sweeps.

The Sweeps periods are February, May, three weeks in July, and November. To the local stations two Sweeps months, February and November, are particularly important because their advertising rates are decided on the basis of audience ratings during these periods. Network affiliated local stations pressure the networks to show blockbusters during the Sweeps to boost their ratings. This skews program scheduling and has a negative effect upon program creators and managers. It has been suggested that continuous measurement of the audience is a more efficient solution to the problem--if the cost were not prohibitive. Probably an ideal solution would be a combination of qualitative and quantitative measurement of the audience (a case in point is a project being tested as Nielsen's A-C people meter). In addition to these techniques, Overnights give quick ratings of a program in some important markets like San Francisco, Los Angeles, Chicago, Philadelphia, and New York.

Arbitron Ratings Company's audience research is mostly confined to local markets. Nielsen has a local service called National Station Index. Both companies conduct client-specific research in which they use telephone interview methods called Telephone Coincidentals.

Thus there are three methods of data collection:

1. <u>Electronic methods</u>: Nielsen uses an audimeter called Storage Instantaneous Audimeter. This is an unobtrusive method which records channel switching, tuning, and stations. Data collection is centralized at Dunedin in Florida and forms the basis of the National Television Index.

2. <u>Diaries</u>: (Audiologs) Sample subjects are asked to list the number of viewers, the duration, and the channel. This is the basis of NAC.

3. <u>Telephone Interviews</u> are used to collect data which NTI and NAC methods cannot collect.

Arbitron also uses similar methods of data collection.

In spite of the most reliable scientific and statistical methodology used in collecting data, audience research has severe limitations and is subject to abuse. While data collection methods could still be refined and may become more reliable, abuse of the system has prompted the Federal Trade Commission, the Electronic Media Rating Council, and the National Association of Broadcasters to issue guidelines regarding deceptive claims of broadcast audience coverage. For instance, the FTC warns stations not to engage in "activities calculated to distort or inflate such data--for example, by conducting a special contest, or otherwise varying ... unusual programming, or instituting unusual advertising or other promotional efforts, designed to increase the audience only during the survey period." Such variation from normal practice is known as "hypoing." NAB, AAAA, and EMRC oppose "any attempt by stations to exhort the public to cooperate with ... audience measurement services whether over the air or by any other means, and recommends to syndicated audience measurement services that the practice be discouraged because of its possible biasing effects."

In short, the public, through its institutional guardians and various trade associations, is seriously concerned about abuse of the rating system through unique contests, on-air announcements, promotions, survey references, and other forms of rating distortions. In a self-regulated society, where the least government is the ideal and the free marketplace is both the ruling symbol and the dominant reality, any attempt, overt or covert, to subvert the basis of society cannot be ignored. The scandals of past decades are still fresh in memory.

WHAT RATINGS MEASURE AND MEASURE NOT

In a society where most human activities are assessed,

measured, and compared, television viewing and performance cannot escape the dominant norm of that society. In fact, television ratings have a very important function because they form a bridge between the leisure time activities and the economic activities of the community. Ratings, in spite of widespread and legitimate criticism, bring the market and the people together in a commercial communion. Like the blueprints of an architect or the genetic code of a species, ratings map out and measure the tastes and trends of television viewers as consumers and assist advertisers and markets in building strategies to deal with uncertain forces or "environmental turbulence," as F.C. Emery and E.L. Trist[16] state. Unlike the theater, the cinema, or the painter's canvas, television is more than a cultural medium--it is a marketplace as well. Anyone who comes to the marketplace will be counted, observed, profiled, and induced to visit again. It is this function of television which the ratings companies observe and quantify. They simplify and tell advertisers that an estimated audience of a few million might have been exposed to their products advertised on a particular time slot. It is a simple economic game, and winning the game is very important, especially when each point drop in rating may mean a loss of $50 million a year to a network. The quest for audiences, as reflected in Nielsen's meter and scale, has become a decisive force in programming; though, as we shall see, there are other forces at work.

Television as a platform, simultaneously for the auctioneer and the poet, has dethroned the elitist critic. When empirical observations become so important, the need for forewarnings or assessment by an ivory tower critic who has contemptuous disregard for the housewife, the teenager, the senior citizen, or the harassed salesman relaxing with a can of beer is not so pressing. The auctioneer and the artist have both benefited from television, but the critic has lost ground. One is awed by the authority of the theater critic of <u>The New York Times</u> or the London <u>Times</u>, but in television Nielsen has usurped the authority of the critic and has relegated him or her to a secondary role. Each medium has its own prophet and critic. Nielsen is the prophet and the critic in a society where an empirical mode of thought is the dominant mode and where measurement, not authority, is all.

What ratings do not measure is also important. Ratings do not tell in absolute terms how valuable or popular a

The Ways of Nielsen

program is. It is only in relation to time slot and competition that we understand ratings. For instance, if "Dallas" were pitted against a highly anticipated mini-series or sportscast, its ratings would reveal its relative strength in a competitive space-time domain. Next week a clawing and wrenching cliffhanger might zoom its ratings against weak competition in the same time slot. Change of time slot changed the ratings of "The Dick Van Dyke Show," "Hawaii Five-O," "M*A*S*H," and many others. Some shows, like "Hill Street Blues," take time to build their ratings; in other words, audiences need time to assimilate the new drama into their existing taste preferences. Low ratings do not necessarily mean failure; probably they mean a need to change programming strategy and to conduct a greater study of the competition, audience demographics, and taste preferences.

Ratings do not assess how deep is the audience's satisfaction with a particular program. But repetitive ratings patterns do show the abiding tastes of the audience, and creators and producers use them as blueprints for future success, and for access to the desired audience. As M.G. Cantor has said, "The system as it exists may be the most efficient for reaching the audience desired, but it allows little direct input from the audience into the creative process."[17]

This blueprinting function of ratings helps the industry to cope with environmental turbulence by suggesting formula programming. Formulas systematize audience tastes into predictable patterns or habitual behavior; a program's success continues so long as a particular mode of consciousness of the audience continues to sustain it. Translated into blueprints and formulas, ratings solve the problem of television's voracious appetite for material. As R.L. Brown has suggested:

> The usual answer to this problem [chronic shortage of new material], of course, has been to reuse the same, basic artistic elements again and again, refurbishing and re-combining them so as to lend the newer versions the required appearance of novelty .... The creative task now becomes that of fitting these elements together (no doubt with the addition of some genuinely new components) into a satisfactory gestalt.... Saleability may also, of course, be

more easily guaranteed if story elements already tested in the market are employed.[18]

This blueprinting function is not necessarily a disadvantage. The artist does not have to devise his or her boundaries because formula provides such constraints, and he or she is free to conjure up new creative possibilities and also to depart from formulaic constraints and create new blueprints.

GUARDIANS OF PUBLIC TASTE

Can the poet's voice be heard in the din of the rat race for ratings? Television imposes so many diverse constraints upon creative artists that it is a tribute to the human spirit that so much remains possible on television. The time itself --a half hour to sixty minutes--is a terrible constraint. But considering television's capacity for narrative compression and viewers' ability to leapfrog and imaginatively close loops and gaps, artists have turned such constraints into opportunities.

The pressure of ratings and the increased risk evidenced by rising program costs have dulled the possibilities for fully exploiting the medium. The ratings war leads to tried formulas for success, and since very few creators have been successful in television dramatic programming, the field is dominated by a handful of people like Aaron Spelling, Grant Tinker, Norman Lear, Garry Marshall, Lee Rich, Bud Yorkin, and Richard Levinson. An individual's or company's past record of success becomes an important determinant for network acceptance of a new series or program. A newcomer has little chance of making a breakthrough in television. It is more important for networks to build and reinforce existing relations with audiences rather than to experiment with new talent. Consequently, the patents, formulas, and blueprints devised by creators and producers to hook audiences have brought about monotony in dramatic offerings. One cannot talk of the artistic growth of Norman Lear in the same way that one traces Shakespeare's growth from the early comedies through the tragedies to his last plays. Hollywood television creators and producers are given to self-imitation, prisoners of their gilded formulas.

The other constraint on programming is the internal

control exercised by the television networks' standards and practices departments. These departments evaluate and make suggestions at various levels of the production process, from the proposal through the final program. All motion pictures are edited for television, and supposedly offensive dialogue and scenes are deleted. The networks' general attitude is that "unless there is an overriding dramatic justification," networks should "avoid the use of profanity, words of obvious disrespect, and obscene or vulgar language."

A network undergoes agonizing internal trials and tribulations when faced with the dilemma of airing a highly promising show which crosses the bounds of decency, according to their standards and practices; such was the case with CBS' decision on the telecasting of Joseph Papp's Broadway play Sticks and Bones and Michael Ritchie's film "Smile." But these qualms vanish very conveniently when networks face the brutal demands of the ratings. There was more sexual explicitness in "Three's Company," "The Dukes of Hazzard," and "Charlie's Angels" than the network's standards and practices would customarily allow, but the highly popular shows brought good ratings, and morality was given short shrift. Only when external pressure groups make demands upon networks do standards and practices departments become aroused to censorial action, usually because these groups threaten to boycott the companies that sponsor the programs or are heavy buyers of TV time. Some victims of pressure groups were programs like "The Untouchables," "Police Woman," Norman Lear's "Mr. Dugan," Arthur Miller's "Playing for Time," "The Promised Land," and "East of Eden." Today pressure groups have become better organized; instead of approaching the networks they launch campaigns against advertisers like General Foods, Procter & Gamble, etc. One such organizer is Reverend Donald Wildmon, whose powerful group, Coalition for Better Television, confronts networks on such issues as sexual permissiveness, religious values, and violence.

Thus Nielsen ratings must be evaluated and understood in the context of the social forces pressuring the networks not to violate public standards. In a society where free speech and free enterprise constitute the controlling center, pressure groups have as much freedom to act as artists have to create; what shapes public communication and commercial television is a series of compromises between the networks' need for ratings, producer-creators' demand for freedom, and audiences' need to protect their traditions.

In spite of these contrary pressures, interference, and informal censorship, television lately has been exploring controversial topics like rape, incest, nuclear war, divorce, and child abuse. Sportscasting of the Olympic Games, documentaries, mini-series, special reports, etc., are some of the proud achievements of commercial television. As channels proliferate and America becomes a wired town, so-called offensive programs will be relegated to specialized channels, and commercial television will be forced to seek out excellence for its survival.

In short, though the ratings play a significant role in determining television programming, other crucial forces cannot be ignored. The artist and the auctioneer both exist in the public domain.

SOME FACTS ABOUT AMERICAN TELEVISION*

- **TV Households**

    There are more than 84.9 million homes equipped with at least one set; 91 percent of these households have color sets, and 57 percent have two or more sets. The total number of viewers is more than 220 million.

- **Peak Viewing Periods**

    Viewing of television programs increases through the day and is highest between 8:00 and 10:00 p.m. Afterwards it decreases. Winter attracts more people to television.

- **Daily TV Viewing**

    Americans viewed television an average of 6 hours and 55 minutes a day during the 1983-84 season. February is the highest viewing month, and July is the lowest viewing month.

---

*Source: Nielsen Report on Television, 1985.

- Older Women and Teens

    Women view more television than men; older men and women view more than young people. Teenagers watch the least.

- Prime Time

    Women have the greatest share of prime-time viewing. From 8:30 to 9:00 p.m. is the heaviest television viewing time. Sunday evenings attract the most viewers.

- The Most Popular Genre

    In 1984 adventure programming was the most popular genre, followed by feature film and suspense/mystery drama.

- Viewing Choices

    There were 1,194 television stations as of January 1985, according to the Federal Communications Commission. Of these, 904 stations are commercial and 290 are public. According to the Nielsen Homevideo Index, there are 9,005 cable systems.

Some 64 percent of U.S. households could receive nine or more TV stations. Considering cable channels and over-the-air station channels, U.S. households have the widest options and choices in the world; 83 percent can receive nine or more channels and 29 percent can receive more than twenty.

NOTES

1. William Stephenson, The Play Theory of Mass Communication (Chicago: The University of Chicago Press, 1967), pp. 64-65.
2. Denis McQuail, Mass Communication Theory (Beverly Hills: Sage Publications, 1983), p. 149.
3. Ibid., p. 153.
4. G.H. Lewis, "Taste Cultures and Their Compositions: Towards a New Theoretical Perspective," E. Katz and T. Szecsko, eds., Mass Media and Social Change (Beverly Hills: Sage Publications, 1980), pp. 201-217.

5. H.T. Himmelweit and J. Swift, "Continuities and Discontinuities in Media Taste," *Journal of Social Issues* 21:6 (1976), pp. 133-156.
6. G.H. Lewis, "Taste Cultures," p. 205.
7. Stephenson, pp. 64-65.
8. Meyer Weinberg, *TV and America: The Morality of Hard Cash* (New York: Ballantine Books, 1962), p. 197-213.
9. *Nielsen Station Index*, (Northbrook: A.C. Nielsen Company, 1981-82), p. 6. Roger D. Wimmer and Joseph R. Dominik, *Mass Media Research* (Belmont: Wadsworth, 1983), pp. 195-271.
10. "Description of Methodology" (New York: Arbitron Ratings Company, Feb. 1, 1985), p. 40.
11. Sydney W. Head, *Broadcasting in America* (Boston: Houghton Mifflin, 1982), p. 294.
12. Sydney W. Head, *Broadcasting in America*, p. 297.
13. Fred F. Kerlinger, *Foundations of Behavioral Research*, 2nd ed. (New York: Holt, Rinehart and Winston, 1973), p. 118.
14. Kerlinger, *Foundations of Behavioral Research*, pp. 123-124.
15. "The Nielsen Ratings in Perspective" (Northbrook: Nielsen Media Research, 1980).
16. F.C. Emery and E.L. Trist, "The Causal Texture of Organizational Environments," *Human Relations* 18 (1965), pp. 21-31.
17. M.G. Cantor, *Prime-Time Television, Content and Control* (Beverly Hills: Sage, 1980), p. 102.
18. R.L. Brown, "The Creative Process in the Popular Arts," *International Social Journal* 20 (1968), pp. 613-624.

Chapter Fourteen

CONCLUSION

The phenomenon of television broacasting in America--with its episodic-serial format; its rhythm and recurrence imitating the hours and the days of the week; its thirty-second commercials; its station breaks and news breaks; its to-and-fro switching between dramatization and monitoring, between mimesis and diegesis, between pictorial representation and verbal narrative--has been determined by the state of technology and the society's controlling center, the centralizing symbol, the free marketplace of goods and ideas. As an interacting whole in a totality, television performs its specific and concrete role by the simultaneity of its differentiation from the other structured wholes and its incorporation of what it differs from. In this mutually conditioning environment, television's freedom is limited by consensus about the normal. In other words, the reality presented on American television about socio-political events is only an American version of reality. It may not have anything to do with the truth. In appearance, an event may not have occurred at all, according to American television, whereas in fact that event may have been of crucial significance for another society.

This reality is beautifully illustrated by Michael Arlen, who, unfortunately, calls it merely American television's parochialism:

> One is what we might call the parochial factor, the continued insistence of television news that complicated international situations be defined in American terms whenever possible. Thirty years ago, in Boston, we used to joke about the parochialism of Hearst's _American_ (with its "Hub Man Lands on

> Omaha Beach" headlines), but the story of our coverage of El Salvador is that nothing really exists there unless an American is involved. Recently, an entire news story revolved around an American soldier who had been shot in the leg. At times like that, you feel the network news reporting on international affairs is on the level of a Mickey Rooney movie....[1]

What Arlen calls American television's parochialism is the fact and the substance of the television phenomenon. Does it mean that truth never gets reported in television? The answer to this question is probably linked with how social change takes place. Primarily, there are two forces which bring about changes in a society: technology and social oppression. Nowadays the development of technology initially is reported in specialized professional journals. But as the industrial and business sectors begin to perceive the technology's advantages for moneymaking (which they shape in terms of public benefits) the facts of the new technology are transformed into news for television. Because of the eternal cycle, the perpetual recurrence of news through the episodic-serialization-dramatization process (another element of television), the new technology is assimilated in the theater of the mind, the public consciousness: it is normalized and domesticated.

Similarly, social oppression remains an unheard cry, a private sigh--unless it is organized into collective defiance with an agenda to threaten the consensus about the normal in society, as happened in the history of the trade unions, Martin Luther King, Jr.'s protest movement of the sixties, the anti-Vietnam War movement, etc. Only when social oppression, generating an organized defiance, begins to threaten some cherished aspect of a society does television becomes its witness, its reluctant spokesman--as happened during the Vietnam War era. As James Reston aptly put it:

> Still in defense of television: The newspapers were onto the tragedies of Joe McCarthy, Jack Kennedy's adventure at the Bay of Pigs, the racial violence in the South and the deception of the U.S. government in Vietnam and Watergate long before the television and radio reporters were paying much attention.

Conclusion

processing. The human mind constantly moves between abstractions and dramatizations, between conceptualization and operationalization; television, because it is the enemy of obscurity, density, and difficulty, dramatizes the most abstruse thought, thus aiding and hastening the assimilation of new facts. Television's impact upon dropouts and minorities (who cannot learn in the class room), on the illiterate masses of Asia and Africa (or functional illiterates in the United States) is unfathomable at present. But one sees great hope for mankind in the industry's profit-motivated need to wed computer technology with television--which will eventually put into question present learning methods and, consequently, the whole print establishment. This conclusion is relevant to the main argument because television is not only a broadcast receiver but also a monitor for video and computers, for live events like a football game, an astronaut's walk in space, the birth of a baby, the death of apartheid, and Live-Aid for Africa. More and more abstract mathematical and scientific theories and concepts are being turned into television images and illustrations, which will facilitate learning and discovery--much as turning abstract human miseries into spoken images increases our understanding and compassion.

With its propensity for serialization and segmentation, television does seem to trivialize life, much as an absurdist dramatist seems to trivialize life by piling up absurdities. But the joke of an absurdist can be as profound as the invocation of an epic poet. Trivialization is a form of redefinition of existing categories. Redefinition threatens the establishment, and the potential for change is established.

The rising tide of expectations from television--stability and change, art and drama, news and entertainment, education and sports--has made inadequate the application of any one theoretical or critical model. A complex phenomenon like television can best be understood and appreciated by investigating the controlling center of American society--the free marketplace of goods and ideas. This calls for a pluralistic approach, an invitation to humanists and empiricists to retool their methodologies and look afresh.

* * *

"That was a way of putting it--not very satisfactory:
A periphrastic study in a worn-out poetical fashion,
Leaving one still with the intolerable wrestle
With words and meanings."
--<u>East Coker</u>

NOTES

1. Michael Arlen, "Post-Vietnam Television News," <u>Harper</u> (August 1984), p. 26.
2. James Reston, "Politics and Television," <u>The New York Times</u> (June 20, 1984), sec. A, p. 27.
3. Glen G. Strodthof, Robert P. Hawkins, and A. Clay Schoenfeld, "Media Role in a Social Movement: A Model of Ideology Diffusion," <u>Journal of Communication</u> 33 (Spring 1985), pp. 134-153.
4. James W. Carey, "A Cultural Approach to Communication," <u>Communication</u> 2 (1975), pp. 1-22.

SELECTED BIBLIOGRAPHY

Abrams, M.H. A Glossary of Literary Terms. 3rd ed. New York: Holt, Rinehart and Winston, 1975.

Adler, Richard P., ed. All in the Family. New York: Praeger Publishers, 1979.

Allen, Robert C. Speaking of Soap Operas. Chapel Hill: The University of North Carolina Press, 1985.

Allison, G.T. Essence of Decision. Boston: Little, Brown, 1971.

Arlen, Michael. "Post-Vietnam Television News," Harper. August 1984.

Ashmore, H.S. "Uncertain Oracles," Center of Magazine. November/December, 1970.

Baldwin, Thomas F., and D. Stevens McVoy. Cable Communication. Englewood Cliffs, NJ: Prentice-Hall, 1983.

Barnouw, Erik. Documentary. New York: Oxford University Press, 1974.

Barrett, Marvin, ed. Survey of Broadcast Journalism, 1970-1971. New York: Grosset and Dunlap, 1971.

Barthes, Roland. Image--Music--Text, Stephen Heath, trans. New York: Hill and Wang, 1977.

Beckett, Samuel. A Collection of Critical Essays, Martin Esslin, ed. Englewood Cliffs, NJ: Prentice-Hall, 1965.

Bennett, W. Lance, Lynne A. Gressett, and William Halton. "Repairing the News: A Case Study of the News Paradigm," Journal of Communication 35, Spring 1985.

Berelson, B. Content Analysis in Communication Research, Glencoe, IL: Free Press, 1952.

Berger, Arthur Asa. Media Analysis Techniques, Beverly Hills: Sage Publications, 1983.

Bluem, A. William, <u>Documentary in American Television</u>, New York: Hastings House, 1965.

Bogart, Leo. "Television News as Entertainment." In <u>The Entertainment Functions of Television</u>, P.H. Tannenbaum, ed. Hillsdale: Lawrence Erebaum Associates, 1980.

Booth, Wayne C. "The Company We Keep: Self-Making in Imaginative Art, Old and New," <u>Daedalus</u>, Fall 1982.

Bottomore, T.B., and Maximilien Rubel, eds. <u>Karl Marx: Selected Writings in Sociology and Social Philosophy</u>, New York: McGraw-Hill, 1964.

Brown, R.L. "The Creative Process in the Popular Arts," <u>International Social Journal</u> 20, 1968.

Buñuel, Luis. "Cinema: An Instrument of Poetry," <u>Theatre Arts</u>, 46, July 1962.

Butcher, S.H. <u>Aristotle's Theory of Poetry and Fine Arts</u>. London: MacMillan, 1923.

Cantor, M.G. <u>Prime-Time Television, Content and Control</u>. Beverly Hills: Sage, 1980.

Cantor, Murial G., and Suzanne Pingree. <u>The Soap Opera</u>. Beverly Hills: Sage Publications, 1983.

Carey, James. "A Cultural Approach to Communication," <u>Communication</u> 2, 1975.

Cawelti, John G. <u>Adventure, Mystery and Romance</u>. Chicago: The University of Chicago Press, 1976.

Chafee, Zachariah, Jr. <u>Government and Mass Communication</u>. 2 vols. Chicago: University of Chicago Press, 1974.

Chatman, Seymour. <u>Story and Discourse</u>. Ithaca, NY: Cornell University Press, 1978.

Christian, Clifford G., and James W. Carey. "The Logic and Aims of Qualitative Research." In Guido H. Stempel III and Bruce H. Westly, eds. <u>Research Methods in Mass Communication</u>. Englewood Cliffs, NJ: Prentice-Hall, 1981.

Culler, Jonathan. <u>Structuralist Poetics: Structuralism, Linguistics and the Study of Literature</u>. Ithaca, NY: Cornell University Press, 1976.

<u>Current Biography Year Book</u>. New York: The H.W. Wilson Company, 1974.

Selected Bibliography

Cussella, Louis P. "Real-Fiction Versus Historical Reality: Rhetorical Purification in Kent State--The Docudrama," Communication Quarterly, 30(3), Summer 1982.

Davidson, Bill. "Fact or Fiction--Television Docudrama." In Richard P. Adler, ed. Understanding Television. New York: Praeger, 1981.

Dickson, Keith. Toward Utopia. Oxford: Oxford University Press, 1978.

Donahue Transcript #05285. Multimedia Entertainment, Inc., 1984.

Doran, Madeleine. Endeavors of Art. Madison: University of Wisconsin Press, 1954.

Edmondson, Madeleine, and David Rounds. From Mary Noble to Mary Hartman. New York: Stein & Day, 1976.

Eisenstein, Sergei. The Film Sense. Jay Leyda, trans. and ed. New York: Harcourt Brace Jovanovich, 1975.

Eisner, Joel, and David Krinsky. Television Comedy Series. Jefferson, NC: McFarland and Company, 1984.

Ellis, J. Visible Fictions: Cinema, Television, Video. London: Routledge & Kegan Paul, 1982.

Emery F.C., and E.L. Trist. "The Causal Texture of Organizational Environments," Human Relations 18:1965.

Esslin, Martin. The Age of Television. San Francisco: W.H. Freeman and Company, 1982.

Esslin, Martin. "Aristotle and the Advertiser: The Television Commercial Considered as a Form of Drama." Horace Newcomb, ed. Television: The Critical View, 3rd ed. New York: Oxford University Press, 1982.

Ettema, James S. "The Organizational Context of Creativity." In James S. Ettema and D. Charles Whitney, eds. Individuals in Mass Media Organizations: Creativity and Constraint. Beverly Hills: Sage Publications, 1982.

Field, Stanley. The Mini-documentary. Blue Ridge Summit, PA: Tab Books, 1975.

Fiske, John, and John Hartley. Reading Television. London: Methuen, 1978.

Foster, E.M. Aspects of the Novel. London: Edward Arnold & Co., 1927.

Freud, Sigmund. Civilization and Its Discontents. New York: W.W. Norton, 1962.

Fromm, Erich. The Forgotten Language: An Introduction to the Understanding of Dreams, Fairy Tales and Myths. New York: Grove Press, 1957.

Frye, Northrop. Anatomy of Criticism. Princeton, NJ: Princeton University Press, 1975.

Gazzaniga, M.S. The Bisected Brain. New York: Appleton-Century-Crofts, 1970.

Gerbner, G. "The Television World of Violence." In Mass Media and Violence, D. Lang, R. Baker, and S. Ball, eds. Washington, DC: U.S. Government Printing Office, 1969.

Gitlin, Todd. Inside Prime Time. New York: Pantheon Books, 1983.

Gross, Lynn Schafer. The New Television Technologies. Dubuque, IA: Wm. C. Brown Company, 1983.

Grotowsky, Jerzy. "Towards a Poor Theatre." In Bernard F. Dukore, ed. Dramatic Theory and Criticism: Greeks to Grotowski. New York: Holt, Rinehart and Winston, 1974.

Guthrie, Tyrone. "Theatre and Television." In The Eighth Art. New York: Holt, Rinehart and Winston, 1962.

Guthrie, Tyrone. My Life in the Theatre. New York, McGraw-Hill, 1959.

Hadas, Moses. "Climates of Criticism." In The Eighth Art. New York: Holt, Rinehart and Winston, 1962.

Hall, Stuart. "Signification, Representation, Ideology: Althusser and the Post-Structuralist Debates." CSMS, 2(2), June 1985.

Hall, Stuart. "A World at One with Itself." In The Manufacture of News, Stanley Cohen and Jock Young, eds. Beverly Hills: Sage Publications, 1973.

Harrington, Michael. The Other America. Baltimore: Penguin Books, 1963.

Head, Sydney W. Broadcasting in America. Boston: Houghton Mifflin, 1982.

Himmelweit, H.T., and J. Swift, "Continuities and Discontinuities in Media Taste." Journal of Social Issues, 32(6), 1976.

Selected Bibliography

Hobson, Dorothy. *Cross Roads: The Drama of a Soap Opera*. London: Methuen, 1982.

Hoffer, Thomas W., and Richard Alan Nelson. "Evolution of Docudrama on American Television Networks: A Content Analysis, 1966-1978." *The Southern Speech Communication Journal*, XLV (2), Winter 1980.

Hotchner, A.H. "One Thing After Another--The Adaptation." In *The Eighth Art*. New York: Holt, Rinehart and Winston, 1962.

Hugh, Arthur. "Trials and Tribulations--Thirty Years of Sitcom." In *Understanding Television*. Richard P. Adler, ed. New York: Praeger Publishers, 1981.

Kahn, Frank J., ed. *Documents of American Broadcasting*. 4th ed. Englewood Cliffs, NJ, Prentice-Hall, 1984.

Kaminsky, Stuart M., with Jeffrey H. Mahan. *American Television Genre*. Chicago: Nelson-Hall, 1985.

Katzman, N. "Television Soap Operas." *Public Opinion Quarterly*, 36:1972, pp. 200-12.

Kerlinger, Fred F. *Foundations of Behavioral Research*. New York: Holt, Rinehart and Winston, 1973.

Koestler, Arthur. *The Act of Creation*, London: Macmillan, 1964.

Kowet, Don, and Sally Bedell. "How CBS News Broke the Rules and 'Got' General Westmoreland." *TV Guide*, May 29, 1982.

Kracauer, Siegfried. *Theory of Film: The Redemption of Physical Reality*. New York: Oxford University Press, 1960.

Krippendorff, K. *Content Analysis in Communication Research*. Glencoe: Free Press, 1952.

Kuhn, Thomas. *The Structure of Scientific Revolution*. 2nd ed. Chicago: University of Chicago Press, 1970.

Langer, Susanne, K. *Feeling and Form*. New York: Scribner, 1953.

Lewis, G.H. "Taste Cultures and Their Compositions: Towards a New Theoretical Perspective." In *Mass Media and Social Change*. E. Katz and T. Szecsko, eds. Beverly Hills: Sage Publications, 1980.

Littlejohn, David. "Thoughts on Television Criticism." In *Understanding Television*, Richard Adler, ed. New York: Praeger, 1981.

Marc, David. *Demographic Vistas*. Philadelphia: University of Pennsylvania Press, 1984.

McLuhan, Marshall. *The Mechanical Bride*. Boston: Beacon, 1978.

McQuail, Denis. *Mass Communication Theory*, Beverly Hills: Sage Publication, 1983.

Meiklejohn, Alexander. *Free Speech and Its Relation to Self-Government*. Reprinted in *Political Freedom*. New York: Harper & Row, 1960.

Meyrowitz, Joshua. *No Sense of Place: The Impact of Electronic Media on Social Behavior*. New York: Oxford University Press, 1985.

Mitz, Rick. *The Great TV Sitcom Book*. New York: Richard Marek, 1980.

Morrow, Lance. "The History Devouring Device: Television and the Docudrama." *Media and Methods* 15, October 1978.

Musburger, Robert B. "Setting the Stage for the Television Docudrama." *Journal of Popular Film and Television* 13, Summer 1985.

Newcomb, Horace, and Robert S. Alley. *The Producer's Medium*. New York: Oxford University Press, 1983.

Nicoll, Allardyce. *British Drama*. 5th ed. New York: Barnes and Noble, 1963.

Ogburn, William F. *On Cultural and Social Change*. Otis Dudley Duncan, ed. Chicago: The University of Chicago Press, 1964.

Pollan, Michael. "Can 'Hill Street Blues' Rescue NBC?" *Channel of Communication*, April/May 1983.

Pool, Ithiel de Sola. *Technologies of Freedom*. Cambridge, MA: The Belknap Press of Harvard University Press, 1983.

Powers, Ron. *The Newscasters*. New York: St. Martin's Press, 1977.

Propp, Vladimir. *Morphology of Folk Tales*. Austin: University of Texas Press, 1968.

Reiss, David S. *M*A*S*H*. Indianapolis: The Bobbs-Merrill Company, 1980.

Reston, James. "Politics and Television." *The New York Times*, June 20, 1984.

Rimmon-Kenan, S. *Narrative Fiction: Contemporary Poetics*. London: Methuen, 1983.

Rotha, Paul. <u>Documentary Film</u>. 3rd ed. New York: Hastings House, 1952.

Sartre, J.P. <u>Being and Nothing</u>. New York: Pocket Books, 1966.

Saussure, Ferdinand de. <u>Course in General Linguistics</u>, New York: McGraw-Hill, 1966.

Stedman, Raymond William. <u>The Serials: Suspense and Drama by Installments</u>. Norman: University of Oklahoma Press, 1977.

Stephenson, William. <u>The Play Theory of Mass Communication</u>. Chicago: The University of Chicago Press, 1967.

Stromgren, Richard L., and Martin F. Norden. <u>Movies: A Language in Light</u>. Englewood Cliffs, NJ: Prentice-Hall, 1984.

Styan, J.L. <u>Drama, Stage and Audience</u>. London: Oxford University Press, 1975.

Southern, Richard. <u>The Seven Ages of Theatre</u>. New York: Hill and Wang, 1961.

Tannenbaum P.H., ed. <u>The Entertainment Functions of Television</u>. Hillsdale: Lawrence Erebaum Associates, 1980.

Thorburn, David. "Television Melodrama." In <u>Understanding Television</u>, Richard P. Adler, ed. New York: Praeger, 1981.

Tocqueville, Alexis de. <u>Democracy in America</u>. New York: Knopf, 1945.

Toll, Robert C. <u>The Entertainment Machine</u>. New York: Oxford University Press, 1982.

Tuchman, Gaye. <u>Making News: A Study in the Construction of Reality</u>. New York: Free Press, 1978.

Turow, Joseph. "Unconventional Programs on Commercial Television: An Organizational Perspective." In James S. Ettema and P. Charles Whitney, eds. <u>Individuals in Mass Media Organizations: Creativity and Constraint</u>. Beverly Hills: Sage Publications, 1982.

Weaver, Paul. "TV News and Newspaper News." In <u>Understanding Television</u>. Richard P. Adler, ed. New York: Praeger, 1981.

Weinberg, Meyer. <u>TV and America: The Morality of Hard Cash</u>. New York: Ballantine books, 1962.

Wertheim, Arthur Frank. <u>Radio Comedy</u>. New York: Oxford University Press, 1979.

Williams, Raymond. *Marxism and Literature*. New York: Oxford University Press, 1977.

Williams, Raymond. *Drama from Ibsen to Brecht*. New York: Oxford University Press, 1968.

INDEX

ABC 156
"A.D." 2
AT&T 43, 83
Accuracy in Media (AIM) 177, 178
"Adam" 3, 189
"Addams Family, The" 103
addressability, television 54
<u>Adventure, Mystery and Romance</u> 22
adventure stories 4
"Adventures of Ozzie and Harriet" 106
advertisers xi
"Advice to a Young Scientist" xiii
aesthetics 18
"After-M*A*S*H" 103
Agricultural Act of 1933 187
AIDS 251
Alda, Alan 111
Aldrin, Edwin 191
Alexander the Great 103
"Alice" 3
"All in the Family" 104, 108, 115-117, 120, 130, 132, 135, 137, 220, 224, 226
"All My Children" 89, 91
Allen, Fred 102
Allen, Gracie 102
Allen, Irwin 204
Allen, Robert C. 9, 10, 11, 22, 84, 86, 87, 97, 124
Allen, Woody 102
Alley, Robert S. 5, 38, 127, 131
Allison, Graham 126
    Allison Model 126
Altman, Robert 110
"America: A Personal History of the United States" 213
American Dream 25, 41, 43
"American Parade" 154
"Amos 'n' Andy" 104, 105, 118, 139
"Anatomy of a Smear" 173
<u>Anatomy of Criticism</u> 2, 22
Andrews, Cecil 159
Andropov, Yuri 177

"Andy Griffith Show" 203
<u>Anna Karenina</u> 223
anthologies, dramatic anthologies 129
Antiope 51
Antonio, Emile de 173
Appalachian 9
Arbitron 234, 238, 241
Archer, Jeffrey 200
archetypal criticism xiv
Aristophanes 103
Aristotle, Aristotelian xii, xv, 2, 3
   Aristotle's model 211
   Aristotelian theatre 187
Arlen, Michael 39, 138, 249, 250
Armstrong Circle Theater 186
Arnold, Matthew xiii
Arthur, Beatrice 139
Aryan Symbol 7
Ashcroft, Peggy 213
Asner, Ed 134
"Atlanta Child Murders, The" 192-193, 195, 203
Auden, W. H. 165
audience, television, as markets of taste 228-233
   audience research 231, 232
   television audience and theater audience 229
Australia 215
author-auteur xiv, 10
authorial approach 5-6

BBC 38
Bacon, Francis 21
Baldwin, Thomas F. 55
"Barney Miller" 103, 108
Barnouw, Erik 170, 171
Barthes, Roland xii, 39
Battle of Britain 201
Bay of Pigs, The 193, 250
Beatles 194
Beckett, Samuel, <u>Waiting for Godot</u> 66, 110
Bedell, Sally 39
Beethoven, Ludwig van 33
Benny, Jack 102
Benton and Bowles 133
Berelson, B. 19, 20, 23
Berger, Arthur Asa ix, 18, 22
Berle, Milton 102
Beta 50
"Betty and Bob" 84
"Betty White Show" 135
"Beverly Hillbillies, The" 104, 107-108

Index 265

Big Apple, the 9
Bill of Rights 55
"Biography" 176
"Biography of a Bookie Joint" 177
Bisected Brain, The 37
black hole 35
blacks iv, 20
Bluem, A. William 171, 188, 189
"Bob Newhart Show, The" 135
Bochco, Steven 5, 75, 130, 132, 136
Bogart, Leo 33, 39, 157
Booth, Wayne C. 180, 203
Bottomore, T. B. 19, 20, 23
Boy George 228
"Brady Bunch, The" 103
Brecht, Bertolt 72, 151, 167, 187, 224
   Caucasian Chalk Circle 77
   "verfremdungeffekt" 80, 188
Britain 13, 25, 167, 210, 211, 214
British Empire 212
British Parliament 178
British Raj xi
Brokaw, Tom 143, 148, 150
Brook-Burns team 112, 113, 114, 134
Brooks, James L. 132
Brown, R. L. 243
Buddha 165
Bureau of the Census, The 237
Burns, Allan 132
Burns, George 102, 121
   "George Burns Comedy Week" 121, 129
Burns, Ken 179

CBN 45
CBS 27, 45, 112, 121, 153, 156, 158, 172, 200
   CBS Evening News 158
   CBS Morning News 158
   CBS News 182
   CBS Sunday News 158
CBS ARTS 45, 83
CBS v. General Westmoreland 60
CNN 30
C-Span 45
cable television 40, 44-46
cablecasting 45
Cambodia 174
Camus, Albert 108
Canada 165
Cantor, Muriel G. 86, 90, 125, 127, 131, 243
Capital City Communication 156

"Capitol" 65
Capra, Frank 167
Carey, James W. xvii, 226
Carrington, Blake 3, 24, 25, 30, 32
Carroll, Lewis, Alice in Wonderland 204
Carson, Johnny 102
Carsonian 24
Carter, President James 176
Catholic Church 215, 216
Cats 229
Cawelti, John G. 4, 6, 22, 65
Ceefax and Oracle 51
censorship 59
Chafee, Zechariah, Jr. 58
Chandler, Adam 3, 30
Chaplin, Charlie 102, 103
Charles, Prince, and Princess Diana 214
"Charlie's Angels" 245
Chatman, Seymour 206
Chicago 43
Chicago School, the xiii
China 4, 13, 25, 43, 64, 110, 156, 176
　　Chinese expansionism 174
Christian, Clifford G. xvii, 226
Christians 8
"Chronicle of a Summer" 170
Cinéma-vérité 169-170
Civilization and Its Discontents 16
cliffhangers 67
Coalition for Better Television 245
coaxial cables 42
Cochram, John 178
cognitive-affective terrain 36
Colby, Alexis 24
"Cold Turkey" 138
"Colgate Comedy Hour" 137
collective creativity 123-142
"Collision Course" 191
"Come Blow Your Horn" 138
commercials, and the structure of television drama 70-74
Communication Act of 1934, The 57
computer shopping 46
COMSAT 48
Conran, Shirley, Lace 207
content analysis xiv, 19-20
Cooke, Alistair 213-215
"Coronation Street" 90
Cosby, Bill 118-120
　　"Bill Cosby Show, The" 118
　　"Cosby Show, The" 70, 105, 118-120
Costello, Robert 188

Index

counter-documentary 177
Course in General Linguistics 22
Cousteau, Jacques 165
"Cover Up" 67
"Creation of the Universe" 181
creativity 123-128
critic, television 218-227
   empirical critic 219
   humanist critic 219
   qualifications 219
critical theory xiii
Cronin, A. J., The Citadel 202
Cronkite, Walter xiv, 152, 153
"Cross Roads" 90
Cuba 156, 193
cultivation analysis 19
cultural lag 41, 52-53
cultural programming 52
cultural text 8
culture, definition 13
Curtis, Dan 201, 205, 210

"Dallas" 12, 65, 68, 90, 92-94, 243
Darrach, Brad 119
Darwin, Charles 14
data processing xv
Davis, Peter 170, 173, 177
"Day After, The" 26
defense mechanism 15
delocalized taste collectivities, television audience as xvi, 228-233
denouement xv
deregulation policy 47
Desdemona 36
Dettlinger, Chet 203
Dewey, John xiii
dialectical tension xv
"Dick Van Dyke Show, The" 243
Diem, President Ngo Dinh 174, 193
Dien Bien Phu, the battle of 174
digital television 40
"Dinosaur!" 179
Direct Broadcast Satellite 48
direct cinema 169-170
Disney Walt 45
   Disneyland 154
"Divorce American Style" 138
docudrama xvi, 129, 130, 184-197
documentaries xvi, 164-183
domestic comedy xv
Dow Jones Cable News 45

drama, Elizabethan 226
dramatic mode of communication xiv, 27-29
dramatic serial 82-99
Drew, Robert 170
"Drifters" 165
"Dugan" 245
"Dukes of Hazzard, The" 66, 245
"Dynasty" 12, 32, 68, 90, 94-96

"E/R" 90
ESPN 45
"E.T." 2, 35
"Early Frost, An" 175
"East of Eden" 245
ecological factor 1
Edmondson, Madeleine 85
ego, defined 15
Egypt 192
Einstein, Albert 14
Eisenstein, Sergei 27, 39, 166, 168, 170
El Salvador 33
Electra complex 14
Electronic Media Rating Council, The 241
electronic technologies 41
Eliot, T. S. 203
Elizabethan era 184
Ellis, J. 76
Ellison, Richard 174
Emery, F. C. 242
Emmy award 106
empiricism xiii
   empirical critic 219
   empirical mode xiv
   empiricist xii, xiii
   empiricist credo xiii
Englishmen 53
Entertainment Channel 45
epic 201
Eros 45
Esslin, Martin 28, 29, 30, 39, 73
Ethiopia 259
Ethiopians 29
ethnic minority xiv
Ettema, James S. 126
Europe 201
   The Europeans 200-201
evangelism 1
Ewing, J. R. 3, 24, 29
"Explorer" 165, 179

Index

FCC, The 47, 48, 57, 124, 221
Fairness Doctrine, The 42, 43, 49, 56-60, 158, 177, 221
"Falcon Crest" 90
Falwell, Jerry 94
"Fatal Vision" 200
"Father Knows Best" 104, 105
"Fear on Trial" 130
Federal Radio Act of 1927 57
Federal Trade Commission 241
Ferris, Charles 54
Ferris, Timothy 181
fiber optics 40
Field, Stanley 176
Fierstein, Harvey 175
Financial Network 45
First Amendment, the 26, 41, 54, 56, 60, 83, 221
"First Camera" 154
"First Hundred Years, The" 85
Fiske, John 9, 38
Flaherty, Robert 54, 165, 180
Ford, John 167
Ford Motor Company 234
"Ford Star Review, The" 137
formulaic literature 4, 5
formulaic television 64-69
   the death of a formula 70
Forsythe, John 94
Foxx, Redd 138
France 5, 13, 201
Frankfurt 25
free enterprise xiv, 144
free marketplace of goods and ideas, the xi, 24, 56, 60, 226, 231, 241, 249, 253
free press 56
   freedom of the press 59
free speech xii, 41, 56, 58
Freud, Sigmund xiii, 14, 15, 16, 17, 22
   Freudian methods xiv
   Freudian psychoanalytical model 14
Friendly, Fred 170-172
Fromm, Erich 15, 22
Frye, Northrop 2, 3, 5, 22
function, functions 8, 17
   the choric-bardic function of television 26
   the delphic-oracular function of television 2

Gadney, Reg 193
Gallup Poll 153
Gandhi 196, 211

Gardner, James E. 121
Gazzaniga, M. S. 37, 39
Gelbart, Larry 110, 132
General Electric 83, 147, 156
General Foods 245
General Motors 7, 234
generic approach 3-5
    generic codes 4
    generic formula xiv
George, Boy <u>see</u> Boy George
Gerbner, George 19, 23
Germans 58
Germany 167, 200
Gestalt 71, 180, 189
Gitlin, Todd 134
Glazer, George 155
Gleason, Jackie 106
"Goldbergs, The" 105
Golden Age of Comedy 121
"Golden Age of Television, The" 5
"Golden Girls, The" 120
"Gomer Pyle, USMC" 104
"Good Times" 137, 139
Gorbachev, Mikhail 177, 178
Gosden and Correll (creators of "Amos 'n' Andy") 118
"Greatest American Hero, The" 2
Greeks 14
    Greek Drama 26, 82
    Greek Theater 229
"Green Acres" 107
Grierson, John 165, 167, 170, 179, 180
Grotowski, Jerzy 82, 189
"Guiding Light" 68, 71, 75, 84, 85, 87, 95-99
Guthrie, Tyrone 62

Hadas, Moses 222
Hagman, Larry 94
Hall, Edward 185
Hall, Stuart 144, 145
Hamel, Veronica 79
Hamner, Earl 5
Hand, Learned xiii
Harrington, Michael 226
    <u>The Other America</u> 226
Hart, Bob 30
Hartley, John 9, 38
"Harvest of Shame" 177, 181
"Hawaii Five-O" 243
Head, Sydney W. 238
"Hearts and Minds" 170, 173

Index   271

hegemony xiv, 6, 13
Helen of Troy xii
Helms, Jesse 3, 147
Hemingway, Ernest 203, 204
　For Whom the Bell Tolls 203
Henning, Paul 108
"Here Comes the Bride" 107
"High School" 170, 176
Hill & Knowlton 155
"Hill Street Blues" 3, 5, 62, 63, 74-80, 132, 136, 169, 220, 243
　as a mock melodrama 76, 96, 99, 130
hillbilly 9
Himmelweit, H. T. 231
Hispanics 230
historical and chronicle plays 184
historical criticism 2
Hitler, Adolf 6, 103, 167, 168, 181, 201
Ho Chi Minh 174
Hoffer, Thomas W. 189
Holinshed, Raphael 185
holistic xiv
Hollywood 13, 52
Holocaust 179, 180, 186
Homer 189
"Honeymooners, The" 103, 105, 106-107, 108
Hoover, J. Edgar 193
Hope, Bob 102
"Hot L Baltimore" 137
Hotchner, A. H. 203, 204
"Hotel" 129
"Huey Long" 171
Huston, John 167

IBM 103
"I Dream of Jeannie" 103, 104
"I Love Lucy" 103, 105
"I Remember Mama" 105
Ibsen, Henrik 113, 168
id 15
ideology 13, 43, 225
"In the Year of the Pig" 173
"Incredible Hulk, The" 2
India 64, 211, 212, 213, 214
Indochina 174
"Inside Nazi Germany" 168
Ionesco, Eugène 115
Iran 25
Iranians 36
Ireland 159
Islamic orthodoxy 25

Israel 64
Italian Commedia xv

J. R. see Ewing, J. R.
Jackson, Michael 228
James, William xiii
Japan 4, 13, 94
Japanese 25
"Jeffersons, The" 104, 108, 118, 137, 139, 140
Jennings, Peter xv, 1, 24, 29
Jerusalem 34
"Jewel in the Crown, The" 198, 199, 205, 211-213, 216
Jews, European 7
"John and Yoko: A Love Story" 193-194, 195
Johnson, Karen 202
Johnson, President Lyndon 172
   The Great Society 174
<u>Jokes and Their Relation to the Unconscious</u> 16
Joyce, James 33
Judeo-Christian God 181

Kaiser, Robert G. 215
Kaminsky, Stuart M. 3, 4, 22
"Kane and Abel" 200
Katzman, N. 19
Keaton, Buster 102
Keats, John 27, 180
Kelly, Richard, <u>The Andy Griffith Show</u> 203
Kennedy, Jackie 193
Kennedy, John F. 30, 174, 175, 178, 250
Kennedy, Robert see "Robert Kennedy and His Times"
"Kennedy" 193
Kennedy clan 167, 195
"Kent State" 189
Kerlinger, Fred F. 238
King, Martin Luther, Jr. 174, 250
"Kino-Pravada" 166
Kinoy, Ernst 191
Kipphardt, Heinar 189
   "The Case of J. Robert Oppenheimer" 189
"Knots Landing" 90
"Kojak" 65, 69
   Theo Kojak 65, 67
Koppel, Ted, "Nightline" 154
Kowet, Don 39, 173
Kozoll, Michael 5, 75, 130, 132, 136
Kracauer, Siegfried xvi, 164
Krippendorff, K. 19, 23
Kuleshov, Lev 166

Index

LPTV 49
"Lace" 198, 199, 200, 207
Lansman, Claude 179
"Larry King Alive" 154
latent meaning 8
Laurel and Hardy 102, 106
"Law and Order" 176
Lear, Norman xv, 5, 117, 124, 132, 136, 224
"Leave It to Beaver" 103, 105
Lebanon 28, 33
"Legacy of Shame" 181
Lennon, John 193
Lévi-Strauss, Claude xiii
Levinson, Richard 224
Lewis, George H. 231
Lewis, Jerry 137
libido 14
Lindbergh child murder case 192
Literary Criticism Approach 1, 2-3
Little, Brown and Co. 202
"Living Newspaper, The" 186, 187
"Lou Grant" 67, 69, 132, 134, 224
"Louisiana Story" 165
"Love Boat, The" 129
Love Canal 28
Luce, Henry 168

MGM-United Artists 45
MTV 45
MTM 132-136
   MTM Enterprises, Inc. 133
MacArthur, General 191
Magid, Frank xii, 33, 153
"Magnum, P.I." 64, 90, 118
"Man from U.N.C.L.E." 105
"Man of Aran" 165
<u>Manchester Guardian</u> 215
manifest meaning 8
Mann, Abby 192, 203
   "Judgment at Nuremberg" 192
Mao Tse Tung 108
Marc, David 25, 38
"March of Time" 167, 168-169, 181, 186, 187
Margulies, Stan 216
Marlowe, Christopher 184
   <u>Edward II</u> 184, 185
Marshall, Garry 124, 224
Martin, Dean 137
Marx, Karl xiii, 11, 12, 14, 22
   Marxism 11

Marxists 11, 12, 156
The neo-Marxist 155
Marxist approach, the xiv, 1, 11-13
Marxist-critical theory 6
Marx brothers 102
"Mary Tyler Moore Show, The" 69, 104, 105, 108, 112-114, 132, 134, 135, 224
"M*A*S*H" 102, 104, 105, 108-112, 243; see also "After-M*A*S*H"
"Masterpiece Theatre" 202, 213
"Matt Houston" 76
"Maude" 137, 139
Maysles brothers (Hillary Harris, Albert, David) 170
McCall, Cheryl 179
McCann-Erickson 133
McCarthy, Joe 35, 250, 251
McCarthyism 145, 170, 171, 180
McCullough, Colleen, "The Thorn Birds" 215
McHugh & Hoffman 153
McLuhan, Marshall 12, 22
McMullen, Jay 177
McQuail, Denis 18, 23, 229
McVoy, D. Steven 55
Medawar, Sir Peter xiii
Meiklejohn, Alexander 57-58
metaphor 8
Metcalf, Burt 110
metonymy 8
"Miami Vice" 65, 72-73, 90
Michner, James 200
Mickey Mouse, Disney's 102
Miller, Arthur, "Crucible" 195
Milton, John 3, 175
mini-documentaries 31, 33, 156, 176
mini-series xvi, 129, 130, 198-217
The narrative structure 206-211
examples cited: "Roots," "Shogun," "Masada," "Jesus of Nazareth," "Nicholas Nickleby," "Brideshead Revisited," "The Thorn Birds," "The Jewel in the Crown," "Holocaust," "George Washington," "Fatal Vision," "Lace," "Mistral's Daughter," "Rich Man, Poor Man," "Rich Man, Poor Man--Book II," "Beggarman, Thief," "Hollywood Wives" 199
Miss America Pageant 19, 226
"Moana" 165
Moby Dick 38
mode of consciousness xi, 35, 36
as a predictor 70
Modleski, Tania 86
Molière 103
Moore, Mary Tyler 133; see also "Mary Tyler Moore Show, The"
Morahan, Christopher 213
"Mork and Mindy" 103, 104

Index

Movie Channel 45
Mudd, Roger 181
Multiple Distribution Service 47
Murdoch, Rupert 60
Murrow, Ed 160, 161, 170-172, 177
"Mussolini: The Untold Story" 196, 208, 210
"My Mother the Car" 104

NASA 43
NBC 5, 75, 83, 147, 156, 177, 178, 208, 215
    NBC Radio Network 133
"Nanook of the North" 165, 181
Napoleon, invasion of Russia 186
narrative structures 210
    the narrator 213-215
narrowcasting 45
Nashville Network 45
Nasser, Gamal Abdel 192
Nathanson, Dr. Bernard 169, 252
National Association of Broadcasters 214
National Conservative Political Action Committee (NCPAC) 177, 178
National Geographic documentary 38
National Geographic Society 165; see also "Explorer"
Nazism 58, 189
    Nazi Germany 7
    Nazi Party, the 7, 167
Negotiated Creativity 123
Nelson, Richard Alan 189
Nero 229
"Never Too Late" 138
New York Times, The 44, 242
New York Times v. Sullivan 59, 172
Newcomb, Horace 5, 22, 38, 97, 127, 131
news and newscasters 143
    news, structure of the 150
    TV news as business 152
news that entertains 32-33
Newscasters, The 33
Newspaper Guild 187
Nickelodeon 45
Nicoll, Allardyce 185
Nielsen, A. C. xii, xvi, 234, 236, 238, 242
    Nielsen ratings 24, 32, 124, 126, 127, 229
"Night Mail" 165
"Night They Raided Minsky's, The" 138
Nixon, President Richard 108, 110, 115, 116
    anti-Nixon 195
Nobel Prize xiii
Norden, Martin F. 64, 169
novels for television xvi, 198-217

O'Brian, Jim 213
O'Connor, Carroll 117
Oedipus complex 14
    oedipal myth 14
Ogburn, William F., theory of cultural lag 53
Olympics 229, 246
Olivier, Laurence 38
"Omnibus" 215
"One Day at a Time" 137, 140
"One Sixth of the World" 166
O'Neill, Tip 30
Ono, Yoko 194
operational definition 19
Oppenheimer, Dr. Robert 172
    "Oppenheimer" 188
oriental theatres 229
Orwellian tradition and "Big Brother" 41
"Overnight" 154

PBS 167, 175, 177, 178, 202, 203, 211, 216
"Painted Dreams" 83, 124
Paley, William S. 59
Papp, Joseph, Sticks and Bones 245
paradigm and syntagm 8-11
    paradigmatic analysis 8
    paradigmatic structure 8
Patchett, Tom 132
Pavarotti, Luciano 230
"payola" 233
Pearl Harbor 20
Peirce, Charles 6
Pennebaker, Don 170
Pentagon 181
    Pentagon Papers 160
Penthouse Entertainment Television 45
people meter 240
"Petticoat Junction" 104, 107
Phillips, Irna 83-84, 85, 99
Piaget, Jean 35
Piggot-Smith, Tim 212
Pingree, Suzanne 86, 90
Pinter, Harold 135
Playboy Channel 45
    philosophy 226
"Playing for Time" 245
plot and characterization in television drama 65
pluralistic approach, plurality xiv
poetics 2, 184
Pol Pot 7
Poland 201

Index

police drama 20
police stories 4
"Police Woman" 245
Pollan, Michael 136
Pope, The 34
Pope, John, as a character in the mini-series "Space" 13
pornography 1
"Portrait of America" 165
Potemkin 166
Powers, R. 39
press, manipulative theory of the 145
   free market model 146
"Primary" 170
primetime drama series and serials 89-92
   primetime television 20
prior restraint 57
Privacy 41, 53-56
   Privacy Act of 1974 55
   Warner Amex's "Code of Privacy" 55-56
private screenings 45
probability xii, 239
Procter and Gamble 82, 85, 245
producer, role of 128
Producer's Medium, The 5, 22
programming xvi, 5, 71
Prokofiev, Sergey 204
"Promised Land, The" 245
Propp, Vladimir xiii, 8, 22
psychoanalytical model, the xiv, 1, 14-17
psychology of TV watching 35-38
Publishers Weekly 203
Pudovkin, V. I. 166
Pulman, Jack 205

quantification xiii

RCA 43, 83, 147
Radio Act of 1927, The 83
Radio Free Europe 133
Radulovich, Lieutenant Milo 171
Randolf, Lillian 118
Rather, Dan xv, 1, 24, 25, 29, 147, 150, 159
Ratings 233-244
   related concepts: share, standard error, HUT, ADI, DMAS, Metro Area, Adjacent ADI, TSA, Cume, Quarter Hour Audience, Television Households, Day part, Sampling, Sweeps, National Television Index, National Audience Composition, National Station Index, Overnights, Telephone Coincidentals 233-244

reader-oriented poetics 9
Reading Television 9
Reagan, President Ronald 30
"Real McCoys, The" 107
Red Lion Broadcasting Co. v. FCC 58
Reiner, Rob 117
Renaissance 184
Reston, James 250
Reynolds, Gene 110
rhetoric 3, 184
"Rhoda" 132
Rice, Elmer 187
Rich, Lee 244
Riefenstahl, Leni 167, 181
right to know 57, 221
Ritchie, Michael 245
   "Smile" 245
"Robert Kennedy and His Times" 193, 196
Robert World Company, The 43
Rochemont, Louis de 168
rock music, video 9
Rogers, Will 102
Roman amphitheatres 228
romances 4
Romans, the 8
Rooney, Andy 28
Rooney, Mickey 250
Roosevelt, President Franklin D. 116
"Roots" 3, 194, 195, 199, 200
Roper xii
Rotha, Paul 165, 166, 167, 168, 179
Rouch, Jean 170
Rounds, David 85
Rousseau's noble savage 107
Rubel, Maxmilien 22
Russia 13, 14, 25, 156
   Russian folklorist 8
   Soviet Russia 166
   U.S.S.R. 201
"Ryan's Hope" 89

Sadat, Anwar as- 34
   "Sadat" 191, 192
Said, Edward W. 224
sampling 238-240
"Sanford and Son" 104, 108, 118, 137, 138-139
Sartre, Jean-Paul 20, 21, 23
satellites 40, 42
   satellite broadcasting 40
   satellite communication 42

Index

Satellite Master Antenna TV 47
Saussure, Ferdinand de 6, 7, 22
scarcity principle 42
Scott, Paul 202
   The Jewel in the Crown 202, 216
   The Raj Quartet 213
Scott, Sir Walter 186
screen realism 62, 63-64
"Search for Tomorrow" 85
Second Court of Appeals xiii
"See It Now" 170-172
Seldes, Gilbert 105
Selleck, Tom 188
"Selling of the Pentagon, The" 177
semiology 6
   semiologist, the 6
   semiological-structural approach 1, 6-11
   semiotics 6
Sennett, Mack 102
serialization of news xvi
serials xv, 128
series 128
series-serials 129
"Sesame Street" 234
Shakespeare, William xii, 5, 103, 104, 185, 189, 215
   Hamlet 38
   Henry IV 184
   Julius Caesar 229
   King Lear 63, 223
   Macbeth 68
   Othello 36
   Richard III 184
   Romeo and Juliet 68, 204
   Troilus and Cressida 109
Shakespearean humor 111, 114
Shakespearean tragedy 3
Shaping the First Amendment xvii
Shaw, David 193
Shaw, George Bernard 109, 113
Sheldon, Sidney 204, 211
"Shoah" 179
"Shogun" 194, 195, 199
Showtime 45
Shroeder, Bill 191
signs xiv
   sign system 6
"Silent Scream, The" 169, 252
Silliphant, Stirling 210
Silverman, Fred 5, 75, 136
Simmons, Ed 137
"Simon and Simon" 90

Singer, Jerome L.   36, 39
Sisyphus, comic   106
sitcom, a typology   101-122
situation comedy   xv, 4, 101-122
"60 Minutes"   148, 150, 156, 158, 160, 161, 167, 171
soap opera   3, 4, 8, 9-11, 82-99
sociological analysis   17-21
sociologists   xiv, 17, 18
"Song of Ceylone"   165
Sontag, Susan   17, 22
Sophocles   5, 215
Southern Satellite System   51
Soviet-German Non-Aggression Pact   201
"Space"   13, 200
Spanish International Network   45
speech, free see free speech
Spelling, Aaron   124, 244
<u>Spirit of Liberty, The</u>   xvii
Stapleton, Jean   117
Statue of Liberty, the   7
Stedman, Raymond W.   83, 84
Stemple, Guido H., III   xvii
Stephenson, William   229, 231
"Steptoe and Son"   138
Steven, John D.   xvii
"Stolen Husband, The"   84
"Story of Louis Pasteur, The"   189
"Streetwise"   179
Stromgren, Richard L.   64, 169
Struthers, Sally   117
subscription TV   46-47
Sumner, Bob   203
super bowl   26, 29, 224
super ego   15
"Superman"   2
Supreme Court   59
suspense, of form, of plot   68, 69, 71
Susskind, David   188
swastika   6, 7
Swift, J.   231
Swiss, The   6
Swit, Loretta   112
symbol   15, 16
syntagm, syntagmatic analysis   8

tables of significance   xiii
Tandem   138
Tarses, Jay   132
taste, markets of taste   230
   taste plurality   231

Index 281

Tchaikovsky, Peter   204
technologies, emerging television, and the cultural lag   40-61
television communication, definition   24
television data base   237
television documentary in American culture   164-183
television drama   11, 19
   dramatic serial   82-99
   form and structure   62-81
television erotica   30-31
television mode, the   24
"Television Vietnam: The Real Story"   178
televisual discourse   28
Ten Days That Shook the World   166
Tet offensive   27
Thackeray, William   186
theory and hypothesis   21
   dissonance theory   232
   the functional theory   231
   learning theory   232
theory of genres   2
Third World, the   11, 14
Thoreau, Henry David   107
"Thorn Birds, The"   215-216
"Three's a Crowd"   3
"Three's Company"   3, 4, 90
"Till Death Do Us Part"   117, 138
Time-Life venture   38
Times (London)   242
"Times of Harvey Milk, The"   167, 175-176
Tinker, Grant   xv, 244; see also MTM
Tocqueville, Alexis de   xii, 54
"Today's Children"   84
topicality in television drama   69
Traub, James   177, 202
Travanti, Daniel J.   78
"Triple-A Plowed Under"   187
Tripper, Jack   30
Trist, E. L.   242
"Triumph of the Will"   187
Truman, President Harry   191
Tuchman, Gaye   145
Turner, Tina   25
Turrow, Joseph   131, 132
Twentieth Century-Fox   110
"20/20"   156, 167, 171
Tylenol, the cyanide lacing of   33

U.S.A. Network   45
U.S.A. Today   44
U.S.S.R.   201; see also Russia

Ulysses 33
unconscious 20
"Uncounted Enemy: A Vietnam Deception, The" 27, 172-173
"United States" 132
University Wits 184
"Untouchables, The" 245
uses and gratification 18

VCRs xv, 49
VHS 50
variety-vaudeville 129
Vatican, The 215
vertical blanking interval 51
Vertov, Dziga 165, 166-167, 168, 170
video data 54
videocassette 40, 49
video-conferencing 43
videodiscs xv, 40
Vidmar, Neil 54
"Vietnam: A Television History" 173-175
"Vietnam OP/ED--An Inside Story" 178
Vietnam War 27, 32, 180, 192, 250

WGBH 202
WGN 83-84
WHMA-TV 202
"WKRP in Cincinnati" 136
WTBS 45
Waiting for Godot 66, 110
Wall Street Journal 44
Wallace, Mike 27, 161, 181
"War and Peace" 186
Washington Post 215
WASP 230
Watergate 116, 145, 160, 161, 250
Watt, Harry 165
Waugh, Evelyn 202
   Brideshead Revisited 202
"We Got Each Other" 135
Weather Channel 45
Weaver, Paul 151
Weber, Max xiii, 226
Weiss, Peter 189
   "Marat/Sade," "The Investigation" 189
Wertheim, A. F. 104
Western Union 43
Westerns 224
Westinghouse 83
Westly, Bruce H. xvii

Index

Westmoreland, General William 160, 170
White, Dan 175
White, Justice 58
"White Shadow, The" 135
Whitman, Walt 162
"Why We Fight" 168
Wicker, Tom 160
Wilde, Oscar 176
Wildmon, Reverend Donald 245
Williams, Raymond 13, 22
Williams, Wayne 192
"Winds of War, The" 198
Wiseman, Fredrick 170, 176
Wolper, David 176, 216
Wood, Peter H. 17, 22
Wood, Robert 132
Wooldridge, Susan 212
Wordsworth, William 107
"World of Plenty" 167
World War II 200, 201
Wouk, Herman 198, 200, 205, 208
Wright, Basil 165

Yorkin, Bud 138, 244
"Young Mr. Lincoln" 189

Ziberg, Michael 132
Zola, Emile 168
    "The Life of Emile Zola: 189

PN 1992 .5 .B36 1987

DATE DUE			
NOV 18 1991			